COOKING WITH NATURAL FOODS

as you search for abundant health

By
Muriel Beltz

TEACH Services, Inc.
Brushton, New York

Copyright © 1996 TEACH Services, Inc.

ISBN 1-57258-110-7
Library of Congress Catalog Card No. 96-60253

PRINTING HISTORY
1st Edition—1978
February 1980
November 1980
September 1981
May 1982
May 1984
August 1986
December 1987
April 1989
October 1990
October 1992
March 1996

Published by

TEACH Services, Inc.
RR 1, Box 182
Brushton, New York 12916

PREVENTIVE CARE

PREVENTIVE CARE is a heart full of love
extended through us from God up above.
It is a freedom, a willingness to tell
of the things we know to keep you well.
We want you to know of our longing to share
God's remedies that are not rare - but
ABUNDANT and SWEET.

PREVENTIVE CARE is a new way of living
Our body responds and keeps on giving
days free of pain and sweet sleep at night,
which make the world more beautifully bright.
Use God's gifts and you will be a better
specimen of humanity.
BE GRATEFUL FOR THIS!

PREVENTIVE CARE will brighten your days and
add joy to your life in many ways.
With it you add a new dimension
life is simple, serene and without tension.
Judicious care has benefits plus,
for God made the rules and God made us.
A MIRACLE INDEED!

PREVENTIVE CARE - God had it in mind
from the very beginning to the end of time.
Eight natural remedies, so simple 'tis true,
and He made them all to care for you.
And now we say "Give God the glory,'' and
share with others this wonderful story.
PRAISE HIS HOLY NAME!

Muriel Beltz

CARVE OUT A NEW LIFESTYLE AT THE

BLACK HILLS HEALTH & EDUCATION CENTER

Member of American Association for Health Promotion

HIGH BLOOD PRESSURE?
HEART DISEASE?
OVERWEIGHT?
SMOKING?
DIABETIC?
Medically supervised
1-3 week programs,
treatments, lectures,
recipes, exercise therapy

HEALTHY CHOICES ENDURE

Be Healthy

Discover a revolutionary new approach. Scientifically designed to help you make healthy choices about your lifestyle.

Be Happy

You will be surprised and pleased with the results. Your friends will notice the difference.

Be Thrifty

This minimum cost program helps you reduce health risks and enjoy a more energetic and productive future.

Write to: Wellness
B.H.H.E.C.
Box 19
Hermosa, SD 57744

or Call: 606-255-4101
800-658-5433 (LIFE)

We have a perfect vacation for you!

BLACK HILLS
HEALTH & EDUCATION CENTER

Black Hills Health & Education Center is a program designed to give people an alternative in the prevention and treatment of disease. Located in the Black Hills of South Dakota, the center is nestled in a valley surrounded with red-rim rock cliffs. A gentle stream flows through the center of the property. The fresh air, sunshine, and scenic beauty of the area make it an ideal place for people to rest, exercise, and learn the proper methods of disease prevention.

In the great majority of cases, disease is brought on by unhealthful life style habits. Generally these habits are formed by following the accepted practices of our society, without understanding their hurtful consequences. We are paying billions a year for health care, forever seeking out doctors to patch up what many of us have done to ourselves by improper diet, smoking, lack of exercise, excessive use of alcohol, and stressful living.

Conventional treatment includes medicine to combat the disease or surgery to repair or remove diseased organs. While this is often a reasonable approach, the patient's long-range, total health is not assured if there is no accompanying change in the offending life style. We need to take care of ourselves and learn how to shoulder more responsibility for our well-being in an intelligent way.

The health education program at Black Hills Health & Education Center is very simple: *CHANGE LIFE STYLE PATTERNS.* Replace debilitating habits with healthful, natural, more therapeutic patterns. Emphasis is placed on health education or life style medicine, an approach that will allow the guest to become a well-informed participant in his or her own recovery. The main theme in this program is to help people develop a life style that will bring the entire body, physically, spiritually, and mentally into optimum health.

Previous experience indicates that persons may be helped - in varying degrees -who come under these general disease categories: cardiovascular (atherosclerosis, hypertension, claudication); inflammatory (arthritis); pulmonary (bronchitis); metabolic (obesity, diabetics, hypoglycemia, allergies); and others. This program is also indicated for post-cardiac surgery rehabilitation. People who have discovered through screening diagnostic procedures, that they are likely candidates for heart attack, stroke, diabetes, or similar preventable diseases, may find this program helpful. However, there is another group of people who can benefit more than any other group — those who choose to invest in preserving rather than recovering their health. Our educational thrust is ideal for those who wish to enhance and retain their good health.

This new life style (new habits) is based upon intelligent application of nature's eight most available healing agencies. You will find a brief synopsis on each of these at the end of this book.

If you need further information about any phase of the **Black Hills Health & Education Center,** or would like to become a guest at a future **Better Living program,** call 605-255-4579 or 605-255-4101. Write to: *Black Hills Health and Education Center, Box 1, Hermosa, South Dakota 57744.*

CONTENTS

COOKING WITH NATURAL FOODS 1

HOLY SCRIPTURES 2

DIET LOW IN FAT 3, 4

IMPORTANT NOTICE OF IDEAL EATING PROGRAM 5

GOOD FOOD-EAT PLENTY 6

IDEAL DIET 7

MENUS 8-11

THERAPEUTIC DIET-DAILY BASIC NEEDS 12

THERAPEUTIC MENU SUGGESTIONS 13, 14

THE PACKED LUNCH 15, 16

EATING BETWEEN MEALS 17

CHARTS OF FOOD COMPOSITION 18-22

BREAK THAT FAST 23

GRAINS 24, 25

BREAKFAST 26-35

MILKS AND CREAMS 36, 37

BREADS 38-43

LEGUMES AND NUTS IN THE DIET 44

MAIN DISHES 45-58, 60

GRAVIES AND SAUCES 59, 60

DRESSINGS AND SPREADS 61-67

COOKING VEGETABLES 68

SEASONING VEGETABLES 69

VEGETABLES-SALADS 70-78

SOUPS 79-83

NATURAL SWEETS 84-97

MISCELLANEOUS 98-100

SPROUTING 102-103

ROASTING CHESTNUTS 103

THE EIGHT NATURAL REMEDIES 104-116

W - WATER 104-105

E - EXERCISE 106

L - LIFE-GIVING AIR 107-108

L - LIMITS 109

N - NUTRITION 110-111-112

E - ESSENTIAL REST 113

S - SUNLIGHT 114

S - SPIRITUAL DIMENSION 115-116

A WORD FROM DR. BELTZ 117

GLOSSARY 118-121

INDEX by sections and alphabetical 122-131

COUPONS FOR ORDERING **Cooking with Natural Foods** 132

COOKING WITH NATURAL FOODS

as you search for abundant health

Compiled by Muriel Beltz
Black Hills Health & Education Center
Box 19
Hermosa, SD 57744

Dear Friends,

Because of the increase in degenerative diseases and other ailments, people all over the world are looking for happier, healthier ways of life.

COOKING WITH NATURAL FOODS is not a diet but a way of life which includes eating well - knowing that you will have adequate nutrition and incorporating all of the eight natural remedies into the life style. (see page 104)

The fine art of cooking with **natural foods** - simple food that is simply delicious — is a comprehensive program for a new start in life.

With simple, tasty recipes and easy to follow instructions, you will enjoy food preparation. It will be exciting, interesting and a real taste treat. However, changing eating habits will be the hardest thing that you have ever done, but the benefits you will receive will be well worth the effort. You will feel more vibrant and alive. Your stamina will increase, your mind will be alert as you get proper nutrition, sufficient rest, daily exercise in the fresh air and sunshine, use water freely, be temperate in all areas of your life and trust in Divine Power.

God made us and He made the food He wants us to eat. We cannot improve the balance of nutrients by refining - taking out many and adding a few. We need to use real foods as grown and as simply prepared as feasible.

I hope that you will find this book to be helpful to you as you study. Be willing to accept new concepts. Develop cheerfulness. Thank God for good food and ask Him to help you like it. May you find that for which you have been searching!

A special "Thank you" to my niece, Carol Pogue, who originally designed the cover of this book and has added the color to make it even more beautiful.

If I can be of any help to you, please feel free to call or write.

Yours for healthful choices,

Muriel Beltz

Muriel Beltz

FROM THE HOLY SCRIPTURES

This is the day, this is the day that the Lord hath made, that the Lord hath made;
We will rejoice, we will rejoice and be glad in it, and be glad in it.
This is the day that the Lord hath made; We will rejoice and be glad in it.
This is the day, this is the day that the Lord hath made.

Psalm 118:24

I beseech you therefore brethren, by the mercies of God, That you present your bodies a living sacrifice, Holy, acceptable unto God, Which is your reasonable service.

Romans 12:1

Know ye not that ye are the temple of God, and that the Spirit of God dwelleth in you: If any man defile the temple of God him shall God destroy; for the temple of God is holy, which temple ye are.

1 Corinthians 3:16, 17

What? know ye not that your body is the temple of the Holy Ghost which is in you, which ye have of God, and ye are not your own? For ye are bought with a price; therefore glorify God in your body, and in your spirit, which are God's.

1 Corinthians 6:19, 20

Beloved, I wish above all things that thou mayest prosper in health, even as thy soul prospereth.

III John 2

If thou wilt diligently hearken to the voice of the Lord thy God, and wilt do that which is right in his sight, and wilt give ear to his commandments, and keep all his statues, I will put none of these diseases upon thee, which I have brought upon the Egyptians: for I am the Lord that healeth thee.

Exodus 15:26

Who forgiveth all thine iniquities; who healeth all thy diseases.

Psalm 103:3

Whether therefore ye eat, or drink, or whatsoever ye do, do all to the glory of God.

I Corinthians 10:31

Behold, I have given you every herb bearing seed which is upon the face of all the earth, and every tree, in the which is the fruit of the tree yielding seed, to you it shall be for meat.

Genesis 1:29

WHY A DIET LOW IN FAT AND CHOLESTEROL CAN HELP YOU

Heart and blood vessel problems, such as angina and hypertension; disorders such as diabetes and hypoglycemia which involve the body's ability to handle sugar - and other ailments as well -are beginning to be recognized as being primarily due to the diet we consume. The diet eaten in advanced countries such as the U.S. has a total fat content of 40-50% of calories consumed. It is also very high in refined carbohydrates. Scientific investigators have found that in poorer countries where the people eat a diet usually under 20% of total calories in fat consisting mainly of unrefined carbohydrates as whole grains, fruits and vegetables, these diseases are almost never found. In countries less poor, but not quite so advanced as ours, where the diet is in between, there is an in between amount of these diseases. The more the fat and refined carbohydrates eaten, the more degenerative disease problems are found.

Other scientist have studied the effects of our typical diet in laboratories and clinics and have confirmed the suspicions that the large amount of fat and refined carbohydrates consumed in this country can bring on these degenerative diseases; whereas a diet in which fat and refined carbohydrates are sharply curtailed can cause these disease symptoms to lessen and even to disappear completely.

The kind of fat does not seem to matter - the fats may be those from dairy products, such as in whole milk, butter, cheese, etc.; or in the form of vegetable fats as found in oil of nuts, seeds, avocados, olives and vegetable oil spreads such as margarine or nut butters; or fat as found in animal foods. It is the total amount of fat of all kinds that is consumed that matters; the more fat, the more disease symptoms.

In addition to the fat contained, animal muscle tissue of all kinds - beef, pork, lamb, poultry, fish, shellfish, etc., but especially organ tissue (liver, brains, kidneys, etc) and eggs (chicken eggs, fish roe, etc.) introduce still another harmful substance into our body -cholesterol. While some cholesterol is needed by the body, the body produces all that it requires. If additional cholesterol is added to the diet it becomes stored in the blood and tissues, since the body is unable to excrete it. In the presence of blood which has a high concentration of fat, the excess stored cholesterol in time causes lesions called plaques to form inside the blood vessels. This condition is known as atherosclerosis.

On our usual high fat diet, these plaques begin to form even in the very young people, gradually building up over a period of time and narrowing the channels in the blood vessels. This narrowing of the blood vessels reduces the amount of blood flow to the tissues served by these vessels and in time the heart compensates by elevating the blood pressure more and more, producing high blood pressure or hypertension.

If the blood vessels that serve the heart (coronary vessels) become sufficiently clogged by plaques, any circumstance which further reduces the already diminished oxygen supply to the heart muscle will cause the heart to "cry out" in pain - the terrible pain of angina. A slight exertion such as running a short distance, an emotional episode, or even a single fat meal, can bring on an angina attack. In one experiment, the subjects, angina patients, did nothing but drink a glass of cream. Even though they were at complete rest, all of them suffered angina attacks.

A fatty meal reduces the oxygen supply to all of the body tissues, not only to the vessels serving the heart. This will happen even if your arteries are not clogged by plaques - though few adults are so lucky, unless they have been on a lifelong low fat, low cholesterol diet. Even in a baby, fat steals oxygen from the body cells. It steals oxygen from the tissues just as the carbon monoxide does when taken in by smoking. In the case of fat, this happens because of several mechanisms. When the digested fat is broken down, it forms tiny fat balls which tend to clump together in the bloodstream. These aggregate with solid elements in the blood and block the blood flow in the tiniest arteries, thus depriving the cells in the tissues fed by those arteries of needed oxygen nourishment. The tiny fat balls also coat these solid elements in the blood. As a result, the red blood cells that are the body's oxygen carriers become stuck together in formations resembling rows of coins. The clumping of the red blood cells further slows the circulation, depriving the tissues of even more oxygen. When the clumped red blood cells reach the lungs where they should take up oxygen from the air breathed in, being clumped together much of their surface area is not free to pick up oxygen. In this way, much less oxygen is carried back into the tissues which are still further deprived of oxygen.

It is because of this process of depriving the body cells of oxygen that fats enables cholesterol to form the atherosclerotic plaques. The artery walls become more easily penetrated by fats and cholesterol when the blood that bathes them is deficient in oxygen, thus encouraging the plaques to form. On a high fat diet, the process of plaque formation goes on hour after hour, day after day, in all of the arterial vessels throughout the body. In the course of many years, the constant narrowing of these vessel channels by the ever-growing plaque formations causes many symptoms. High blood pressure and angina are two of the common symptoms; others include a gradual deterioration in hearing and vision and even senility and impotency.

In many studies, it has been shown that by going on a diet in which fat and cholesterol intake are sharply reduced, the plaque-forming process can be reversed and the symptoms produced by the artery damage lessened or even eliminated. Refined carbohydrates and added salt have been found to contribute significantly to the development of heart and blood vessel problems. On a low fat diet, the plaques or sores that are narrowing your arteries should gradually begin to disappear so that near normal circulation will be restored.

This same diet has proved successful in reversing diabetes and hypoglycemia. Hypoglycemia is a pre-diabetic stage, caused by similar abnormal conditions in the blood that bring about diabetes; both respond to the same dietary therapy—a low fat diet. Diabetes and hypoglycemia appear under the circumstances which occur when the concentration of fats in the blood is very high. By lowering the blood fats by a diet low in fats of all kinds, and low in simple carbohydrates, like sugar, honey, and molasses which become converted, a Canadian investigator, Dr. I.M. Rabinowitch, treated 1,000 diabetics over a five year period and had a high rate of success. Even insulin-dependent diabetics no longer required insulin or other drugs in 25% of the cases. Had the diet been even lower in fat content, Dr. Rabinowitch would have obtained an even higher reversal rate, based on the experiences of others.

High blood fats bring about a situation where the insulin from the pancreas is unable to effectively act upon blood sugar. Studies have been done where perfectly normal young men were made diabetic in a period of days or even hours, depending upon how fast fats were introduced into their blood. When fats were introduced very rapidly, by injection into the bloodstream instead of by diet, they became diabetic in two hours. The scientists who did this study were also able to reverse diabetes by chemically lowering the blood fats.

You would lower your blood fats by a gradual and permanent means, by your diet and the fast results you could obtain would surprise you, if you adhered to the diet closely.

Certain kinds of arthritis also respond well to a diet by which blood fats are reduced. High blood fat levels cause the watery part of the blood (plasma) to seep out of the tiniest arteries (capillaries) at an abnormally high rate, due to the pressure built up in the capillaries when the circulation becomes slowed. The resultant swelling or edema produced in the tissues provides the environment conducive to the development of arthritic symptoms. When the edema and slowed circulation in the capillaries are improved, marked relief and recovery can occur. Other diseases also have shown an improvement on this type of diet such as colitis, gallbladder disease, hypertension (high blood pressure) and obesity.

FOR REASONS STATED ABOVE, we suggest a diet without cholesterol, fat 10%-20% of the calories, approximately 10% of the calories in protein and about 70% of the calories from unrefined carbohydrates. Salt should be one-half teaspoon or less per day.

IMPORTANT NOTICE
ABOUT THE RECIPES IN THIS BOOK

This is an **IDEAL EATING PROGRAM** for a preventive lifestyle,
weight control,
and stress control.

FREE FROM *Cholesterol and Refined Sugars*

LOW in *Fat*

HIGH in *Natural Protein, Vitamins, Minerals, Bulk, Fiber, and Complex Carbohydrates (the efficient energy source).*

Many, many people have received tremendous benefit from following a good eating program as suggested in **"Cooking with Natural Foods"**—using the recipes and menu guides.

*IF...*one is wishing to lose weight more rapidly or wanting less natural fat for other reasons, it may be necessary to cut down on the quantity of nuts in the recipes or use only the therapeutic recipes. The same would apply to olives, avocados and seeds. Good results can be obtained in some products by substituting oatmeal for one-half of the nuts. HOWEVER, the pie crusts that include more nuts will produce a nice, tender crust.

Remember that much of your meal should be grains with fresh fruits or fresh vegetables.

THE MANY THERAPEUTIC RECIPES included in this book are nutritious, tasty and satisfying. **Therapeutic recipes will be marked (T).**

Therapeutic Recipes are those which are approximately 10 percent protein, 10 percent fat and 80 percent complex carbohydrates and should be used exclusively in REGRESSION diet programs for heart problems, obesity, diabetes, arthritis, or any other degenerative disease.

For significant weight loss or regression, choose 250-300 calories for breakfast, 250-300 calories for the noon meal and 200 or less calories for the evening meal.

When using whole, natural foods, the bulk and fiber produce a fullness and satiety which continues until the next meal which should be between five and six hours. The evening meal should be light so the stomach will be empty when it is time for sleep and the entire body can be at rest.

When the body has been rejuvenated (is back to normal, weight, etc.), other recipes may be brought into the dietary which use foods high in natural fat—nuts, avocados, coconut, and olives.

HAPPY EATING!

GOOD FOOD, EAT PLENTY

I. Good Food

A. Looks good
B. Smells good
C. Tastes good
D. High-quality nutrients
E. Inexpensive
F. Easy to prepare
G. Harmless
H. Served on schedule

Vitamin & Mineral Sources

A. Fruits and Vegetables
B. Whole grains, both breads and cereals; legumes; raw foods.
C. Citrus, tomatoes, cabbage, potatoes, raw fruits and vegetables, etc.
D. Sunshine. Through action on skin.

II. Dangerous Foods (The Cancer Threat):

A. Pressed or ground meats, rare meats, treated meats, aged or cured meats.
B. Products from diseased animals.
C. Spoiled, rotted or fermented foods.
D. Irritating or stimulating foods.

III. Foods to be used with restraint

A. Refined foods (carbohydrates, fats, proteins, minerals, vitamins).
B. Concentrated foods (nuts, seeds, tofu).

IV. Techniques

A. Preparation & storage: preserve color, flavor, nutrients.
B. Serving & eating: dignity, beauty, order, punctuality, cheerfulness.
C. Combinations: Restrain the appetite, eat slowly, and only a limited variety at one time. It is better to serve fruits and vegetables at different meals.
D. Meal planning & menus: all four taste experiences: sweet, sour, salt; bland or bitter.

Breakfast	Dinner	Supper
Main dish	Main dish	Fruit
2 or 3 Fruits (one raw)	2 or 3 Vegetables (one raw)	Grains (Cereals or breads)
Bread	Bread	
Spread - Fruit, Nut	Spread - Legume, Olive, Melty Cheese	

IDEAL DIET

GENEROUS BREAKFAST

Breakfast Main Dish
Raw Fruits - One Citrus
Other Fruit (may be raw, also)
Whole Grain Bread
Spread (dried fruit, nut, avocado, olive)

GOOD DINNER

Dinner Main Dish (grain, legume or combination)
Raw vegetables or salad
Cooked vegetable
Whole Grain Bread
Spread (legume, nut, olive, melty cheese)

SPARE SUPPER

Fresh Fruit and/or fruit sauce
Grains (bread, crackers, cereals)

BASIC PRINCIPLES AND GUIDE LINES

A. Eat three kinds of whole grains each day.
B. Eat dark green and yellow vegetables, raw and cooked each day. May eat potatoes every day, if you wish.
C. Eat two or three kinds of fresh fruit each day.
D. Add beans or other legumes three or four times a week, or less if they are not agreeable.
E. Eat sweet potatoes or yellow squash once or twice a week.
F. Maintain your ideal weight by eating two or three meals a day with nothing but water between meals.
G. Eat slowly, chewing your food well.
H. Vary your diet from meal to meal, but do not eat too many varieties at any one meal. Keep both meals and dishes simple.
I. Eat at regular times and allow at least five hours between meals.
J. Eat all you need to maintain health, and enjoy your food, but don't overeat. Too much food dulls and depresses the mind, causes disease and fatigue, and shortens life.
K. Eat with thanksgiving praising God for His goodness.
L. Limit rich foods. Eat sparingly of nuts, seeds and avocados.
M. Limit salt to ½ teaspoon or less per day.
N. Fruit juices and concentrated foods usually should be taken in small quantities.

"BLESSED ART THOU, O LAND, WHEN...THY PRINCES EAT...FOR STRENGTH, AND NOT FOR DRUNKENESS!" Ecclesiastes 10:17

MENUS

These suggested menus are guidelines for you to use in selecting foods for your family. **DO NOT** try to follow them exactly - you may find it necessary to substitute often. Use foods in season.

Set aside one day a week for baking bread, waffles, granola, rolls, crackers, pita, etc. Make two or three products a week and freeze the surplus for future use.

Set aside one day for making salad dressings, mayonnaise, nut butters, cashew jack cheese, spreads.

If you want a dessert, use one of your choice from the NATURAL SWEETS section or some fresh fruit.

Foods never improve by canning or freezing, so use fruits and vegetables fresh as much as you can. For example, in strawberry season, use strawberries in fresh fruit pie, fruit salad, on your cereal or just as they come from the market or garden.

Use a variety of foods. **Learn** to like food that is good for you. **Try** different vegetables and fruits. **Be thankful** for good, natural foods.

BREAKFAST	*DINNER*	*SUPPER*
	SUNDAY	
Waffle Perfect	Garbanzo Roast	Cornmeal Rice Cakes
Currant Delight or any	Escalloped Potatoes	with gravy
Unsweetened fruit juice	Barley Salad	Orange, apple,
thickened - add fruit.	Scottish Oat Crisps	banana salad
Fresh fruit in season		
	MONDAY	
Delicious Millet	Lima Bean Tomato Casserole	Cream of Potato Soup
Almond Milk	Fresh Corn Sauté	Whole wheat English
Fresh fruit	Tabuli Salad	muffins with jack
Whole grain toast	Whole grain rolls or bread	cheese & tomato
Nut spread or jam		Grapes
	TUESDAY	
Cashew French Toast	Chili	Tomato Soup
Spicy Apple Syrup	Sprout Salad	Herb Bread Toast with
Fresh Fruit	Whole grain bread with	spread
	avocado spread	Fresh peaches
	WEDNESDAY	
Granola	Tamale Pie	Fruit Salad
Cashew or almond milk	Eggplant Casserole Deluxe	Whole grain toast
Strawberries	Gazpacho Salad	Strawberry jam
Cantaloupe	Whole grain bread	
	THURSDAY	
Fruit Toast	Baked Potato (no oil gravy)	Corn Chowder
Whole grain Toast with	Zucchini and Tomatoes	Corn Dodgers
nut spread	Lentil Roast	Blueberries, raspberries,
Fresh fruit	Lettuce with Avocado Dressing	strawberries

FRIDAY

Baked Oatmeal
Strawberry - coconut cream
   or nut milk
Fresh fruit
Whole grain toast with nut
   spread or jam

Tomato-Lentil Delight
Brown Rice
Green beans Almondine
Lettuce & onion salad with
   Italian low cal. dressing
   made with lemon juice.

Your choice Pita filled
   with green pepper, tomato,
   onion, rice, cucumber
   sprouts, avocado,
   jack cheese, etc.
Fresh fruit

SATURDAY

Apple-oatmeal muffins
   (make day before / Re-heat)
Fruit sauce
Fresh fruit

Skillet Spaghetti
Toss salad
Peas
Whole grain bread
Carob pie

Fresh fruit salad
Oatmeal Raisin bread
   toasted

SUNDAY

Corn Bread
Creamed Tomatoes
Fresh fruit - peel and
   cut oranges, apple
   banana

Baked Potato with
   green onion dressing
Green beans
Sliced tomatoes
Whole grain rolls
Banana Nut cake

California Fruit
   soup
Coconut - sesame
   sticks

MONDAY

Millet-Rice Pudding
Fresh fruit, peaches, berries
Whole grain bread toasted

Nut spread

Navy bean soup with
   Dumplings
   (make day before and
reheat)
Toss salad - lettuce, onion,
tomato, dill, with dressing

Creamy Coconut Fruit
   Soup

Oatmeal Gems

TUESDAY

Apricot Kuchen
   (make day before)
Orange slices
Fresh fruit

Spanish Rice
Carrot Loaf
Gaspacho Salad
Whole grain rolls

Pat's Fruit Soup
   cold or hot
Date muffins

WEDNESDAY

Onion French Toast
Sliced Tomatoes
Fresh Fruit

Lentil Patties or Roast
Whole Wheat Spaghetti with
   Broccoli Sauce
Carrots steamed
Cucumbers, tomato, onion,
   diced and sliced with salt
   and lemon juice

Fruit Shakes
Scottish Oat Crisps

THURSDAY

Oatmeal-Raisin Toast
Canned fruit or frozen
Fresh fruit

Soy-Oat Patties with
   Tomato Sauce
Peas
Baked Potato with Cashew
   Gravy
Sliced tomatoes and green
   pepper strips

Pizza
Toss Salad
   No oil Italian
   dressing

Potato & Rice Patties
Fresh Fruit
Whole grain toast with
    spread, savory or
    Hommus

FRIDAY

Macaroni - Cabbage Dinner
Zucchini dinner salad
Whole grain bread with
    avocado spread

Apple Rice Betty
Cantaloupe

Date Rolls
    (made day before & reheat)
Fresh fruit - bananas,
    peaches
Small glass orange juice

SATURDAY

Potato Salad - make
    day before to blend
    flavors
Creamed celery
Cabbage, carrot, onion slaw

Melon Ball Rainbow
Fresh Fruit Muffins

Soy-Oat Waffles
Orange Sauce
Fresh Fruit

SUNDAY

Pizza
Tossed Salad
Sliced Tomatoes
Carob Fudge

Baked Nut Rice
Fresh Fruit Pie

Scrambled Soy Cheese
    (Tofu)
Sliced Tomato & Avocado
Grapefruit
Whole grain toast with
    olive spread

MONDAY

Baked Stuffed Potato
Summer Squash Casserole
Rosy Crunch Salad

Wheat Casserole
Banana Logs
Small glass of fresh
    fruit juice or an
    orange

Hot Soupy Beans over
    whole grain toast
Olives
Pineapple, fresh or canned
    in own juice

TUESDAY

Millet Loaf
Cheese-Broccoli Casserole
Sesame-Spinach Salad

Peachy Crumb Cake
Fruit Soup, cold

Corn Chowder
Whole grain toast with
Cashew
    Jack cheese and tomatoes
Fresh Fruit

WEDNESDAY

Enchiladas

Stuffed green peppers
Olives, celery and
    carrot sticks

Fresh Fruit Salad

Cashew French Toast

Brown Rice or any cooked
    whole grain cereal
Two kinds of fruit in
    season
Toast with nut butter and
    jam

THURSDAY

Cheese-A-Roni
Eggplant Casserole
Green Beans
Sprout Salad

Waffles - Berry Topping
Fresh Pineapple

FRIDAY

Grapenuts or Shredded
Wheat
Almond Milk
Strawberries
Whole grain toast

Bean-Oat Patties
Rice Oriented
Peas
Tomato-Lettuce Salad

Apple Bread Pudding
Fresh Papaya

SATURDAY

Raisin-Nut Roll
  (see Date Roll recipe)
Fresh peaches
Fresh cantaloupe
Whole grain toast with
  cashew jack cheese and
  sliced tomatoes

Country Potato Patties
Garbanzo Salad
Cucumbers-onions with
  Mayonnaise dressing

Mixed cooked vegetables

Corn Soup
Rice Cakes

Pineapple in own
  unsweetened juice

THERAPEUTIC DIET BASIC DAILY NEEDS

FRUIT: one citrus serving
        one or two servings of any fruit (exclude olives and avocados)

VEGETABLES: one serving green and one serving yellow
           variety of raw salads (include edible raw vegetables, greens and herbs)

LEGUMES: three or four times a week (include garbanzos, lentils, all beans, peas, etc.)

CEREAL: three servings of whole grains daily (include wheat, rye, oats, millett, brown rice,
        barley, buckwheat)

TUBERS: use as desired (yams, potatoes, turnips, beets, etc.)

**Use whole foods. The whole fruit has 6-10 times as much fiber as the juice.

The **FOUR FOOD GROUPS**—fruits, grains, nuts and vegetables—provide the requirements in protein, fat and carbohydrates, minerals, vitamins, bulk and fiber.

If no refined foods are added, the above guide becomes the basis for a good eating program. It also is an excellent reducing program.

When the body has been reconditioned, with all the functions in good working order, the nuts and seeds, avocados, olives, and coconut may be included in small amounts. For weight control, **calories in** must equal **calories out.**

Good Nutrition will be a beautiful picture instead of a puzzle if we remember the **FOUR FOOD GROUPS.**

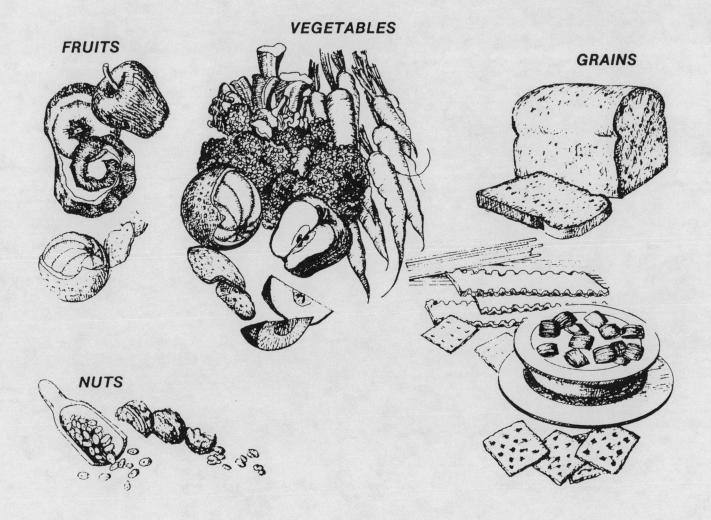

FRUITS

VEGETABLES

GRAINS

NUTS

THERAPEUTIC MENU SUGGESTIONS

BREAKFAST

Food Item	Serving	Calories
Cornmeal	½ cup	60
Cracked Wheat	½ cup	90
Four Grain Cereal	½ cup	90
Granola	½ cup	100
Grapenuts	¼ cup	100
Oatmeal	½ cup	80
Rice	½ cup	115
Rice, millet	½ cup	90
Rolled Wheat, rye	½ cup	80
Rolled Triticale	½ cup	80
Shredded Wheat	½ cup	80
Whole Grain (oat, wheat triticale, millet, rye	½ cup	90
Fruit Milk	¼ cup	25
Rice Milk	¼ cup	30
Apple Sauce	¼ cup	25
Dates	1 T.	30
Date Sugar	½ T.	30
Fruit Sauce	¼ cup	25
Raisins	1 T.	30
Corn Bread (39)	1 slice	50
Corn Crisps	1	30
Date Muffin	1	175
Pita Crisps	½ pita	35
Rice Cakes	1	30
Toast	1 slice	70
Wheat-Oat Muffin	1	100
Jam (all)	1 T.	30
Apple	1 med.	90
Banana	1 med.	100
Cantaloupe	¼ (5" dia.)	40
Fruit, canned in own juice	½ cup	50
Grapefruit	½	40
Grapes	10	35
Orange	1 med.	65
Pear	1 med.	100
Tomato	1 med.	25
Hash Browns	½ cup	50
Ketchup	1 T.	10
Pinto Beans	¼ cup	65
Scrambled Tofu	½ cup	65

DINNER

Food Item	Serving	Calories
Beets	½ cup	20
Bread Dressing	½ cup	80
Broccoli	½ cup	20
Brussel Sprouts	½ cup	30
Cabbage w/dill	½ cup	25
Carrot-Bean Croquette	¼ c. pattie	95
Carrots	½ cup	25
Cauliflower	½ cup	25
Chard (greens)	½ cup	20
Chinese Vegies	½ cup	20
Corn	½ cup	65
Garbanzo-Rice Loaf	½ cup	100
Garbanzos	¼ cup	60
Gravy	½ cup	50
Green Beans	½ cup	15
Kidney Beans	¼ cup	55
Lasagne	½ cup	150
Lima Beans	½ cup	25
Navy Beans/onions	¼ cup	60
Pizza	1/8	170
Potato, Baked	1	100
Potato Balls	3	60
Potato, Mashed	½ cup	60
Potato, Pattie	1	50
Potatoes, Peas	½ cup	70
Rice, Oriental	½ cup	115
Spaghetti	½ cup	60
Squash, Baked	½ cup	65
Tamale Pie	½ cup	50
Tomato-Lentil Delight	½ cup	80
Tofu in Pita	½ cup	95
Vegetable Stew	½ cup	80
Yams, Baked	½ cup	95
Zucchini	½ cup	10
SALAD BAR		FREE
French Dressing	1 T.	FREE
Italian Dressing	2 T.	FREE
Ketchup	1 T.	10
Lemon		FREE
Bread or Roll	1	70
Bean Spread	2 T.	30
Garbanzo Spread	1 T.	30
Millet Spread	1 T.	30

SUPPER

Food Item	Serving	Calories
Best Barley Soup	½ cup	50
Corn Chowder	½ cup	65
Minestrone Soup	½ cup	40
Potato Soup	½ cup	70
Split Pea Soup	½ cup	80
Tomato-Rice Soup	½ cup	50
Tomato Soup	½ cup	40
Vegetable Soup	½ cup	40
Zucchini Soup	½ cup	40

Bread Sticks	3	70
Corn Crisps	1	30
Crackers	1	10
Croutons	½ cup	70
Fruit Crisp	½ cup	75
Pita Crisps	½ Pita	35
Rice Cake	1	30
Toast	1	70
Popcorn	1 cup	25

Apple	1 med.	90
Apple Sauce	½ cup	50
Banana	1 med.	100
Canned Fruit in own juice	½ cup	50
Fruit Malts	½ cup	50
Fruit Salad	1 c.	100
Jam (all)	1 T.	30
Orange	1 med.	65
Pears	1 med.	100
Sliced Tomatoes	3 slices	15

High Fat Foods

Almonds	10	90
Almond Butter	1 T.	90
Avocado Spread	2 T.	50
Cashew-Pimiento Spread	1 T.	20
Olives	5	30
Peanut Butter	1 T.	55
Pizza Bun Topping	1 T.	20
Sunflower Seeds	1 T.	50

THE PACKED LUNCH

A PACKED LUNCH SHOULD—
Be a substantial balanced meal with a significant part of the day's calories.
Should be carefully planned and prepared so that it is a pleasure to eat.
Should be varied from day to day so that it will be anticipated.
Should not include "junk" and empty calories.

PLAN AHEAD—
Plan all meals a week ahead, including lunches, and make definite plans to have needed lunch supplies on hand:

A good quality lunch box, chosen to fit your luncher's personality. The man on the road may want a thermal controlled container (styrofoam, etc.)

Assorted thermos bottles—wide and narrow-mouth

Assorted plastic containers with tight fitting lids. Little jars also are handy.

Waxed paper, sandwich bags, platic wrap and foil.

A bread knife for splitting sandwiches.

Small spatula for spreading fillings.

A re-freezable ice bag from camper's store.

Supply of paper bags.

WORK AHEAD—

Plan the lunches and have them written for easy referral

Lettuce, celery, carrots, radishes, etc., should be washed and stored in the crisper in plastic bags or containers, ready for use.

Some sandwiches may be made ahead and frozen, if necessary; however, fillings with celery, parsley, sprouts, etc., do not freeze well.

Fruits should be washed and stored in refrigerator. Could be divided, such as grapes, and put into individual servings in bags ready to use.

Clean thermos containers as soon as you can with warm soapy water and bottle brush.

Rinse with soda water and then clear water.

Sandwich Fillings:

Peanut butter goes nicely with any of the following: finely chopped apples, dates, crushed pineapple, raisins and bananas sliced in at the time of eating; chopped or sliced dill pickle made with lemon juice; sliced tomato and lettuce (add just before eating); finely shredded carrot and cabbage; thinly sliced zucchini or radishes; sprouts.

Tofu: Mash the tofu and add any of the following or several at one time: olives, celery, minced onion, parsley, sprouts, cucumber; chopped nuts, crushed pineapple, raisins, chopped apples, dates, figs, apricots, prunes.

Chopped nuts combined with oil-free mayonnaise and celery, celery and olives, grated carrots, dates, raisins, etc.

Left-overs moistened with oil-free mayonnaise make fine sandwich fillings: eggplant, baked beans, lentil roast, patties, etc.

Avocado with a little onion salt and a little fresh lemon juice (and you may also add fresh tomato). This a delightful spread for bread, but due to its fragile qualities, it is best to serve freshly-made at home.

—15—

Variety In Sandwiches:

Raisin bread, banana bread go well with the fruit combination.

Oatmeal bread, rye bread (rye may not be acceptable with peanut butter combinations) different whole grain breads, Pita bread, use whole grain crackers with stews or fruit salads instead of sandwiches.

Fill the Thermos with:

Vegetable stews, all soups, creamed vegetable or casserole dish, beans, fruit salad, applesauce, etc.

The Naturals for Lunches:

Fresh fruit, lots of it. Include a sharp knife if needed. Nuts, preferably dry roasted or raw, whole grain crackers, wafers sticks, rolls.

Carry in a sealed cup or container:

Baked beans, any salad combination, canned or frozen fruit, canned tomatoes.

Specials:

For children: Keep container servings small, be generous with sandwich filling, pre-cut fruit for easy eating, place sandwiches in sandwich bag which will protect the luncher while eating the sandwich. Send plastic spoons and forks when needed, use pretty napkins often. Add a surprise from time to time: a little bag of salted nuts, small box of raisins, health cookie or candy, a little note.

EATING BETWEEN MEALS

Snacks are Detrimental to Health for a Number of Reasons.

1. They deprive the stomach and other organs of the rest they normally require.

2. They retard digestion and thus give rise to flatulence (gas) and related symptoms.

3. They tend to increase the total calorie intake beyond actual need.

4. Since snacks are high in sugar and simple carbohydrate content, they deprive the body of necessary elements such as Vitamins and Minerals found in a balanced diet.

5. Snacks tend to lessen the desire and enjoyment of regular meals and thus reduce digestibility.

X-ray studies conducted to determine the emptying time of the normal stomach shows the average to be between four and five hours. A study was run using several persons who were given a routine breakfast consisting of *cereal and cream, bread, cooked fruit* and an *egg.* Their stomachs were x-rayed and found to be empty in *four and one-half hours.*

A few days later these same persons were given the same type of breakfast and two hours later they were fed snacks, their emptying time was checked. The results are shown on the following chart.

Normal Breakfast	2 hours later	Results
Person No. 1	Ice Cream Cone	Residue in the stomach after 6 hours
Person No. 2	Peanut Butter Sandwich	Residue after 9 hours
Person No. 3	Pumpkin Pie, Glass of Milk	Residue after 9 hours
Person No. 4	Half slice of bread & butter repeated every 1½ hour interval and no dinner	More than half his breakfast in stomach after 9 hours
Person No. 5	Twice in the morning, twice in the afternoon a bit of chocolate candy	13½ hours later more than one-half the morning meal was still in the stomach.

The key to regularity in eating lies in having a good breakfast. When the morning meal is omitted, one tends to become hungry before noon and hence resorts to a snack. The snack slackens the appetite for lunch; less is eaten, but before long, hunger returns. Snacking in the afternoon becomes the logical solution, then there is no desire for food at six p.m., so dinner is delayed until later. This requires the stomach to work during sleeping hours, and a restless night follows.

FRUITS

	Edible Calories per 100 grams (3 1/2 oz.)	Protein %	Fat %	Carbohydrate %
Apples	58	1.2	8.7	90.1
Apricots	51	6.6	3.3	90.1
Avocados	167	4.2	82.2	13.6
Bananas	85	4.3	2.0	93.7
Blackberries	58	7.0	13.0	80.0
Blueberries	62	3.8	6.9	89.3
Breadfruit	103	5.6	2.4	92.0
Carob	180	8.4	6.5	85.0
Cherries, sweet	70	6.3	3.7	90.0
Cranberries	46	2.9	12.7	84.4
Dates (dried)	274	2.7	1.5	95.8
Figs (fresh)	80	5.0	3.1	91.9
Figs (dried)	274	5.2	4.0	90.8
Gooseberries	39	6.9	4.4	88.7
Grapefruit	41	4.1	2.0	93.9
Grapes, American	69	6.4	12.1	81.5
Grapes, European	67	3.0	3.7	93.3
Guavas	62	4.4	8.1	87.5
Kumquats	65	4.6	1.3	94.1
Lemons	27	14.2	9.5	76.3
Lemon Juice	25	6.7	6.7	86.6
Limes	28	8.7	6.1	85.2
Loganberries	62	5.4	8.1	86.5
Loquats	48	2.7	3.5	93.8
Lychee Nuts (fresh)	64	4.7	3.9	91.4
Mangos	66	3.6	5.1	91.3
Muskmelons				
Cantaloupes	30	7.7	2.8	89.5
Casabas	27	14.3	0.3	85.4
Honeydews	33	8.1	7.6	84.3
Nectarines	64	3.2	0.6	96.2
Oranges	49	7.0	3.4	89.6
Papaya	39	5.2	2.1	92.7
Peaches	38	5.3	2.2	92.5
Pears	61	3.9	5.4	90.7
Persimmons	127	2.1	2.6	95.3
Pineapples	52	2.6	3.2	94.2

	Edible Calories per 100 grams (3 1/2 oz.)	Protein %	Fat %	Carbohydrate %
Plums	66	2.5	0.4	97.1
Pomegranates	63	2.7	4.0	93.3
Quinces	57	2.4	1.5	96.1
Raisins	289	2.9	0.6	96.5
Raspberries, red	57	7.1	7.3	85.6
Strawberries	37	6.4	11.4	82.2
Tangerines	46	5.8	3.6	90.6
Watermelons	26	6.5	6.4	87.1

GRAINS

Barley, pearled (light)	349	8.3	2.4	89.3
Buckwheat, whole grain (kasha)	335	11.8	6.0	82.2
Buckwheat flour, dark	333	11.8	6.3	81.9
Cornmeal, whole ground	355	7.1	9.2	83.7
Millet	327	12.1	7.9	89.1
Rolled Oats	390	12.6	15.9	71.5
Rice, brown	360	7.1	4.4	88.5
Rye Flour, dark	327	14.8	6.7	78.5
Triticale	329	14	5.7	80.3
Wheat, whole grain (hard red winter)	330	13.3	4.6	82.1
Wheat flour (whole), hard wheats	333	14.4	5.0	80.6
Wheat, shredded or wheat flakes (whole)	354	10.0	4.7	85.3
Wild Rice	353	14.2	1.7	84.1

LEGUMES, NUTS, SEEDS

Legumes

Beans, lima	123	23.6	3.4	75.6
Beans, lima, dried	345	20.5	3.9	73.0
Beans, red, dried	343	22.8	3.7	73.5
Beans, pinto, dried	349	22.8	2.9	74.3
Chickpeas (garbanzos), dried	360	19.8	11.2	69.0
Lentils, dried	340	25.3	2.7	72.0
Peanuts	582	15.6	70.0	14.4
Peanut Butter	581	16.6	71.2	12.2
Peas	84	26.1	4.0	69.9
Peas, dried	340	24.6	3.2	72.2

	Edible Calories per 100 grams (3 1/2 oz.)	Protein %	Fat %	Carbohydrate %
Soybeans	134	28.2	31.8	40.0
Soybeans, dried	403	29.4	36.8	33.8
Soy sauce	68	28.2	15.9	55.9
Tofu	77	38	51	11

Nuts and Seeds

Almonds	598	10.8	75.9	13.3
Brazil Nuts	655	14.2	66.9	10.9
Cashews	561	10.6	68.1	21.3
Chestnuts, fresh	194	5.2	6.5	88.3
Coconut, fresh	346	3.5	85.4	11.1
Coconut, dried	662	3.8	82.1	14.1
Filberts	560	12.1	60.0	16.0
Pecans	696	7	85	8.4
Sesame seed, dried	563	11.5	73.0	15.5
Sunflower seeds, dried	560	14.9	70.6	14.5
Walnuts	628	11.3	79.1	9.6

VEGETABLES

Asparagus	26	23.5	6.4	68.9
Bamboo Shoots	27	23.5	9.3	68.9
Bean sprouts (mung beans)	35	26.6	4.9	67.4
Beans, green (snap beans)	32	14.5	5.3	80.0
Beets (raw)	43	10.2	1.9	88.4
Beets (cooked)	32	9.4	2.6	86.2
Broccoli	32	27.5	7.8	65.9
Brussel sprouts	45	26.7	7.3	65.8
Cabbage	24	13.3	7.1	80.4
Carrots	42	7.4	4.0	88.8
Cauliflower	27	24.4	6.3	68.9
Celery	17	12.9	4.9	81.8
Cucumbers	15	14.7	5.6	80.7
Eggplant	25	11.6	6.8	80.0
Jicama	25	—	—	—
Kale	38	26.8	17.6	56.3
Kohlrabi	29	16.9	2.9	81.0
Leeks	52	12.0	4.8	83.2

	Edible Calories per 100 grams (3 1/2 oz.)	Protein %	Fat %	Carbohydrate %
Lettuce, Romaine	18	17.8	12.9	69.4
Lettuce, Iceberg	13	16.9	7.0	75.3
Mushrooms	28	25.4	8.9	54.7
Okra	36	16.4	7.0	75.3
Onions	38	11.0	2.2	87.8
Parsley	44	20.0	11.4	68.9
Parsnip	76	6.2	5.5	88.4
Potatoes	76	7.6	1.1	90.7
Potatoes, baked in skin	93	7.7	0.9	91.4
Pumpkin	26	9.4	3.2	89.2
Radishes	17	16.3	4.9	81.2
Squash, summer varieties	19	14.2	4.4	79.0
Squash, winter varieties	50	6.8	5.0	88.6
Rutabagas	46	6.7	1.8	91.7
Sweet potatoes	114	4.1	2.9	93.0
Sweet potatoes, baked in skin	141	4.1	3.0	92.9
Tomatoes	22	12.3	7.7	76.4
Tapioca	352	.5	.5	98.9
Turnips	30	9.3	5.7	84.3
Watercress	19	28.4	13.2	56.3
Water chestnuts	79	4.9	2.2	92.4
Olives	191	4.0	98.0	2.0

MEATS, FISH, DAIRY PRODUCTS

Meat, Poultry

Beef rib, roasted	241	50.0	50.0	0
Hamburger, lean, raw	179	49.9	50.1	0
Hamburger, lean, cooked	219	53.4	46.6	0
Sirloin, choice grade (raw)	313	23.1	76.9	0
Sirloin, choice grade (broiled)	387	25.4	74.6	0
Chicken, light meat (roasted)	166	81.5	18.5	0
Turkey, light meat (roasted)	176	80.0	20.0	0
Leg of lamb, roasted (prime gr)	319	32.1	67.9	0
Pork loin, roasted	362	28.9	71.1	0

Fish, Shellfish

Cod, raw	78	96.5	3.5	0

	Edible Calories per 100 grams (3 1/2 oz.)	Protein %	Fat %	Carbohydrate %
Cod, cooked (canned)	85	96.5	3.2	0
Crab, steamed	93	79.4	18.4	2.2
Flatfish, raw (sole, sand dab, flounder)	79	90.5	9.5	0
Halibut, raw	100	89.1	10.8	0
Salmon, canned (Red or Sockeye; solids and liquid)	171	50.7	49.3	0
Scallops, steamed	112	88.7	11.3	0
Shrimp, canned, drained	116	89.0	8.5	2.5
Tuna, canned in oil, drained	197	62.5	37.5	0
Tuna, canned in water, not drained	127	94.2	5.8	0

Eggs, Milk

Eggs, whites	51	93.2	1.0	5.8
Eggs, poached	163	34.0	64.2	1.8
Milk, whole (3.5% fat)	65	23.0	47.6	29.4
Milk, skim	36	42.8	2.5	54.7
Milk, goat	67	20.4	52.8	26.8
Milk, human - 1 cup	192	5.0	45.0	48.0

Cheeses

Cheese, blue or roquefort	368	24.9	73.0	2.1
Cheese, cheddar	398	26.8	71.1	2.1
Cheese, uncreamed	86	84.4	3.1	12.5
Cheese, parmesan	393	39.1	58.1	2.8

Source of Information:

Edible calories per 100 grams: directly from data in U.S. Dept. of Agriculture Handbook No.8, Table 1.

Percent of total calories of protein, fat and carbohydrate: Computed from data in U.S. Dept. of Agriculture Handbook No.8, Table 1 and Table 6.

All figures given are for uncooked foods, unless specifically mentioned as cooked.

BREAK THAT FAST!

Breakfast is literally breaking a fast - an overnight fast. The need for an adequate breakfast is little realized by the vast majority of Americans who either skip or skimp on their morning meal. Let us look at some of the reasons why eating a nutritious breakfast is important.

Physiologists and nutritionists at the State University of Iowa did a study on the subject which came to be known as the "Iowa Breakfast Study." From their research these scientists concluded that "when you eat an adequate breakfast you can turn out more work during the late morning hours, you are quicker in your reactions, and you do not tire as easily."[1]

Junior high school boys taking part in this experiment showed better attitudes and scholastic attainments when they ate breakfast. On the other hand, workers who omitted breakfast suffered from increased fatigue, irritability, reduced work output, increased tremors, and slowed reaction time. During these conditions, strain is placed on the body, proneness to accidents is increased, and the 10 o'clock slump occurs.

Contrary to popular opinion, the coffee break is not a solution to the problem. In fact, because it is a stimulant and contains little nutritive value, coffee may cause a deeper drop in physical and mental efficiency after its 'lifting' effects have disappeared.

Many skip breakfast with the mistaken idea that it will help them lose weight or that if they eat breakfast they will gain weight. But this is not true. In fact, eating a good breakfast will aid in the maintenance of appropriate weight because it will alleviate ravenous hunger throughout the day. It is between meal snacks and late, high caloric suppers that result in excess fat.

How can one get a nutritionally adequate breakfast? First of all, breakfast should be the heartiest meal of the day. At breakfast time the stomach is in a better condition to digest more food than at the second or third meal of the day. The habit of eating a small breakfast or no breakfast and a large dinner is not healthful. It is a poor way to treat the stomach. Because the stomach plays such an important part in handling all the food one eats, and in preparing it for assimilation into the body, one must take proper care of it to expect good performance. **So make breakfast your heartiest meal, supplying at least ⅓ of the day's calories and nutrients.** It is simple to do this by eating whole grain cereals, waffles, and breads; milk or soy milk; nuts or nut butters; and delicious fresh or dried fruits.

To avoid the morning rush with its temptation to skip breakfast, you may find it helpful to prepare some of the food, or perhaps set the table, the night before.

It is never too late to begin a healthful routine of "breaking the fast." At first, you may find it difficult to enjoy eating in the morning. But keep up the endeavor. Soon you will love it! Remember — *Breakfast in the morning starts your day out right and keeps it going that way!*

[1] Cereal Institute Inc., *Breakfast Source Book*, Chicago, IL

GRAINS

THE MOST IMPORTANT FOOD

Grains represent the most important single item in the diet. For many nations grains in some form represent the main dish at all meals. For us, personally, we can expect to have a better disposition, greater ambition, increased ability to successful work production, and greater ability to experience happiness. With all of these benefits, it is important to carefully examine the grains and study how they can be used in our own menus.

TWO MISTAKES

Most people make *two mistakes* in their use of grains in that they *use them polished,* and they *fail to cook them long enough.* Grains are packaged in such a way that the vitamins and minerals are carried almost entirely on the outer shell. Milling generally removes this outer shell, leaving a white, easily ground central kernel, which is almost devoid of vitamins and minerals. The central portion has the starch and the protein, but both of these are difficult for us to metabolize without the accompanying minerals and vitamins. The B vitamins are required, also certain other vitamins, in the metabolism of protein. We can easily see that grains are made to order when used as the whole grain but become much less efficient in the body metabolism when polished. Bleaching is another thief of the vitamins and minerals of the grain.

LONG, SLOW COOKING

Many people fail to cook the grain long enough to release the chemical bonds between the small units of the molecules. Our digestion is not strong enough to entirely split many molecules in grains, thereby causing us to suffer some distress in the colon, to form gas or to fail to receive all the benefits possible from the whole grains. The *harder grains* need more than an hour of cooking, *preferably several hours.*

THE REAL STAFF OF LIFE

There are a number of grains, each having individual chemical characteristics and flavor qualities, that make a whole new world of eating experiences with each line of grains. Rice, for instance, can be cooked out dry and used with a number of sauces, spreads, gravies, and soups. By simply increasing both the cooking time and the amount of water, the end product is creamy and can be used as a porridge for breakfast; can be congealed, sliced, and baked; or can be shaped while still hot into patties after seasoning with a variety of herbs and diced vegetables. For each grain, the number of different styles of cooking is as varied as the number of grains. A cookbook having a good section on grains is a valuable asset to any kitchen, as valuable as the stove and the blender.

HEALTH STORES

Special food stores carry many of the grains, whole, flacked, cracked, etc.

THE GRAINS

BARLEY: This grain grinds into a very fine, white flour which can be used to make white gravies and to vary whole grain breads. It must be used with wheat to make a light, yeast bread. It is high in malt and has a delightful, mild flavor. When dextrinized before use, the flavor is enriched.

BUCKWHEAT: This seed is not actually one of the grains, but because of its chemical content is widely used in the same fashion that grains are used. It has a fairly strong flavor, and when used whole or as the flour, it is well to mix it with one of the more bland grains such as corn, rice, or millet. It has a high biologic value, being rich in vitamins and minerals, it deserves much greater popularity than just as buckwheat griddle cakes.

CORN: Corn was first grown in North America, and continues to be our most widely used grain in this hemisphere. Being a large grain on a large ear, it grows luxuriantly and is an important seed crop. When used in rotation with the other grains, it is an important nutrient. It should be considered, as with all the grains, to be one among many, and not a steady diet. Corn can be used in the "milk stage" as whole kernel or cream corn, and served as a vegetable in the menu. It has many uses as the hoecake, griddle cake, waffle, mixed with soybean flour to make a raised cornbread, chapitis, fritos, enchilatas, and tortillas. By using a coarse grind, grits are produced which can be used in a variety of ways: 1. breakfast porridge, 2. congealed porridge sliced and baked. 3. mixed with other grains, etc. Serving grits and gravy, a variety of fruit sauces, numberous nut or soy spreads such as peanut butter or almond-date jam, no-oil soy mayonnaise, tomato gravy, etc. are delicious with grits.

MILLET: Millet is a cereal commonly used in Europe and gaining much popularity in this hemisphere. It has a bland flavor and can be used in much the same way as corn or rice. Many recipes are included in this book.

OATS: This is one of our more common cereal grains of quite high biologic value. It can be used as the whole grain, the rolled grain, grits or coarse cracked oats, flour or meal. The flours can be used in breads, and the other forms can be cooked as breakfast foods, or used to give body to casserole dishes and stews, and to make patties or burgers. This important grain has many uses, and should not be thought of merely as "oatmeal". Try the oatburgers.

RICE: The most important grain in the economy of the orient, rice has kept much of China alive and healthy for the last three centuries. Not until polishing the grain became a common practice did nutritional deficiencies exist in China when rice was abundant. It has a very high quality protein, and many essential vitamins and minerals. One who is on a varied diet of fruits and vegetables will have his diet completed by rice. The great travesty against this grain is polishing. Use brown rice.

RYE: This hardy cereal grain is widely grown for its grain as well as it straw. It makes a quick growing pasture grass in some of its species. The flour made from rye should be used to vary the nutritive content of breads, to make gravies, and to thicken soups and casserole dishes. Very delightful breakfast cereals can be made by using several kinds of grains together.

WHEAT: There are many grains in this group of cereal grasses. Each of the different species has somewhat different amino acid content as well as vitamin and mineral spectrum. Generally, when bread is spoken of, one thinks of wheat bread. Like rice, it has been subjected to a great injustice in that the major nutritive properties are removed in the milling process for the production of a finer flour and a product that will keep for long periods on the grocery shelf. The long keeping quality of white flour is due to the separation of the rich vitamin and mineral bearing oils which are likely to become rancid. Bugs do not so readily attack the white flour products since the bugs recognize that the product is inferior and will not support their lives.

BREAKFAST

COOKING WHOLE GRAINS

3 METHODS

(T) THERMOS METHOD

Use one quart thermos

1-1/3 c. wheat, rye, barley, oats,
   or a combination of any of these.
2-2/3 c. water
1 t. salt

COMBINE whole grain, water and salt and soak 8-10 hours. **DRAIN** water into kettle and bring to boil and add whole grain. **PLACE** all back into thermos and screw cap on tightly. **LAY** thermos on its side for 8 hours.

CROCK-POT METHOD

Same amount of ingredients as above.

In the evening, place grain, salt and warm water in crock pot.

TURN to low and let it cook all night.

BOILING METHOD

Same amount of ingredients as above.

SOAK grain 8 hours.

COVER and allow to boil gently until tender and kernels break open.

Grains can be toasted before cooking. See rice recipe.

(T) BROWN RICE CEREAL
    8%   4%   86%

WASH rice lightly in warm water. Toasting the rice is optional, but it seems to bring out the flavor. To do this, place washed rice in a dry skillet and place over heat, stirring constantly, until lightly toasted.

COOK rice, use 2½ c. water and ½ t. salt for each cup of rice. Bring salted water to a boil. **ADD** rice, **STIR, TURN HEAT DOWN** to low, **COVER** and simmer until water is absorbed. **DO NOT STIR AGAIN.** Either long or short grain rice can be used, depending upon personal preference. Short grain seems to be more tender.

7-⅓ c. servings   95 calories per serving

(T) WHOLE OATS, BARLEY, AND RICE

½ c. cut oats   ½ c. rice
½ c. whole barley   3 c. water

MIX all together and **STEAM** for 1 hour. Can add fruit.

(T) ROLLED FOUR GRAIN CEREAL

½ c. rolled barley   ½ c. rolled wheat
½ c. rolled oats   ¼ t. vanilla
½ c. rolled rye   4 c. water

BRING water to a boil and add the grains and cook until done. Makes 4 cups.

(T) ROLLED WHEAT AND OATS

4 c. water
1 c. rolled oats
1 c. rolled wheat

ADD the rolled grains to boiling water and cook until done.

(T) DELICIOUS MILLET

1-1/8 c. millet
3 c. water
½ t. vanilla

STEAM about 40 minutes until millet is done. **ADD:**
½ c. pineapple
¾ c. chopped dates
STIR in and **STEAM** another 5-10 minutes. Makes 4 cups.

REMINDER

(T) Recipes are Therapeutic

(T) Therapeutic Recipes will not include nuts, seeds, avocados, olives or coconut.

For many of the following recipes, percentages are given. They represent protein, fat, and complex carbohydrates respectively.

   Example: Protein-7%   Fat-30%   C.C.-69%

MILLET BREAKFAST DISH

½ c. cornmeal   ½ c. chopped dates
½ c. millet   3 c. water

SIMMER millet and cornmeal in the water for about 1 hour. **ADD** rest of ingredients and serve hot.

(T) WHOLE MILLET CEREAL

1 c. millet
4 c. water
1 t. salt

COMBINE, bring to boil, cover and simmer until water is absorbed.

12-1/3 c. servings   52 calories per serving

GROUND-GRAIN TYPE CEREAL

GRIND whole grain (wheat, rye, barley, oats, millet, etc., or any combination of these) in Moulinex grinder or blender. For each cup of ground grain, use 2½ c. water. Bring 2 c. of the water to a boil. **MIX** the other ½ c. of water with 1 c. of the grain. **ADD** ½ t. salt to the water and stir in moistened grain. **STIR** until it begins to boil again. Turn off heat, cover and let stand 10 minutes. A mixture of grains provides a tasty and nutritious cereal.

(T) TRITICALE

4 c. water   ½ t. vanilla
3 c. triticale   few drops of almond extract

ADD triticale to boiling water. **ADD** flavorings and **COOK** until done. Makes about 5 cups.

(T) OATMEAL

1½ c. oats   1 t. vanilla
3 c. water   drops of almond extract

BRING water to a boil, then **ADD** oats and flavoring. **COOK** till done. Makes 3 cups. Can add raisins or dates.

(T) BAKED OATMEAL

2 c. rolled oats
1 med. apple, shredded
¼ c. raisins
1/16 t. coriander
1/8 t. cardamon
1 t. vanilla
1/16 t. pure coconut extract
6 c. water

COMBINE all ingredients and **BAKE** 1 hour at 350°. For a variation, substitute ¼ cup crushed pineapple for the apple and eliminate the coriander and cardamon. Yield: 6 cups.

BAKED OATMEAL
7%   30%   69%

3 c. regular oatmeal (may use quick oatmeal)
½ c. coconut
1 t. salt
¾ c. chopped dates
6 c. boiling water

MIX first four ingredients. **ADD** boiling water all at once. **BAKE** at 375 degrees for 35 to 40 minutes. May be baked in oven. Prepare night before using **COLD** water. Set timer for an hour before you wish to serve.

12-½ c. servings   78 calories per serving

(T) WHEAT BERRIES

2 c. wheat berries
4 c. water

PUT in steamer for 2 hours or until soft.

(T) CORNMEAL DELIGHT
7%   8%   90%

1 c. cornmeal
4 c. cold water
1 t. salt
2 c. chopped apple
¼ c. raisins

STIR cornmeal into cold water. **COOK** and add other ingredients. **PUT** into baking dish. **BAKE** 45 minutes to 1 hour at 350 degrees.

VARIATIONS:
     ¼ t. cardamon or
     ¼ t. anise or
     1 t. vanilla

12-½ c. servings   55 calories per serving

DELICIOUS MILLET
9%   34%   65%

1 c. millet
4 c. water
1 t. salt
½ c. coconut
½ c. toasted cashews
¾ c. chopped dates

COOK first 3 ingredients one hour. **SHORTLY** before serving, stir in last 3 ingredients.

10-½ c. servings   163 calories per serving

ONION FRENCH TOAST BATTER
10%   62%   32%

1 c. water
¼ c. cashews
1 T. arrowroot or cornstarch
1 t. onion powder
¼ t. salt

Follow instructions for "Cashew French Toast"
SERVE with fresh-sliced tomatoes

4-¼ c. servings   59 calories per serving

(T) CORN MEAL WITH CORN
11%   9%   86%

1 c. cold water
1 c. yellow corn meal
2 c. boiling water
1 t. salt
1 c. corn (frozen or canned)

STIR corn meal into cold water. **POUR** this into boiling water and stir to prevent lumping. **ADD** corn and reduce heat to simmer. Continue to cook for 30-45 minutes. This could be put into a casserole and baked for 45 minutes at 350 degrees.

10-⅓ c. servings   58 calories per serving

MUSELI

This can be a quick, nutritious breakfast with each person selecting the items of his or her choice. Mix it right in the cereal bowl. Use pineapple juice or apple juice, or nut milk for liquid.

Rolled oats, quick
  (grains should be lightly
  browned in oven or
  dry fry pan)
Rolled wheat
Almond meal or
Sliced almonds
Shredded fresh apple
Raisins
Dates
Sliced filberts
Currants

Cocount, plain or toasted
Sunflower seeds
Crushed pineapple
Sprinkle of salt
Drop or two of vanilla or
  almond extract
Pineapple juice
Apple juice - unfiltered
Nut milk

CASHEW FRENCH TOAST BATTER
10%   50%   46%

1 c. water
½ c. raw cashews **(omit for Therapeutic)**
4 dates
½ t. salt
1 T. whole wheat flour
3 T. Orange juice concentrate
1 banana (optional)

WHIZ in blender until smooth. **POUR** into shallow bowl. **DIP** slices of bread into it and place on cookie sheet and bake until golden brown. Turn and brown other side. May use teflon griddle. **TOP** with applesauce or fresh fruit.

6-½ c. servings   145 calories per serving

COCONUT-MILLET WAFFLES

6 dates
a little water to blenderize
3 c. oatmeal
½ c. millet flour
½ c. coconut   Blenderize with enough
1 t. salt   water to make 6 cups
1 t. vanilla

Bake in preheated iron on hottest setting for 8-10 minutes. If lid sticks at 8-10 minutes, wait a little more. **Cool** separately on racks. Good to make ahead the night before and make lots. **FREEZE** with wax paper in between.

SOY-OAT WAFFLES
19%   33%   70%

3¼ c. water (or more, to equal medium-thin batter)
1½ c. rolled oats (oatmeal)
2 T. sunflower seeds
1 c. soaked soybeans
½ t. salt
½ c. cornmeal
¼ c. coconut (optional)

SOAK soybeans several hours or overnight in sufficient water to keep covered. **DRAIN** and discard water. **COMBINE** all ingredients and blend until light and foamy, about half a minute. Let stand while waffle iron is heating. The batter thickens on standing. **BLEND** briefly. Pour into a pitcher for convenience. **BAKE** in hot waffle iron 10-15 minutes or until nicely browned. If waffle iron is hard to open, leave a few seconds longer.

NOTE: When serving a large number, bake waffles ahead of time. Stack separated with waxed paper. Just before serving, reheat in hot waffle iron just long enough to heat through for soft waffles or longer to make crisp. Do not allow to dry.

6 waffles   219 calories per serving

(T) TOPPING
3%   2%   98%

1 c. grape juice
1 c. apple juice
1 c. berries

28 calories per serving

12-¼ c. servings

THE WAFFLE PERFECT
13%   24%   65%

2½ c. oatmeal
¾ c. cornmeal
¾ c. whole wheat flour
⅓ c. nuts blended in
1 t. salt
1 c. water

STIR in 4 to 4½ c. hot water. **BATTER** will be thin as this makes a lighter waffle. **BAKE** in hot waffle iron 8-12 minutes. (Do not peek until at least 8 minutes). **SERVE** with 1 c. thickened grape juice, 1 c. applesauce, 1 c. blueberries or other fruit topping or spread. Waffles may be made ahead and frozen, then heated briefly in toaster. Batter may be mixed the night before and refrigerated.

6 waffles   278 calories per serving

(T) MULTI-GRAIN WAFFLES

3 c. water
2 c. rolled oats
½ c. rolled wheat
½ c. rolled rye
½ c. soy flour

COMBINE all ingredients in blender and blend until smooth. **LET** batter sit for about 5 minutes before spooning it into the hot waffle iron. **BE SURE** batter is not too thick; it's better a little thin than too thick. For variation you may add ¼ c. of date butter.

Yield: 6 waffles

(T) YUMMY GRANOLA

8 c. rolled oats (rolled rye or barley may be substituted for 2 c. of oats)
½ c. cornmeal

COMBINE above in large bowl and add the following:
Whiz in blender:

2 ripe bananas
½ c. water
1 c. chopped dates
1 T. vanilla

MIX well. **SPREAD** on cookie sheets ½ inch thick. **BAKE** at at 275⁰ approximately 90 minutes, stirring every 30 minutes until golden and dry. If not quite dry, turn oven off and leave pans in oven to complete drying. **STORE** in airtight container

(T) GRANOLA

6 c. old fashioned rolled oats
6 c. rolled wheat
1½ c. flaked rye
¾ c. soy flour

SIMMER until soft:

1½ c. apple juice
1 c. chopped dates

ADD: 1 T. vanilla

STIR thoroughly. **BAKE** 200° for 2 hours, **STIRRING OCCASIONALLY.** If not dry enough, turn off oven and leave in until crisp.

CRUNCHY GRANOLA

| 10% | 61% | 35% |

MIX all together:
3½ c. oatmeal
1/8 c. soy flour
½ c. w.w. flour
½ c. broken nuts (filberts - walnuts)
½ c. sunflower seeds

BLEND:
1 c. coconut
¼ c. sesame seeds, ground
½ c. water
½ c. dates
1½ T. vanilla
1 t. salt

MIX all ingredients well. **SPREAD** ½" thick on two cookie sheets. **BAKE** in preheated oven at 225 degrees for 1 hour and 20 minutes to 1 hour and 40 minutes, or until golden and crisp or slightly browned. **STIR** twice and trade position of cookie sheets during baking to ensure even baking. Keep fresh by freezing part of it.

20-⅓ c. servings   104 calories per serving

FRUIT - NUT GRANOLA

| 10% | 30% | 64% |

HEAT electric fry pan to 350 degrees
1 c. water
1 c. dates

COOK until dates are soft and can be stirred into smooth paste.

ADD
1 pound 2 oz. quick oatmeal
¼ c. each, cocunut, sunflower seeds, rolled wheat

STIR for 7-10 minutes. **TURN OFF HEAT** and **STIR** in:
½ c. mixed dried fruit (raisins, apricots, apple)
½ c. chopped nuts (almonds, cashews, walnuts, filberts)

COOL COMPLETELY. Try this as a topping for banana ice cream.

20-¼ c. servings   137 calories per serving

GRANOLA

| 13% | 36% | 55% |

6 c. old fashioned rolled oats
6 c. rolled wheat
1½ c. flaked rye
2 c. raw sunflower seeds
2 c. coconut
2 c. nuts (pecans, walnuts, almonds - one kind or mixed)
¾ c. soy flour (optional)
1 T. salt
1½ c. apple juice
1 c. chopped dates
1 T. vanilla

SIMMER apple juice and dates until dates are soft. **COOL** and **STIR** all ingredients together and **BAKE** in oven 190 degrees to 200 degrees for two hours stirring every one-half hour. If not dry enough, turn off oven and leave it in oven for a while. **SHOULD BE CRISP.**

60-⅓ c. servings   134 calories per serving

SCRAMBLED SOY CHEESE

1 c. soy cheese
1-2 T. homemade Veg. broth (see recipe) or water
2 t. food yeast
Salt or vegesal to taste
Onion powder to taste or small onion, chopped
2 t. chicken style seasoning
½ t. soy sauce (optional)
¼ c. chopped green pepper and, or , 2 T. pimiento

COMBINE all ingredients and mix well. **TO HEAT** - Place in dry skillet over very low heat, stirring frequently. Optional -¼ c. chopped green pepper, 2 T. pimiento. (Use in place of scrambled eggs, or eggs in potato salad, or mixed with olives for sandwich spread, or mixed with a mayonnaise for "cream cheese" or "cottage cheese".)

(T) FRUIT TOAST

1 QUART OF ANY KIND OF FRUIT (cherries, apricots with pineapple, peaches, berries.) Arrowroot powder or cornstarch to thicken.

PUT fruit in kettle and heat. When hot ADD cornstarch mixed smooth with cold water, stirring constantly until mixture thickens. PUT over hot homemade Whole Wheat toast. Amount of cornstarch used will vary according to the amount of juice in the fruit.

(T) CHERRIES ON TOAST

5 c. cherries, pitted-with juice, if canned
¼ c. dates
1 t. vanilla
¼ c. orange juice

HEAT and serve over toast or waffles. Can place cherry mixture in baking dish and cover with granola for a crisp.

TOMATO SOUP
14%   51%   42%

1½ c. cashews
2½ c. water
1 qt. tomato sauce
1 qt. canned tomatoes
¼ t. garlic powder
½ t. salt
¼ t. sweet basil flakes

BLEND cashews and water until smooth. ADD rest of ingredients and bring almost to boil, but do not boil.

20-½ c. servings   87 calories per serving

COTTAGE FRIES

SLICE peeled, raw potatoes as cottage fries. Put on Pam-sprayed pan. Sprinkle with a combination of 1/8 t. garlic and onion powder, mixed, and 2½ t. nutritional yeast flakes. BAKE for 20 minutes. BROIL to brown.

(T) HASH BROWN POTATOES
10%   1%   89%

SHRED raw, scrubbed potatoes. BAKE either on a teflon griddle or a waffle iron lightly sprayed with Pam. Crispness is determined by the amount you put into the waffle iron or on the griddle. SEASON with salt, onion salt, etc. or grated onion and paprika or taco seasoning.

½ c. servings   75 calories per serving

(T) GOLDEN BREAKFAST POTATOES

COOK six large potatoes. While still warm, CUT into 1" cubes. Place on large, baking sheet. Sprinkle with chicken-like seasoning and Vegit. BAKE at 400° to brown.

(T) BREAKFAST BEANS

3 c. great northern beans, soak, freeze overnight. Cook with Indo (see page 45)
1 c. water
1 clove garlic
1 c. chopped onion

STEAM all ingredients until tender. Makes 6 cups.

SCRAMBLED TOFU
42%   48%   18%

Tofu is a concentrated food and should be used only occasionally. It is made from soybeans and can be made at home or purchased in food stores. Some of the nutrients as well as the fiber has been removed from the soy bean.

1 cube tofu - 1 lb.
1 T. soy sauce
½ c. chopped green onions or 1 T. onion powder
1½ t. chicken-like seasoning
1/8 t. paprika, or cumin

COMBINE ingredients in teflon skillet, breaking the tofu into particles the size of peanuts or larger if you wish. HEAT through. May be served as the hot dish for breakfast with whole grain toast or added to soup made with garbanzos, onion, chicken style seasoning, and noodles. Also good for sandwiches with sprouts and tomatoes. FOR VARIATION, add chopped tomato, diced green pepper, chopped black olives, chopped green olives, and pimiento.

4-½ c. servings   89 calories per serving

(T) RICE BREAKFAST PATTIES

20 c. cooked rice, unsalted, well done
1½ c. flour
1 c. date butter
1½-3 c. water

MIX all ingredients. Mixture should be stiff. ADD only enough water and flour so you can make patties. Form into ¼ c. patties. BAKE in a 350° oven 45-60 minutes or to a golden brown. Makes 80 patties.

(T) CRANBERRY FRUIT SAUCE
2%   6%   99%

1 lb. cranberries
1 qt. water, Cook to pop. Pour off liquid. Save.
4 apples, sliced
½ c. water
¼ c. frozen apple juice concentrate. Cook until apples are soft.
1 can crushed pineapple - 20 oz.

COMBINE all and cook for a few minutes. Good on toast, pancakes, waffles, or for holidays. Juice from cranberries may be used adding equal parts of apple, pineapple and orange juice. Use as base for pudding, etc., or as jelly for toast. Thicken with arrowroot starch, cornstarch or tapioca.

12-¼ c. servings   72 calories per serving

(T) PINEAPPLE-ORANGE SAUCE
4%   2%   98%

1/3 c. orange juice concentrate
1 c. pineapple juice
2 c. chunky pineapple
1 small banana
2/3 c. water

BLEND and **HEAT. THICKEN** with starch if necessary. Makes 4 cups.

16-¼ c. servings   39 calories per serving

(T) LEMON SAUCE

1 c. unsweetened pineapple juice
1 T. lemon juice
1 t. vanilla
2 T. cornstarch

MIX ingredients in saucepan and cook over medium heat until thick; stirring as necessary to keep smooth. **POUR** over baked apple dish. Serve hot or cold.

(T) ORANGE DATE SAUCE

2 c. dates
2 c. water
½ c. orange juice

COOK until soft. **BLEND** date mixture with 1 c. orange juice. Serve over waffles, French toast, etc.

(T) APRICOT PINEAPPLE SAUCE

2 c. apricots blended or apricot puree

ADD 2 c. apricots cut in pieces and 2 c. crushed pineapple. **HEAT** in kettle until boiling. **ADD** arrowroot or cornstarch to thicken. Serve over toast, waffles, or French toast.

(T) BLUEBERRY SYRUP

3 c. unsweetened grape juice
3-4 T. arrowroot or cornstarch
2 c. fresh or frozen blueberries
1/8 t. lemon juice

COMBINE juices and thickners in saucepan. **COOK** until thickened. Sauce should be thin like a syrup. If it gets too thick, add more grape juice. **ADD** blueberries. Serve warm or hot. Good over waffles, pancakes, and french toast. Can blend blueberries and add to thickened juice, but will need more thickener.

(T) STRAWBERRY SAUCE

2 c. pineapple juice
1/5 c. arrowroot or cornstarch
3 c. strawberries

MIX starch with some of the pineapple juice. **HEAT** rest of pineapple juice to boiling point then add the starch mixture. **STIR** until thick. **ADD** strawberries and serve. Makes 5 cups.

(T) STRAWBERRY PINEAPPLE BANANA SAUCE
(Fruit Sauce)

BLEND strawberries, crushed pineapple, and bananas in blender. **HEAT** adding arrowroot or cornstarch to thicken. (Mix starch with water before adding to hot mixture). Serve over waffles or toast.

(T) PEACH BERRY SAUCE

THICKEN canned peaches with the juice with tapioca or cornstarch. Just before serving, **ADD** a few blueberries.

(T) CURRANT DELIGHT
1%   —   100%

1-½ c. unsweetened grape juice (purple)
1 c. currants
1 T. minute tapioca

PLACE ingredients in a saucepan. **BRING** to a simmer, then turn off heat. Cover and let stand 30 minutes. Then turn on heat and simmer very slowly about 5-7 minutes until tapioca turns translucent. **REFRIGERATE** and use as a topping for waffles, Cashew French Toast, or as a spread for bread. This is best if made the evening before you need it as the currants hydrate more and appear like little berries. **VARIATIONS:** omit currants and use any juice. Thicken with 1 T. cornstarch or 2 T. tapioca per cup of juice.

16-1/8 c. servings   18 calories per serving

(T) SPICY-APPLE SYRUP
—   —   100%

1-½ c. apple juice
1 T. arrowroot powder or cornstarch
2 T. lemon juice
1/8 t. cardamon

BRING to boil, stirring constantly, until clear.

12-1/8 c. servings   15 calories per serving

(T) RICE CRACKERS

1 c. short grain rice
3 c. hot water
1 t. salt

COOK 45 minutes - until rather soft.

1 c. rice, **MASH** and taste for salt—add if needed. Put rice on wax paper by heaping tablespoonfuls and put wax paper on top and roll out. Rice may stick a little. **SPRINKLE** corn meal lightly on baking sheet. Transfer rice cakes to baking sheet. Bake 300 degrees for 45 minutes or until brown and crisp. Makes about 25 crackers, 2x2 inches.

(T) ONION CRISPS
8%   4%   86%

1 c. cooked rice
½ t. dried onion flakes

MASH onions into rice and prepare as for Rice Crackers.

4 servings   44 calories per serving

(T) CORN CRACKERS
10%　　10%　　83%

1 c. freshly ground cornmeal
¾ t. salt
½ c. boiling water

MIX AND ROLL thin as you can. *BAKE* in 350 degree oven until crisp and brown. Check in 20 minutes.

4 servings　　　　　　　　　104 calories per serving

SESAME CRACKERS
21%　　32%　　53%

1/3 c. almonds
1/3 c. sesame seeds

GRIND almonds and sesame seeds, each one separately, in Moulinex grinder until silghtly pasty. *PUT* into blender and add 2/3 c. water and blend until very smooth. *PUT* the following in a bowl and mix well:

½ c. whole wheat flour
½ c. barley flour (or whatever available)
¼ c. rye flour
½ c. rolled oats
½ t. salt
1/3 c. full fat soy flour (sift)

ADD blended mix to dry ingredients that have been thoroughly mixed together in bowl. *MIX* well and knead lightly. Dough should not be sticky when all dry ingredients are kneaded in. If it is, add a bit more w.w. flour as needed. *ROLL* between wax paper until very thin (1/8" or less). Put on a cookie sheet. *CUT* in squares and prick with fork. *BAKE* at 400 degrees until lightly browned and crisp. Walnuts, pecans or cashews can be substituted for almonds. *NOTE:* The crackers on the outer edges of the pan will brown more quickly than those in the middle. *REMOVE* them when brown and continue baking the rest until they are brown.

11 servings　　　　　　　　78 calories per serving

SESAME CRISPS
11%　　55%　　38%

1 c. cooked rice
3 T. sesame seeds, ground

PREPARE as Rice Crackers.

4 servings　　　　　　　　　122 calories per serving

(T) INDIAN CORN CRACKERS OR CORN CHIPS
11%　　9%　　83%

1 c. corn flour (freshly grind the Indian Corn)
½ t. salt
1-2 T. flax meal or whole wheat flour
enough water to hold it together

ROLL OUT between sheets of wax paper. *PLACE* on cookie sheet lightly sprinkled with corn meal. *CUT. BAKE* in moderate oven until lightly browned.

4 servings　　　　　　　　　121 calories per serving

JEAN'S CRACKERS
17%　　34%　　55%

2 c. rolled oats
1½ c. whole wheat flour
½ c. ground sunflower seeds (optional)
1/3 c. ground almonds　　½ t. salt
1/3 c. coconut　　　　　　1 c. water or more

MIX lightly. *DIVIDE* dough and place on 2 non-stick baking sheets. *COVER WITH CLEAR WRAP AND ROLL OUT.* Cut in squares. *BAKE* at 325 degrees until brown 20-30 minutes. *REMOVE* edge squares as they brown.

20 servings　　　　　　　　101 calories per serving

CRACKERS
14%　　48%　　42%

2 c. oatmeal
½ c. cashew nuts (blenderize oatmeal and cashews until fine)
1 c. whole wheat flour
½ c. sesame seeds (grind half of the amount in seed grinder)
½ c. sunflower seeds, ground　1 t. vanilla
1 c. water　　　　　　　　　　1 t. salt

MIX dry ingredients in a bowl. *ADD* liquid and mix. *ROLL* out very thin between sheets of wax paper and put on cookie sheet. *CUT* in squares, salt lightly and bake at 350 degrees for 15 minutes. *WATCH* carefully. You may have to remove the outer edges if they become brown first. *BAKE* until nice, light brown.

10 servings　　　　　　　　227 calories per serving

COCONUT OR SESAME STICKS
15%　　43%　　47%

1½ c. whole wheat flour
½ c. soy flour
1 T. date sugar or 3 dates blended in the water
1/3 c. shredded unsweetened coconut
1/3 c. sesame seeds
½ t. salt
1/3 c. walnuts ground fine in nut grinder
¾ c. cold water

MIX w.w. flour, soy flour, coconut, date sugar and salt. *ADD* walnuts and blend in well with fork. *ADD* water. *MIX* well and roll up into a ball and *KNEAD* until all dry ingredients are well moistened and stay together in a smooth ball. *ROLL* into lengths about ½" around and *CUT* into 3" sticks. *BAKE* at 350 degrees about ½ hour or until golden brown.

8 servings　　　　　　　　　193 calories per serving

(T) BURRITOS OR WHEAT LEFSE
16%   5%   85%

3 c. whole wheat pastry flour
½ c. nuts and seeds ground fine (brazil and sunflower seeds
  work well.)
1 c. water
½ t. salt

ADD salt to flour. **COMBINE** all ingredients, stirring to combine flour and water evenly. **MAKE** into ball. **DO NOT KNEAD** as this develops gluten and will make the product tough. You may need to add a bit more water. **ROLL OUT** thin or pat out with fingers until thin and nicely rounded. **BAKE** on a teflon griddle or silver stone pan, medium hot, as the product should be pliable enough to roll. **SERVE** with mashed beans, green onion, tomatoes, olives, chopped green peppers, guacamole, chopped lettuce, sprouts—whatever you enjoy. **TOP** with cashew jack cheese, taco sauce (mild), homemade catsup, or use the No-Oil Soy Mayonnaise with chopped green onion.

12 servings-1 large   100 calories per serving

APPLE-OATMEAL MUFFINS
9%   36%   60%

1 c. finely shredded apples
1½ c. rolled oats
½ t. salt
½ c. raisins or chopped dates
½ c. chopped nuts (use Moulinex to get them fine)

SOFTEN dates in small amount of water and mash. **COMBINE** all ingredients. Let stand until moisture is absorbed. **MIX** together lightly with fingers or fork. With spoon, pack lightly into muffin pans. **FILL WELL** and **ROUND** nicely. **BAKE** at 375 degrees for 25 minutes.

12 servings   98 calories per serving

(T) SPROUTED WHEAT BREAD

2 c. wheat soaked in 1½ c. water for 12 hours.

DRAIN and rinse twice daily until sprouts are the length of the grain. **DON'T RINSE** the last day so the sprouts will be as dry as possible. **PUT** sprouted wheat through food grinder and **ADD** 1 c. raisins alternately with the wheat. You may add any additional dried fruit that you wish such as dates, apples, apricots, etc. **PUT** into a small pan which has been sprinkled with cornmeal. **FORM** the loaf as it will not rise. **BAKE** at 250 degrees for 2 hours. **SERVE** warm or toasted. You may add whole raisins instead of ground raisins if you wish.

(T) APPLE SAUCE MUFFINS

2-3 c. applesauce
3 c. rolled barley and wheat
3 c. chopped dates
1 c. orange juice concentrate

COMBINE all ingredients and let stand for a few minutes to allow absorption of moisture. Place papers in muffin tins or spray with PAM and coat with bran. **FILL** using a #16 scoop. **BAKE** at 350° for 25 minutes or until lightly browned.

Yield: 16 muffins

FRESH FRUIT MUFFINS
10%   24%   72%

STIR together:

½-¾ chopped dates or any other dried fruit
2 c. rolled oats
1 T. vanilla
1 c. coconut (optional)
3 c. crushed fruit (pulp and juice)
2 c. whole wheat flour
½ t. salt

May need more flour or liquid depending on how juicy your fruit is. Be sure to **THAW FROZEN FRUIT** before using. **PUT** in pan (muffin or cake) and **BAKE** at 350 degrees for about 50 minutes or firm to touch.

24 servings   108 calories per serving

(T) TACO CHIP SEASONING
45%   5%   43%

½ c. chicken-like seasoning
1 c. food yeast
1 t. onion salt
1 t. garlic salt
1 t. paprika
½ t. cumin
½ c. dried parsley   Sufficient for 96 Tortillas

SHAKE the seasoning mixture from a sieve over the whole tortilla, **STACKING** them on top of each other. The tortilla is damp and the seasoning will stick to both top and bottom of the tortilla. **CUT** 4 or more at a time in the size you wish or leave whole. **SPREAD** singly on cookie sheet and **BAKE** in oven until crispy done, but not too brown. These may be done under the broiler for a more tender product, but they must be watched very closely! A toaster-oven also works well.

96 Tortillas   90 calories per tortilla

OATMEAL GEMS
15%   27%   62%

3 c. oatmeal
1 c. millet four
1 t. salt
1/3 c. full fat soy flour
1/3 c. sunflower seeds or cashews
1¼ c. water

COMBINE dry ingredients except sunflower seeds. **MIX** well. **BLEND** well the sunflower seeds in 1¼ c. water. Add liquid mixture to dry ingredients. Let set about 10 minutes. **SPOON** into little mounds or shape like biscuits on prepared cookie sheet. **BAKE** at 350 degrees until lightly browned - about 1½ hour. (More water can be added if dough does not stick together.)

12 servings   177 calories per serving

CORN DODGERS
9%   22%   72%

3 c. cornmeal
½ c. unsweetened coconut
1 t. salt
2¼ c. boiling water

MIX and *SPOON* onto non-stick cookie sheets. *BAKE* at 375 degrees for about 30 minutes. Makes 10 dodgers.

10 servings   155 calories per serving

CORNMEAL RICE CAKES
15%   47%   42%

1 c. cornmeal   1 c. cooked rice
4 T. soy flour   ½ c. ground sunflower seeds
½ t. salt

MIX cornmeal, flour and salt. *ADD* 1 c. boiling water. *MIX* well until moisture is absorbed. *ADD* rice and sunflower seeds. *MIX* and *PLACE* in mounds on cookie sheet. *FLATTEN* to about ½" thickness. *BAKE* at 400 degrees for 30 minutes or until brown. May serve with gravy.

12 servings   127 calories per serving

QUICK CORN BREAD
16%   37%   52%

2 c. water
1 t. salt
2 t. nut butter or equivalent
2 T. sesame seeds, ground in nut grinder
½ c. soy flour
¼ c. fine coconut
1½-2 c. cornmeal (use 1½ c. to begin and add if necessary)

COMBINE all ingredients and, using an electric mixer, beat well. *ADJUST* the cornmeal to make a soft batter. *HEAT* heavy muffin pan—I use the heavy iron pan—sprinkle a little corn meal in bottom of pan for each muffin and *SPOON* batter into the hot pan. *BAKE* immediately at 400 degrees for 35 minutes. This bread will actually rise about ¼ inch. Flavor is especially good if you use freshly-ground corn.

12 servings   72 calories per serving

CORN BREAD
22%   29%   53%

1-1/3 c. soaked soy beans
2 c. water
2 T. sesame seeds, ground
1 t. salt
1 t. date sugar or equivalent of dates
1½ c. cornmeal

LIQUIFY soy beans, sesame seed, salt, dates, or date sugar and *PUT* in bowl and *ADD* cornmeal and mix thoroughly. Bake in prepared corn stick pans or muffin tins for 35-45 min. at 400 degrees. *SUGGESTION:* serve with creamed tomatoes. Make a white sauce (cashew gravy) add tomatoes and heat.

12 servings   134 calories per serving

(T) TORTILLAS
13%   12%   79%

5 c. flour (half golden and half whole wheat)
1 t. salt
4 T. cashew butter (grind cashews in nut grinder)
2 c. water

ROLL out thin on floured board or *MAKE* in tortilla maker. *BAKE* on non-stick griddle a few minutes.

If you do not wish to make Tortillas, they may be purchased in most markets. EL MOLINO makes a tortilla of corn, salt, water which is very nice.

30 Tortillas   74 calories per tortilla

NATURAL CORN CHIPS

1½ c. water   1 t. salt
¼ c. walnuts   ¼ c. oat flour
2 T. sesame seeds   1¼ c. cornmeal
1 T. coconut

BLEND all in blender. *SIFT* cornmeal lightly on non-stick baking sheets. *POUR* blended mixture thinly and spread evenly. This takes two pans. *BAKE* for 10 minutes at 350 degrees. *SCORE* with plastic knife and finish baking, 5-10 minutes more or until crisp and light brown and loosened from the pan.

CRISPY CORN BREAD

1 ¾ c. cornmeal
1 c. oatmeal
½ c. ground cashew nuts
¼ c. date sugar
1 t. salt
¼ c. coconut
2 c. water
1/8 c. ground sesame seeds

MIX well and *POUR* out onto baking sheet sprinkled with cornmeal. *TOP* with

2 T. coconut
¼ c. sesame seeds
½ c. chopped cashew nuts

BAKE 40-60 minutes at 375 degrees. Best when eaten warm the first day.

CORN CRISPS

1½ c. fine corn meal   ½ T. vanilla
1 c. water   ½ c. almonds, ground fine
little salt

BLEND and let set a few minutes. Blend again and drop in circles on a non-stick baking pan. Batter will be thin. *BAKE* 5-10 minutes in a 350 degree oven. They should be light brown and crisp.

(T) SOUTHERN PANCAKES

2 c. cornmeal
1 T. date sugar
1 t. salt

½ c. rice milk
2 c. boiling water

MIX and **ADD** more water if necessary to make pancake consistency. **BAKE** on hot griddle. **TURN ONCE. SERVE** with thick applesauce or fruit syrups.

(T) EARLY MORNING PANCAKES

5-7 potatoes (may use leftovers)
⅓-½ c. rice milk
1 t. onion powder
3-4 freshly chopped parsley (or dried)

STEAM potatoes until tender. **MASH** until smooth with potato water or soy milk, parsley, salt, and onion powder. Should be moist to form into patties. **PLACE** on well-sprayed baking sheet. **BAKE** at 400° for 20-40 minutes, turning once. Pancakes should form a brown crust. **SERVE** with fresh parsley and tomatoes. A complement to tofu.

Yield: 1 dozen
1 pancake

Total Recipe 580 calories
49 calories

(T) CRISPY CORN CHIPS

Tortilla shells

PLACE each tortilla shell on baking sheet. Place another identical baking sheet over to top. **BAKE** in 350° oven until crispy. Good when used with soup or for tostados. May season with taco chip seasoning (page 33). Spray with water if not damp enough to hold the seasoning.

MILKS AND CREAMS

SESAME MILK

11%	66%	31%

½ c. sesame seeds
5 dates

¼ t. salt
4 c. water

SOFTEN dates by simmering in ½ c. water. GRIND sesame seeds in nut grinder until finely ground. PUT simmered dates, ground seeds, salt, and 2 c. water in blender and blend until smooth. POUR into container and add remaining 1½ c. water (use to rinse blender). STIR well. Delicious on cereals or as a beverage. Toasting the sesame seeds enhances the flavor and is said to make them more digestible. (250 degrees for 1-2 hours. Check occasionally as they should be just slightly brown.) Seeds may be browned in a dry fry pan.

16-¼ c. servings   34 calories per serving

SESAME MILK
for use in cooking

12%	82%	12%

GRIND ½ c. seeds. BLEND in 2 c. water until smooth. POUR into container and add 2 c. water. This can be used in place of milk in almost any recipe and has a comparable nutritive value.

16-¼ c. servings   27 calories per serving

SUNFLOWER SEED MILK

17%	76%	14%

The night before, put 1 cup of shelled sunflower seeds and 3½ cups water in the blender. COVER. Before breakfast, BLEND until you have a white milk and seeds are reduced to pulp. POUR into a fine wire strainer or strain through a thin cloth. The seeds can be soaked only a few hours, if you need the milk during the day. To retain all bulk and fiber, do not strain milks.

14-¼ c. servings   58 calories per serving

(T) BASIC RICE MILK
For General Cooking

2 c. brown rice (cooked very well)
2 c. hot water

Place rice and water alternately in blender and blend until smooth. This will be quite thick and gets even thicker as it sets. It may be used in gravies, sauces, and soups in place of milk.

RICE MILK

9%	45%	49%

1 c. cooked rice
2 c. water
½ t. salt

2 T. malt (optional)
½ c. cashews
4 dates (optional)

PUT all ingredients into blender. Blend until smooth. POUR into container and add enough water to make a total of 6 cups. STIR WELL when using, as it settles.

24-¼ c. servings   27 calories per serving

NUT MILKS - ALMOND OR CASHEW

almond: 11%	70%	27%
cashew: 10%	63%	33%

1 c. raw cashews or almonds
1 quart water
¼ t. salt

6 dates (optional) put in blender with cashews, if sweet milk is desired. May add bananas or other fruit for flavor.

PUT nuts, salt and 1½ to 2 c. water in blender and blend until smooth. POUR into container and add remaining water. Shake well each time before pouring into anything as it settles. This is not a drink but can be used over hot cereals.

24-¼ c. servings   Almond, 38 calories per serving
                          Cashew, 28 calories per serving

COCONUT MILK

4%	88%	13%

2 c. hot water
1 c. macaroon coconut (ground, unsweetened)
Dash of salt

ADD coconut to hot water and let stand for 20 minutes.

BLEND a few minutes. This is delicious on cereal, and can be used as milk in recipes. Strain only if necessary for a smooth product.

8-¼ c. servings   62 calories per serving

(T) OATMEAL MILK

13%	19.7%	69%

1 c. quick rolled oats
4 c. water
¼ c. soyagen (soy milk powder) or soy flour and a date
1 t. vanilla
1/8 t. salt
1-3 T. date sugar or equivalent of dates

BLEND until smooth. ADD 2 or more cups of water depending on richness you wish. May blend in fruit or coconut. Frozen fruits are nice blended in milk for use on cereals. To retain all bulk and fiber—do not strain.

24-¼ c. servings   19 calories per serving

CASHEW NUT CREAM

11%	68%	28%

¾ c. raw cashews or almonds
1 c. water
6-8 dates
½ t. vanilla
Pinch of salt

BLEND until smooth. Will thicken in refrigerator.

16-1 T. servings   86 calories per serving

COCONUT CREAM

7%   40%   54%

1 c. water
½ c. unsweetened coconut
¼ c. whole grain flour (barley best)
3 dates
¼ t. salt

LIQUIFY water, coconut and dates for 1 minute. Use unsweetened shredded or fresh coconut. *ADD* remaining ingredients and mix. *STIR* until thickened over medium heat. *COVER* and simmer very gently for 10 minutes. *SERVE* hot over fruit as dressing.

32-1 T. servings   101 calories per serving

CASHEW CREAM

12%   73%   21%

1 c. white grape juice
½ c. cashew nuts
¼ t. vanilla

BLEND until smooth and creamy. *SERVE* as topping for fruit pie or puddings.

16-1 T. servings   28 calories per serving

STRAWBERRY CREAM

9%   47%   49%

BLEND:
1½ c. water (cold)
½ c. cashews
½ c. cooked rice
1 c. frozen strawberries
¼ c. dates
Pinch of salt
1 t. lemon juice

CHILL until served.

VARIATIONS: Use any other frozen fruit in place of strawberries.

48-1 T. servings   9 calories per serving

(T) FRUIT MILK

2 c. pineapple juice
1 banana

BLEND
May use any blend of fruit and juice you wish. May soak dried fruit in water and blend as part of milk.

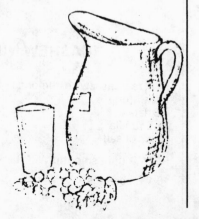

BREADS

BREADMAKING — EASY AND FUN

TIPS FOR SUCCESS

Read the recipe all the way through and know that you have the proper ingredients or suitable substitutes.

Understand the mixing method.

Use the freshest and best quality of flours. Grind your own if possible.

Keep temperature right. Too cold prolongs the rising. Yeast plants grow best at about 80 degrees.

Develop gluten by beating thoroughly a part of the wheat flour.

Dough should be about double in bulk when ready for baking.

Prepare pans with a very thin coating of lecithin and a layer of bran or corn meal on sides and bottom. This will prevent free fat from coating the bread, but will allow the product to be released from pan.

Bake until well done, about 45 minutes to an hour depending on size of loaf.

All yeast breads are more healthful when 2-3 days old. Slice, reheat (400° for 15 minutes for a loaf). It will be even tastier than fresh baked.

(T) WHOLE GRAIN BREAD
         15%   11%   77%

This recipe was developed especially for use in my breadmaking classes. It is a simple recipe and the bread is light, fine grained, and delicious.

2 c. whole wheat flour (100%) ½ c. oatmeal
2 T. date sugar   2 c. hot water
1 T. yeast   2½ c. whole wheat
1 t. salt   flour
¼ c. ground sunflower seeds

MIX first six dry ingredients together, stirring very well to thoroughly mix the yeast with the other ingredients. *ADD* 2 c. hot water and beat it for 200 strokes by hand or 2 minutes if you use an electric mixer. This mixture should be soupy and we mix it to develop the gluten. *ADD* 2½ c. whole wheat flour and mix to a firm dough. *LET IT REST* for 6-10 minutes. *SPRINKLE* a little flour on the table and empty the dough onto the table. *KNEAD* to a soft dough that bounces back almost instantly when tested. *MAKE* into two loaves. *PREPARE PANS* with Pam and bran flakes or if using teflon pans, just sprinkle the bran in the bottom of the pan and put a bit of bran on the sides and ends of the loaf and place the loaf in the pan to rise. *PLACE* the pan in the oven. *SET* the oven at 150 degrees and let the bread rise for 20 minutes or until it is to proper size. *TURN* the oven temperature to 350 degrees and bake the loaf for 45 minutes—or until well done. Remove from pan and cover with damp towel to soften crust.

30 slices   76 calories per slice

(T) WHOLE WHEAT BREAD
         15%   9%   82%

3 T. yeast
½ c. warm water - mix and set aside.

MIX 4 c. of hot water with 1 T. salt in mixer

PLACE in blender and blend thoroughly.

1 c. grape juice
16 pitted dates
½ avocado or ½ c. ground sunflower seeds

ADD this to the mixture in mixer.

1 c. apple sauce
9 c. whole wheat flour

THOROUGHLY beat this mixture for several minutes. *LET* this *RISE* for 1½-2 hours. *ADD* in about 1 cup whole wheat flour. *THOROUGHLY* knead and mix until smooth and elastic. *ADD* about 6 c. whole wheat flour. Knead down and shape into six loaves. *PLACE* in pans, sprinkled with cornmeal, and let rise until about double in size. *BAKE* at 350 degrees for 40 minutes.

90 slices   85 calories per slice

WHOLE WHEAT BREAD II
16%   21%   69%

½ c. warm water, 1½ T. yeast. Dissolve it in water. Let stand while other ingredients are mixed.
3 c. warm water
2 t. salt
½ c. ground almonds
½ c. sunflower seeds, ground
½ c. apple sauce or blended peaches
3 T. gluten flour

MIX all together along with yeast mixture. *ADD* 5 c. whole wheat flour. *KNEAD* and stir until it is thoroughly mixed. If more flour is needed, add about 2 or 3 cups to make a firm dough. *LET SET* for about three hours. Place a damp cloth over bread to keep from drying. Punch down and knead it again, then form it into loaves and place in prepared pans. *LET RISE* again from three to six hours. Bake in 350 degree oven for about an hour. Makes three large loaves or four small. Raisins or other fruit may be added to this bread.

60 slices   71 calories per slice

HERB BREAD
15%   18%   72%

3 T. apple juice concentrate (2 dates whizzed in blender or one apple blended may be used instead of the apple juice.)
½ c. fresh parsley, blended or 1 T. dried
1¾ c. water
½ c. cashew nuts blended in the water (warm)
2 T. yeast (Stir together and wait for yeast to dissolve)
½ c. sunflower seeds ground fine in seed grinder or could be blended with the above ingredients.
1 t. salt
½ t. dill weed
¼ t. sage
¾ c. cornmeal
4 c. whole wheat flour (or use half golden white)

KNEAD until smooth and elastic. *FORM* into 2 loaves and drop into the tall cans which have been thinly coated with Crisco and cornmeal. *LET RISE* double in size. *BAKE* at 350 degrees for one hour.   *(use juice cans)*

30 slices   82 calories per serving

(T) SWEDISH LIMPE BREAD
14%   7%   84%

6 c. warm water   4 t. anise seed
2 T. yeast   1 T. caraway seed
1 c. packed dates   Grated rind of 4 oranges
3 t. salt
8 c. rye flour and 12 c. whole wheat flour. A little more if needed.

DISSOLVE yeast in 1 cup warm water. *BOIL* together for one minute: 5 cups water, dates, salt, caraway and anise seed. *COOL*. *ADD* other ingredients and *KNEAD* well. *LET RISE* for 2 hours. *PUNCH DOWN* and let rise another hour. *KNEAD* and make into 6 loaves. *PLACE IN PANS* sprinkled with cornmeal. Let rise one hour or longer. *BAKE* in 375 degree oven for 45 minutes.

90 slices   119 calories per slice

(T) APPLE BREAD
15%   6%   84%

6 t. diastatic malt (opt.)
3 T. dry yeast
5 c. very warm water
2 apples
1 T. salt
8 c. whole wheat flour
1 c. rye flour
1 c. oatmeal

PUT malt, yeast, and 1 c. of very warm water in bowl. *BLEND* apples in 2 c. very warm water. In a large container. *MIX* 7 c. whole wheat flour, 2 T. salt and blended apples, 2 more c. very warm water and yeast mixture. *BEAT* with electric mixer for 2-3 minutes or very briskly by hand for 5 to 10 minutes or until very elastic. *ADD* 1 c. whole wheat flour, 1 c. rye flour, 1 c. oatmeal (any other flours may be used in the same amounts.) *STIR* vigorously until well blended. *COVER* and *LET RISE* until double in bulk. *DIVIDE* into equal parts (3 or 4 loaves). Take each part individually and place on floured board. *KNEAD* in more whole wheat flour to reach desired consistency. (It should be smooth, elastic and a little on the soft side). Too much flour makes it heavy and too little makes it fall. *PLACE* in pans sprinkled with cornmeal and let rise until double in bulk. *PLACE* in 400 degree oven. Turn down to 350 degrees and bake 1 hour. Loaf should sound hollow when tapped on top with fingers. Remove from pans and cool.

90 slices   65 calories per slice

(T) MULTI-GRAIN BREAD
7%   7%   81%

5 c. warm water (use ½ cup to soften 3 T. yeast)
¾ c. dates
4 c. whole wheat flour
¼ c. cashew nuts ground fine
1 T. salt
4 c. whole wheat flour
¾ c. gluten flour (opt.)
½ c. oatmeal
½ c. cornmeal (whole, ground)
½ c. rye flour

LIQUIFY dates in water. Cashews may also be liquified if you do not have a nut grinder. *ADD* to the 4 c. flour and yeast mixture. *BEAT* with mixer for five minutes. *ADD* whole wheat flour as needed and knead until firm and elastic. *SET* in a warm place to rise until double in bulk. *KNEAD* down. *FORM* into loaves. Let rise until double. *BAKE* for 10 minutes at 425 degrees and 40-45 more at 350. *REMOVE* from pans and cool on rack or turn loaf on side.

90 slices   72 calories per slice

(T) FAST WHOLE WHEAT BREAD
16%   5%   85%

4 T. dry yeast
½ c. warm water. Stir and set aside to work.

COMBINE in a bowl 5 c. hot tap water, 7 c. freshly ground whole wheat flour and 1 T. salt. **BLEND** ¼ c. dates in ½ c. water and add to the bowl mixture. Mix until well blended. **ADD** one cup flour to mixture and the yeast mixture and blend thoroughly. **ADD** 4 or 5 more cups flour and knead well. If using electric mixer, knead for 10 minutes on low speed. Shape into loaves and place dough in pans that have been sprinkled with cornmeal. **LET RISE** until double in bulk. **BAKE** at 350 degrees for one hour if loaves are large.

90 slices   60 calories per slice

(T) CRACKED WHEAT BREAD
16%   5%   84%

½ c. bulghur wheat soaked in ½ c. hot water *or*
  1 c. cracked wheat soaked in 1 c. hot water
2 T. yeast
½ c. water
2 c. whole wheat flour
2 c. unbleached white (may use all w.w. or some
  golden wheat)
¼ c. gluten flour (optional)
2 t. salt
2½ c. hot water with 1/3 c. dates blended or date sugar

BEAT the flour, salt and water with dates for about five minutes to develop the gluten. **ADD** yeast mixture and the soaked wheat to the bowl and mix. **ADD** 4 c. w.w. flour. It may need an extra cup of flour. **SET** it aside to rise for 30 to 40 minutes. **MAKE** into loaves. **LET** rise. **BAKE** 325-350 degree oven for almost an hour. Cover the last 15 minutes if getting too brown. May use tall juice cans.

60 slices   64 calories per slice

(T) CORN BREAD
14%   5%   86%

½ yeast cake
¼ c. lukewarm water
½ c. corn meal
1¼ c. water
1 t. salt
4 dates blended in 1¼ c. boiling water
2¾ to 3 c. flour (use whole grain flours of your choice or
  unbleached white for part of it)

COOK corn meal in 1¼ c. boiling water for 10 minutes stirring occasionally. When cool, **ADD** softened yeast and beat well. **ADD** flour and salt and mix well. **KNEAD** using as little flour as possible. Let rise. **MAKE** into loaves and let rise until double. Bake at 350 degrees. Makes two loaves. *A lovely bread!*

30 slices   51 calories per serving

(T) PEASANT BREAD
15%   6%   84%

1 heaping T. dry yeast
1 t. salt
1 T. dates blended in 2 c. warm water
  (may use ½ apple instead of dates)

STIR all together and then **ADD**
1 c. whole wheat flour
1 c. unbleached white flour or golden wheat

BEAT a few minutes to develop gluten. Then **ADD**
1 c. rye flour
1 c. w.w. flour
1 c. cornmeal

MIX and add flour until dough is no longer sticky. **KNEAD** until smooth and **LET RISE** until double. **PUNCH DOWN** and divide into two long loaves. **PLACE** on cookie sheet sprinkled with cornmeal and let rise. You may make cuts across the top of the loaves. **BAKE** 400 degrees for approximately 45 minutes—until nicely browned. May add caraway seeds and more rye flour for a rye loaf. May use some cracked wheat berries in a wheat loaf. A nice crusty bread.

30 slices   69 calories per slice

(T) GARLIC FRENCH BREAD

SHAPE Apple Bread dough as for French bread. **ROLL** top in sesame seeds. When baked and sliced, sprinkle each slice on one side with garlic powder and put back into oven wrapped in foil to rehead. **SERVE** warm.

(T) BROWN BREAD
17%   6%   82%

8 c. warm water
4 T. yeast
3/8 c. date sugar

MIX and set aside until foamy.
1 c. gluten flour
6 c. whole wheat flour

MIX with the yeast mixture and **BEAT** three or four minutes with electric mixer.
½ c. barley flour
½ c. millet flour
½ c. soy flour
½ c. cornmeal

ADD and continue to beat with mixer. If you have a bread mixer, you can finish by machine; otherwise you will knead by hand.

10 c. whole wheat flour—**MIX** in a little at a time using as much of the flour as you need. Let rise 30 minutes. Place pan in sink of warm water. **FORM** loaves—6. Let rise 20-30 minutes. **BAKE** 350 degrees, 45-50 minutes. Keep flour and pans warm at all times in bread making.

120 slices   71 calories per slice

(T) WHOLE WHEAT BREAD III
15%   11%   79%

Group 1
1 c. water
2 apples (core, not peel) blend with water
Group 2
2 T. diastatic malt
2 T. yeast
½ c. warm water. Place all in cup and let rise
Group 3
3½ c. very hot water from tap
½ c. ground sunflower seeds
1 c. oatmeal
1 c. flaked rye
10 c. freshly ground whole wheat flour
1 T. salt

In mixing bowl, *PLACE* group 1 and group 3. *BEAT* well and *ADD* group 2 and continue to mix for 10 minutes. *ADD* more flour if necessary to make a soft, non sticky dough. *MAKE* dough into 4 loaves. *PLACE* in pans with cornmeal or bran on the bottom. *PUT* cornmeal or bran on sides and end of loaf unless using non-stick pans. *PLACE* loaves in oven at 150 degrees for twenty minutes or longer if necessary until the loaf has risen to proper size. *TURN UP* oven to 350 degrees and bake for 45-55 minutes. *TAKE OUT* of oven and *COVER* with damp towel so the crust will soften. This bread is of a very fine texture and comes out perfect every time (so far). I've made it about ten times. I grind my flour fresh and use the Kitchenetic Bread Maker.

60 slices   89 calories per slice

OATMEAL RAISIN BREAD
13%   24%   69%

4 c. rolled oats
4 c. boiling water   *MIX* oats and boiling water
1 T. salt
1 c. dates blended in 1 c. water
3 c. raisins
1½ c. water - 2 T. yeast
2 c. walnuts
1 c. rolled barley
1 c. soy flour
2 c. whole wheat flour
6 c. white flour unbleached or golden flour

KNEAD until smooth. *LET* double in size. Makes 8 small loaves. *BAKE* at 400 degrees oven for 40-50 minutes. *BAKE* one hour or more if you make larger loaves.

80 slices   98 calories per slice

(T) WHOLE WHEAT ENGLISH MUFFINS
15%   16%   75%

2 T. yeast
2 c. cashew milk (1¾ c. warm water, ½ c. cashews blended)
2 dates added to blender mixture. Then mix with yeast and let stand till bubbly.
1 t. salt
½ c. cracked wheat
4½ c. whole wheat flour or part golden white (contains germ & some bran)

ADD half of the flour, the salt and cracked wheat to the liquid mixture, beating, mixing and stirring for a few minutes. This can be done in the mixer ½ minute at low speed scraping the sides of the bowl and then beat three minutes at high speed. *CONTINUE TO ADD* the flour and knead until smooth and elastic. *LET RISE* until double. *PUNCH* down and *LET REST* ten minutes. On a lightly floured surface, roll dough to slightly less than ½" thick. *CUT* with 4" round cutter, rerolling scraps. *DIP* top and bottom of muffin in cornmeal. *COVER* and let rise for 30 minutes or until very light. *BAKE* at medium low heat on ungreased griddle covered or ungreased fry pan covered or may be baked in 350 degree oven 25-28 minutes or until muffins are done. If not in oven, turn when half done. *COOL* on rack. To serve, split and toast.

12 muffins   199 calories per muffin

(T) PEAR BREAD
13%   6%   89%

2 c. chopped dried pears
4-5 fresh grated pears
4 T. frozen pineapple juice
2 cups each of the following:
    whole almonds, raisins, dats (made into butter), millet flour
3 T. grated lemon peel
4 c. whole wheat flour
½ c. soy flour
½ c. gluten flour
6 c. golden wheat flour (this includes the germ, but not all the bran)
4 c. warm water
4 T. yeast

DISSOLVE yeast in warm water with pineapple juice. Mix as for other bread. *LET RISE* once. *FORM* into loaves. *ROLL* top in almond slices. Let rise again. (Approximately 20 minutes.) Bake for 1 hour at 350 degrees.

80 slices   109 calories per slice

(T) DOUGH FOR COBBLER
15%   5%   86%

½ c. warm water
2 T. yeast
6 dates blended in

Then **ADD:**
½ c. warm water
2 t. salt
6¾ c. flour, plus enough flour to make a soft dough

ROLL out dough (flour board and rolling pin) and place on top of fruit thickened with cornstarch or arrowroot powder. **LET** rise and bake at 400 degrees until brown, then at 325 degrees for a total of 40 minutes. Makes enough for 2 large or 4 small pans of cobbler.

4 small   75 calories each

(T) DATE ROLLS
9%   3%   96%

dough for cobbler   1½ c. water
1½ c. dates   1 t. lemon flavoring

BRING to a boil and mash until smooth. **ROLL** out a piece of bread dough 12"x18" about ½" thick. **SPREAD** with date butter and roll up like jelly roll. May bake in a loaf pan as bread or cut with sharp knife into 1½" circles and place on pan. Let rise until double in size. **BAKE** these at 375 degrees for 20-25 minutes.

VARIATIONS: Instead of date mixture—1 c. raisins and 1 c. nuts. Sprinkle with anise, coriander and a little carob powder.

18 rolls   82 calories per roll

(T) SCOTTISH OAT CRISPS OR BISCUITS
14%   10%   78%

1 ¾ c. warm water
¼ c. dates blended in ¼ c. water
1 T. yeast

COMBINE in a large bowl. **SIFT** over yeast mixture and mix well:

3 c. oats, ground to flour in blender
1 t. salt

SIFT in 2 c. whole wheat flour until dough is not sticky and can be kneaded. **FORM** into soft ball and cover. Let rise to double. **TURN** out on board. Flatten to ¾" and cut out rounds with a glass for biscuits. For crisps, **ROLL** each round very thin. **PLACE** on cornmeal-sprinkled baking sheet and let rise 30 minutes. **BAKE** at 350 degrees until delicate brown.

20 crisps or biscuits   94 calories per crisp or biscuit

(T) OATMEAL CRACKERS
16%   16%   69%

1 T. yeast   ½ c. hot water
½ t. salt   1 t. dried onion flakes
1½ c. rolled oats (add as much as needed)

ROLL thin. Cover with dry towel and let rise one hour. Won't rise much. Place in cold oven. Set oven for 250 degrees for 15 minutes. Increase heat to 350 degrees. Bake until crisp and done—around 15 minutes.

6 servings   81 calories per serving

(T) PITA
16%   5%   84%

3-4 cups flour. (Use unbleached wheat flour or golden flour with some whole wheat mixed in or you may use whole wheat pastry flour exclusively)
½ T. salt

1 T. dry yeast dissolved in 2 cups water. **ADD** salt and flour and knead in additional flour if necessary until smooth. **CUT** into 24 balls; knead each ball until smooth and round. **COVER** and let rise about an hour. **FLATTEN** out balls on floured board with rolling pin and **COVER** to **LET RISE** about 45 minutes more or until slightly puffed. **PLACE** flat breads, bottom side on top on baking sheet. **BAKE** in very hot oven 550 degrees or as hot as oven will go for about two minutes or until browned and puffed in center. These may be opened in half and filled with any sandwich mixture you like. Good with lentils, beans, sprouts, cashew cheese, etc.

24 Pita   68 calories per pita

ANOTHER FILLING FOR PITA
57%   11%   34%

PUT 1-20 oz. can Loma Linda Vegeburger in fry pan over medium heat. **ADD** diced onion and season salt, a little basil. **SAUTE** gently and turn so it does not stick to the pan. **ADD** three or four cups of shredded cabbage and cook until barely done. **SERVE** hot in warmed pita.

12-½ c. servings   65 calories per serving

(T) FRUIT POCKETS

Use bread dough or dough for cobbler and roll it out thin. **CUT** circles the size of a tortilla tin, using the can for a cutter. **FILL THE CENTER** with chopped dates for sweetening or raisins and **ADD** apples, blueberries, coconut, blackberries, or whatever you would like or have on hand. Date sugar is good with any fruit. **DAMPEN** the outer edge of the circle with water and fold it in half. **USE** a fork to go around the edges to make a seal to keep in the juices. **PRICK THE TOP** with a fork to allow the steam to escape. The more fruit in the center, the better. These are great for breakfast, supper or fellowship dinners. **HEAT** and **SERVE.**

(T) NO KNEAD BREAD
16%　　　13%　　　76%

8 c. whole wheat flour　　　　　　　2 t. salt

MIX and warm. Also warm bread pans. Then mix:
2 T. yeast
1 c. water
1 T. diastatic malt or date sugar or both. *SET* aside until frothy. *ADD:*
½ c. sunflower seeds ground fine
3 c. warm water
1 c. each rye flour and oatmeal

PUT all together and mix until flour is evenly wetted. Resulting dough should be wet enough to be slippery. Most bread is too dry. *SPOON* dough into pans prepared with cornmeal. *LET* rise to almost double. *BAKE* 350 degrees for one hour.

60 servings - 1 slice　　　　74 calories per slice

CORN BREAD II
13%　　　19%　　　72%

2½ c. warm water
1 T. dry yeast
2 dates
2 c. cornmeal (whole, ground)
⅓ c. sunflower seeds ground fine and blended
1 c. whole wheat flour
1¼ t. salt

BLEND dates in warm water and *ADD* yeast. *LET STAND* until it foams. *MIX* dry ingredients and add water and yeast mixture. *STIR* well. *POUR* into shallow baking pan. Let stand 10 minutes. *BAKE* at 375 degrees for 45 minutes.

16 servings　　　　100 calories per serving

(T) WHEAT-OAT MUFFINS
11%　　　6%　　　89%

1¼ c. water　　　　　　½ t. vanilla
3 T. date sugar　　　　½ t. grated orange rind
2 t. yeast　　　　　　　1 c. oatmeal
½ t. salt　　　　　　　1 c. whole wheat flour
¾ c. raisins or blueberries or ½ c. dates

DISSOLVE yeast in water with date sugar. *ADD* other ingredients. *PREPARE* muffin tins with a very thin film of oil or lecithin dusted with cornmeal or bran. Fill 2/3's full and let rise 10 minutes. *PREHEAT* oven to 425 degrees. Bake at 375 degrees for about 15-20 minutes.
Yields 10-20 muffins

(T) BROWN BREAD MUFFINS

2 c. whole wheat flour
1 c. warm water
1¼ c. raisins
½ c. dates blended with some of the water
2 T. lemon
¼ t. salt
1 T. yeast

MIX all ingredients well and put in muffin pans sprayed with Pam and coated with bran. Let rise 30 minutes. Bake 350° for 20-30 minutes.

(T) DATE MUFFINS
12%　　　9%　　　87%

2 T. yeast
½ c. lukewarm water
1½ c. chopped dates
2 t. salt
2 c. hot water
3½ c. whole wheat flour
2 c. oatmeal

SOFTEN yeast in lukewarm water. *MIX* together dates, salt and hot water. *ADD* flour and oatmeal. When cool enough, *ADD* yeast. Stir well. *FILL* muffin cups one-half full. *LET RISE* until double. *BAKE* at 350 degrees for about 20-30 minutes. (You may have to add ½ c. more water to get right consistency). Reheat before serving.

16 servings　　　　175 calories per serving

ONION BREAD

Use favorite bread recipe. Use equivalent to one loaf—*ROLL* into rectagle. *SPREAD* with 1 c. sauted onion, 2 T. ground sesame seeds. *CUT* into three long strips. *ROLL* into three long rolls and *BRAID. BAKE* at 350° for 25-30 minutes.

(T) CORN-OAT MUFFINS

1 T. yeast softened in ¼ c. water. Add this to
1 c. apple sauce
1¾ c. hot water and mix with
1 t. salt
2 c. cornmeal
1 c. quick oatmeal
1 c. whole wheat flour

FILL muffin tins ¾ full. These should have been prepared with the cornmeal sifted in the bottom. Let rise for 20 minutes. Bake for 20 minutes at 375.

LEGUMES AND NUTS IN THE DIET

Weight for weight, ordinary dry beans, peas and lentils contain about the same percentage of protein as does fresh meat (or about twice as much as do grains), peanuts and peanut butter contain rather more; and soybean flour contains much more. Protein should be about 10% of our total calories.

Peas, beans (including soybean flour) and peanuts, (including peanut butter) are outstanding economical foods in view of their nutritive values, while the tree nuts, though not quite so cheap, are of such a high nutritive value as to make them economical as well as attractive and convenient foods.

The most economical source of protein is from legumes, whole grain products, and vegetables. Nuts and seeds are also economical as only a small quantity is used at a meal. Protein is found in every natural food. Eat a variety to maintain health.

Comparisons: For a mere fraction of the cost of a sirloin steak, the housewife can give her family the same amount of protein plus essential trace elements, vitamins, and minerals not found in meat.

Example:
Beans at 80¢ per lb.   8¢ per serving
Milk at 55¢ per quart   16¢ per serving
Eggs at 98¢ per dozen   18¢ per serving
Beef at 99¢ per lb.   47¢ per serving

Advantages of non-animal protein: No cholesterol; no infectious diseaes.

MAIN DISHES

Good sources of protein, natural fats and complex carbohydrates

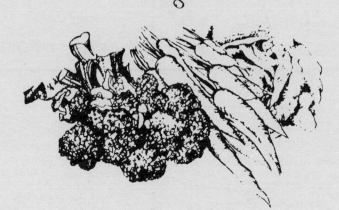

Grains
Corn
Rice
Wheat
Oats
Buckwheat
Millet
Rye

Other Foods
Food yeast
Olives

Certain Vegetables
Asparagus
Broccoli
Brussel Sprouts
Spinach
Corn
Green Peas
Mustard greens
Squash (winter and summer)
Green beans

Nuts & Seeds
Nuts
Sunflower
Sesame
Pumpkin

Legumes
Beans
Peas
Lentils
Garbanzos

Certain Tubers
Potatoes
Carrots
Sweet Potatoes
Beets

HOW TO COOK DRY BEANS

Measure desired amount of beans (1 c. dry beans yields about 2½ c. of cooked beans). Remove all particles of dirt, sand or damaged beans. Wash several times rubbing between palms. You may use a large colander for this.

Cover with water and soak overnight if desired. Soybeans and garbanzos cook faster if frozen after being soaked. Other beans need not be frozen after being soaked, but it will shorten cooking time.

To one cup of beans, add 4 c. water (for lentils use 3 c. only). Bring to boiling point and reduce heat just to keep a constant simmer. Add more boiling water as necessary until beans are at desired tenderness. Lentils may be cooked in less than one hour, and should not be soaked, however, other beans may vary up to 2 hours or more. (Soybeans and garbanzos will take up to 5 or more hours to be palatable and tender.) When tender, add salt to taste, more or less ½ t. to each cup of dried beans. Additional seasoning is advised as your taste indicates.

Many people do not eat beans because they cause flatus or gas. This can be overcome by preparing them properly. "The substance in beans which produce gas—two unusual starches, stachyose and raffinose—are not broken down by the starch digesting enzymes normally present in the digestive tract. Thus, they remain in the tract to come in contact with certain bacteria which react to break them down to carbon dioxide and hydrogen, which are the two main components of gastrointestinal gas. The method to be used to break down these starches so that they can be digested is as follows. *IN THE MORNING,* wash the beans. Then place them in the amount of water needed for cooking them. Let them soak all day. Before going to bed, place them in the freezer. The freezing process breaks up the starch molecules mentioned above. Cook them in the same water that is now ice, but do not add any salt. Use the meat tenderizer that contains papain, which comes form papaya. This tenderizer contains salt, therefore it takes the place of salt. The papaya enzyme gets through to these starches and breaks them down. They will not cause any gas. If you cannot find meat tenderizer with papain, then use six papaya enzyme tablets, crushed. These are equivalent to one teaspoon of meat tenderizer. Papaya enzymes do not contain salt. Therefore, you will have to add salt.

The *INDO* meat tenderizer is available in most nutritional centers and is free from harmful additives. Be sure to check the label as not all are acceptable.

OTHER METHODS TO HELP ELIMINATE DISTRESS from eating beans, are the following:

1. Soak overnight, drain. Cover with water and cook.
2. Soak overnight, drain. Cover with water and bring to boil. Let set one hour. Drain, add water and cook.
3. Soak overnight, drain. Cover with water. Add 1-2 T. fennel seed. Cook.
4. Soak overnight, drain. Freeze overnight. Rinse. Add water and cook.

Seasoning Suggestions:

To all *WHITE BEANS,* at the time of salting, add few sprinkles of garlic salt. *LENTILS AND BLACK BEANS* are good this way, too. Simmer for 15 minutes more. *RED BEANS AND SOYBEANS* are tasty with a sauce made of ½ onion diced and sauteed in water. Add 1 clove garlic diced, 1 T. pimiento diced, 2 T. tomato paste (for soybeans use ½ c. tomato paste and more onion and a bit of lemon juice). Simmer these together and add to beans. Cook beans until soupy thickness. Pinch of sweet basil, oregano or Italian seasoning may be added for variation. *GARBANZOS* are excellent simmered with chopped onions, a little food yeast and salt.

(T) GARBANZO ROAST
   16%   10%   75%

2 c. garbanzos	½ c. green pepper
2 c. bulghur wheat	½ c. celery
½ diced onion	½ c. pimiento, diced
¼ t. sage	½ c. olives
¼ t. salt	

SOAK garbanzos overnight and then cook. *BLEND* half the garbanzos with one cup water. Cook the bulghur wheat with 2 c. water and sage, oregano and salt. *SAUTE* in a little water, the onion, green pepper, celery and mix all ingredients. Bake for 1 hour at 350 degrees.

24-⅓ c. servings   120 calories per serving

(T) QUICK PINTO BEANS
   26%   3%   73%

1 c. dried pinto beans
3½ c. hot water
½ t. salt, scant
½ t. onion salt

BOIL beans in water for 5 minutes. *TURN* off heat and soak one hour. *PRESSURE* cook for 45 minutes. *ADD* salts and simmer a few minutes. May serve over waffles or whole wheat toast for a breakfast that gives stamina or southern style with greens or cornbread.

8-½ c. servings   83 calories per serving

SOYBEANS
28%   29%   50%

1 c. dried soybeans
3½ c. water
1 chopped onion, sautéed in water
1 clove garlic, minced
1 t. salt, scant
6 oz. tomato paste, scant
2 t. date sugar or date butter

SOAK beans in water overnight. **PRESSURE** cook for 1 hour and 20 minutes. **ADD** rest of ingredients and cook together.

12-¼ c. servings   98 calories per serving

(T) BUSHNELL'S BEANS
24%   4%   75%

SOAK overnight and cook until just tender (about three hours):

1 lb. mixed beans (pinto and great northern)
5 c. water (may need more during cooking)

ADD and cook one hour longer (or until very tender):

1 large chopped onion
1 large chopped green pepper
1 clove minced garlic
4 c. canned tomatoes
2½ t. salt
½ t. each: savory and marjoram
1 bay leaf

ADD during the last 30-40 minutes of cooking:

4 large stalks chopped celery

VARIATION: ADD chopped parsley at the end of cooking time.

20-½ c. servings   83 calories per serving

(T) LIMA BEAN AND TOMATO CASSEROLE
21%   4%   78%

1 lb. dry lima beans   2 sliced onions
2 c. tomatoes   salt to taste
½ c. diced celery

SOAK the dried beans overnight. Drain and cover with water. Boil them until tender or nearly done. **ADD** remaining ingredients. Place in a casserole and add more water if necessary. Bake slowly 1 hour at 325 degrees.

10-½ c. servings   89 calories per serving

(T) CHILI
26%   3%   76%

3 c. chili beans or pinto beans

SOAK overnight in 9 c. water. **COOK** beans until tender. **ADD** and let simmer:

½ c. chopped onion
1 can tomato paste   ¼ t. garlic powder
3 c. tomato juice   2 t. cumin
1½ t. salt   ¼ t. coriander (opt.)

12-1 c. servings   200 calories per serving

SOYBEAN SOUFFLE
33%   37%   36%

1 c. dry soy beans soaked overnight in 1 quart of water. **DRAIN** then **ADD:**
2 c. hot water or more to blend beans until smooth.
1 T. minced parsley
1 small onion, chopped
1 T. food yeast
1 T. soy sauce
1 pkg. G. Washington broth, Golden
½ t. salt

MIX all ingredients. **PLACE** in 9x12 baking dish. **BAKE** 45-50 minutes in a 350 degree oven. Good hot with gravy or cold as a sandwich filling. May be mixed with olives and cashew mayonnaise.

12-⅓ c. servings   76 calories per serving

SOY BEAN LOAF
23%   44%   39%

1 c. soy beans, soak overnight
1½ c. water
3-4 stalks diced celery
1 diced onion
2 diced pimientos
1 can sliced pitted olives
Fresh or dried parsley
¼ t. garlic powder
½ t. salt
¼ t. paprika
½ t. sage
1 T. soy sauce
1 T. food yeast flakes
½ c. bread crumbs or *oatmeal*

BLEND soy beans and seasonings in water. **ADD** the other ingredients and put in a casserole baking dish. Bake at 300 degrees for 2 hours.

12-½ c. servings   127 calories per serving

DRIED LIMA BEANS & RICE
13%   16%   71%

1 c. lima beans (soaked)   ½ c. cashews
1 med. onion   5 c. cooked rice

COOK lima beans and onions. **ADD** some blended cashews to beans and serve over brown rice.

10-½ c. rice & 1/3 c. beans   227 calories

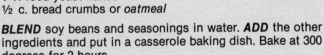

(T) BEAN BURGERS
15%   5%   82%

1 c. baked beans or seasoned cooked beans
½ c. bread crumbs
1 onion chopped fine
2 carrots grated fine
½ t. sage
Tomato sauce to moisten
Salt to taste

MIX and shape into patties. Brown on teflon griddle and serve with tomato sauce or home-made catsup.

8-¼ c. servings   95 calories

SOYTEENA
22%   45%   38%

1 c. dry soy beans, cleaned and soaked
1 c. tomato juice
½ c. peanut butter
½ med. onion
1 stalk celery
1 T. food yeast flakes
2 T. soy sauce
¼ t. garlic salt
1 c. cornmeal

COMBINE all ingredients except cornmeal and **BLEND** until smooth. **STIR** in cornmeal. **STEAM** in cans for 2 hours. **COOL. CUT** out bottom of can and run knife around the edge to release. **USE** within few days or may be frozen.

16-¼ c. servings   140 calories per serving

SOY BEAN LOAF II
24%   51%   55%

1½ c. vegetable juice
1 c. raw soy beans, soaked and ground (may be done in blender)
2 med. potatoes, shredded, raw
1½ c. dry oatmeal
1 c. onions, chopped
1 t. salt
1 t. celery salt
1 t. onion salt
¼ t. garlic salt

MIX all ingredients and **BAKE** in loaf pan sprinkled with cornmeal, 350 degrees for one hour.

12-1/3 c. servings   139 calories per serving

BEAN OAT PATTIES
17%   29%   57%

1½ c. cooked beans, any kind with liquid
1 c. rolled oats   2 T. food yeast
¼ c. nuts, chopped   ½ t. sage
½ c. chopped onions   ½ t. salt or to taste

Have beans a bit soupy. **MASH** beans or whiz in blender. **ADD** other ingredients. **MIX** well. Let stand for 5-10 minutes. **SHAPE** into patties and bake in covered pan at 350 degrees for 30 minutes. **TURN** patties after 15 minutes. **SERVE** with tomato sauce or brown gravy.

12-1/3 c. servings   69 calories per serving

(T) SOYBEAN PATTIES

1 c. dry soybeans
3 c. water

SOAK soybeans overnight. **DRAIN** and whiz with water.

ADD:
2 c. oatmeal
2 c. chopped celery
2 med. chopped onions
1/3 c. dry green peppers
1 t. Italian seasoning
3 t. sweet basil
2 T. food yeast flakes

MIX all ingredients and **FORM** into patties using #12 scoop. Makes 15 patties.

SOYBEAN OMELETTE
33%   38%   34%

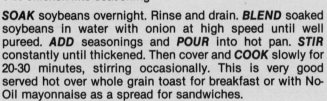

1 c. dry soybeans
¼ c. chopped onion
2 c. cold water
1 t. garlic salt
1 T. food yeast flakes
1 T. chicken-like seasoning

SOAK soybeans overnight. Rinse and drain. **BLEND** soaked soybeans in water with onion at high speed until well pureed. **ADD** seasonings and **POUR** into hot pan. **STIR** constantly until thickened. Then cover and **COOK** slowly for 20-30 minutes, stirring occasionally. This is very good served hot over whole grain toast for breakfast or with No-Oil mayonnaise as a spread for sandwiches.

6-1/3 c. servings   146 calories per serving

SOY-OAT PATTIE WITH TOMATO SAUCE
The Patties   28%   30%   46%

1 c. soaked soybeans
½ c. water
2 T. food yeast flakes - 1 T. if powdered
1 T. soy sauce
1 t. Italian seasoning
¼ t. salt
¾ c. regular rolled oats
½ t. onion salt
¼ t. garlic salt

COMBINE all ingredients except the oats in blender, chopping fine. **POUR** over oats and stir lightly—and let stand ten minutes to absorb moisture. **DROP** on teflon griddle or pan from tablespoon or ¼ c. scoop. **COVER. BAKE** at 350 degrees for 10 minutes or until nicely browned. **TURN** and bake ten more minutes. Serve with tomato sauce.

8-¼ c. servings   86 calories per serving

(T) *Tomato Sauce*   13%   5%   89%

½ c. onions, chopped and sautéed in a small amount of water
½ c. green pepper, chopped (fine)
2 c. cooked tomatoes
½ t. salt
1 t. sweet basil
1-2 dates, chopped
1½ T. cornstarch, mixed in small amount of cold water or tomato juice.

CUT the tomatoes in small pieces or use sliced canned tomatoes. *ADD* all ingredients and simmer for ten minutes to combine flavors. You may want to use stewed tomatoes and just add the sweet basil. Serve over patties.

10-¼ c. servings   22 calories per serving

(T) REFRIED BEANS I

1 c. dry beans—cook in usual manner until soft.
Blend with one can tomato sauce.

1 clove garlic	1 small onion
¼ t. cumin	1/3 t. salt
½ t. oregano	¼ c. green pepper

BLEND all together. *BAKE* at 325° for 2 hours in casserole dish.

(T) REFRIED BEANS II
25%   3°   74%

1 c. pinto beans, soaked overnight. *ADD:*
1 finely minced onion
1 finely minced clove garlic

SIMMER one to three hours until thoroughly tender. *ADD* salt and mash with potato masher. When semi-mashed, stir and cook until desired consistency. *ADJUST* seasoning.

8-¼ c. servings   92 calories per serving

(T) BAKED BEANS
23%   5%   77%

3½-4 cups cooked navy beans
1 med onion, whole
3 T. lemon juice
3 T. date sugar or 3-4 dates, chopped
1½ pint (3 cups) blended tomatoes
¼ t. oregano
¼ t. garlic
½ t. chicken-like seasoning

COMBINE all but the first 2 ingredients. *ADD* beans. *SALT* to taste. *PLACE* whole peeled onion in center. *BAKE* at 300 degrees to 325 degrees for 2 hours.

12-½ c. servings   101 calories per serving

(T) CHILI BEANS

5 c. cooked beans-kidney, pinto mixed
4 c. tomatoes
Sauté
1 large onion chopped
1 large clove garlic minced
1 med. sweet pepper, chopped
¼ t. each sweet basil and oregano
1 T. cumin
½ t. paprika
¼ t. salt or to taste

COOK for a few minutes. For those not on therapeutic diet, ½ c. sliced olives may be added. *BAKE* for 30-60 minutes, 350 degrees.

20-½ c. servings   84 calories per serving

TOSTADA WITH BEANS

Heat corn tortillas in a very warm pan without oil. When hot, place in towel in a pan in warm oven until ready. Prepare shredded lettuce, mashed pinto beans, sliced tomatoes, shredded carrots, chopped onions, sliced avocado, sliced olives. When ready, place hot tortillas on warm plate and assemble in layers. (Let each person prepare his own). May top with Cashew-Pimento Cheese Spread or Soy Mayonnaise. Serve with rice, beans, soup, etc.

VARIATION: Cut tortilla in pieces. Season by shaking them in a plastic bag with seasonings of onion salt, garlic salt, food yeast, or others to suit your taste. Bake in oven to use as corn chips.

(T) CARROT-BEAN CROQUETTES
21%   4%   76%

1 medium onion, diced
1 c. mashed pinto beans
1½ c. raw carrots, grated
½ c. breadcrumbs
¼ t. sage and a little salt

COMBINE all ingredients and *MIX WELL. FORM* into balls and roll in fine bread crumbs. Bake on ungreased baking sheet for 15 to 20 minutes at 375 degrees. Serve with your favorite sauce.

10-¼ c. servings   94 calories per serving

(T) GREEN AND WHITE BEANS
26%   4%   73%

SOAK 2 c. small white beans. *COOK* in crockpot overnight with 4-5 c. water and 1 T. savory. Next morning, prepare 1 pkg. green beans (Italian). When tender, add to white beans and also add:

1-2 T. chicken-like seasoning
2 T. onion powder
3 T. food yeast flakes
dash of garlic powder

SIMMER and *SERVE.*

12-½ c. servings
126 calories per serving

BARLEY CASSEROLE
13%   20%   71%

1¾ c. barley, raw, toasted slightly
5 c. very hot water
2 c. cubed eggplant
2 T. parsley
2 onions, chopped
6 pkg. G. Washington Golden Seasoning
½ c. slivered almonds

COMBINE all ingredients, except the nuts. **PLACE** in casserole. **BAKE** 1¾ hours at 350 degrees, covered. **SPRINKLE** nuts on top of barley and bake an additional 15 minutes to toast almonds.

10-½ c. servings   186 calories per serving

BARLEY-GARBANZO PATTIES
26%   17%   58%

1 c. each cooked barley and mashed garbanzos
½ c. quick oats
2 stalks celery, finely chopped
1 small onion, finely chopped
1 clove garlic, chopped
3 green onions with tops, chopped
1/8 t. salt
1 t. paprika
2-3 T. soy sauce

Mix well. If dry, add a little tomato juice or water. Let stand a few minutes and then shape into patties. Cook on T-Fal griddle. (Should be covered part of the baking time).

10-1/3 c. servings   65 calories per serving

(T) BARLEY PATTIES

2 c. cooked barley-well done
1 chopped onion
1 c. chopped celery (fine)
½ c. grated raw potato
½ t. thyme
½ t. sage
1 t. sweet basil
bread crumbs - enough to hold shape

PLACE patties on baking sheets and bake in 350° oven until brown. **SERVE** with gravy.
Yield: 16 patties

BRAZIL NUT CASSEROLE

COOK two cups of noodles or small macaroni (whole wheat, whole corn, spinach, sesame, or a mixture). **MAKE** a white sauce a bit thinner than gravy using the Cashew Gravy recipe. Place a layer of the white sauce in a casserole, add the cooked macaroni or noodles, ½ cup of sliced brazil nuts sprinkled over the macaroni and ½ c. of sliced olives and the rest of the white sauce on top. The white sauce should be thin enough so it will filter down through the pasta. **SPRINKLE** with seasoned bread crumbs and a few more sliced brazil nuts. Bake for 30 minutes or until warmed through in a 350 degree oven.

(T) BREAD DRESSING
13%   10%   76%

12 c. whole grain bread cubed and toasted lightly (1 loaf)

COOK together:

2 c. water
2 large onions, chopped fine
3 stalks celery plus leaves chopped
3 t. dried parsley
2 T. chicken-like flavoring
2 t. thyme
1 t. savory
1 t. marjoram
2 t. sage
½ t. rosemary
½ t. garlic powder
½ t. salt

BOIL together 15 minutes. **TOSS** with fork into bread cubes. **BAKE** covered 1 hour in pan of water at 400 degrees. Serve with brown gravy.

24-1/3 c. servings   147 calories per serving

GARBANZO NOODLE CASSEROLE
14%   21%   65%

3 c. whole wheat or soy noodles
1 medium onion, chopped
1 stalk celery, diced
1 c. cooked garbanzos
2 c. soy, nut, or sesame milk
3 T. flour
¼ c. water
½ t. salt
2 t. chicken-like seasoning (see recipe)

COOK noodles in lightly salted water. **DRAIN. SAUTÉ** onions and celery until tender. **ADD** milk to onions and celery and bring to boiling point. **MIX** flour with the ¼ c. water until smooth and slowly add to milk, stirring contantly. Continue to cook and stir until thickened. **ADD** salt and seasoning. **COMBINE** cooked noodles, garbanzos, and milk sauce. When thoroughly mixed, put into casserole and sprinkle with sesame seeds. **BAKE** 35-45 minutes at 325 degrees.

10-½ c. servings   156 calories per serving

GARBANZO BURGERS

2 c. soaked garbanzos
1 small onion or ½ t. onion powder
1 t. garlic powder
¾ c. water
1½ c. soaked soybeans
½ c. water

BLEND soaked garbanzos, water, onion, and seasonings. **GRIND** or blend soybeans and **ADD** to garbanzo mixture. **FORM** into patties and **BAKE** in 350° oven till brown and set. Makes 8 servings.

GARBANZO POT PIE
17%   18%   69%

2 c. potatoes, diced small
1½ c. carrots, diced small
½ c. onions, chopped
1 pkg. frozen peas, or 1 c. fresh
1-2 c. cooked garbanzos
2 c. soy or nut milk
2 T. flour
3 t. chicken-like seasoning

MAKE 3 c. medium cream sauce - 2 T. flour and 2 c. milk to make sauce. *ADD* juice from garbanzos and 3 t. chicken-like seasoning. Steam potatoes, carrots, onions, and peas until tender. *ADD* garbanzos and sauce; mix lightly. Pour into casserole. Cover with ¼ recipe of cobbler dough (see recipe in Breads) and bake in hot oven 450 degrees for 20 minutes or until nicely browned.

16-½ c. servings   147 calories per serving

GARBANZO SAUCE
15%   19%   68%

2 c. canned tomatoes or equal of fresh
2 medium diced onions
2 t. salt
1 bay leaf
3 c. cooked garbanzos
½ c. tomato sauce
½ c. water
1/3 c. chunky peanut butter
Hot brown rice

SAUTÉ onion in a little water until tender. *BLEND* by hand the hot water and peanut butter. *ADD* all ingredients except peanut butter mixture and rice. *COVER* and *SIMMER* 15 minutes. *ADD* peanut butter and simmer 10 minutes longer. Serve over brown rice.

10-½ c. servings   328 calories per serving

(T) HAYSTACKS

Corn chips from corn tortillas, toasted until crisp in 250-300° oven between 2 cookie sheets.
pinto beans
chopped lettuce
chopped tomatoes
chopped onions
tomato sauce
olives (if diet permits)

LAYER corn chips, beans, lettuce, tomatoes, onions, etc.
BEANS:

3 c. soaked pinto beans
5 c. water
1 c. green pepper
1½ c. chopped onion
1 t. cumin

COMBINE all ingredients and simmer until beans are tender. Makes 6 cups.

LASAGNA
19%   31%   57%

1-8 oz. pkg. lasagna (whole wheat or whole corn is good). *DO NOT COOK.* Use uncooked. Make tomato sauce thinner by adding extra tomato juice.
½ c. cashew jack cheese
1-20 oz. can tofu or 1 lb. block
1 pkg. chopped spinach or fresh-thawed if frozen. May use other green or omit.

Sauce:
1 can (2½) whole tomatoes
1-8 oz. can tomato sauce
1 small can tomato paste
1-2 large onions
½ c. chopped olives
1 clove garlic
½ t. oregano
¼ t. sweet basil

SAUTÉ onions and garlic, in water—few tablespoons—to soften onion. *ADD* tomatoes, sauce and paste and all seasonings. Cover bottom of 9x12 baking dish with *HOT* tomato sauce. *PLACE* lasagna noodles on sauce. *CRUMBLE tofu in small pieces and spoon over pasta. ADD* thin layer of spinach, and then the tomato sauce. Should make two or three layers of each depending on size of the baking dish. Thread Cashew Pimento Cheese over the top. Bake at 375 degrees for 45-60 minutes or until hot and bubbly. The cashew cheese may be put on each layer if you wish. Cut in squares and serve.

12 servings   192 calories per serving

PIZZA
15%   29%   64%

Crust:
1 package dry yeast - 1 T.
1½ c. warm water
2½-3 c. whole wheat flour (a little more or less to make soft dough)
½ t. salt.

SPRINKLE yeast on warm water. *STIR* to dissolve. *ADD* 2 c. flour and the salt. *BEAT* thoroughly. *STIR* in rest of flour. Place in bowl and cover with a damp cloth and let rise ½ hour. *MAKE* into pizza crust. Use thin coat of crisco on pans. Makes 2 large. Use your favorite pizza sauce or use this Pizza sauce which is very good. You may also wish to try shredded, steamed cabbage on the top of the sauce and then dribble with the Cashew Jack Cheese. *BAKE* at 450 degrees for 20-25 minutes or until the crust is brown and cheese bubbly.

16-1/8 pizza   171 calories per serving

PIZZA SAUCE
15%   20%   75%

SAUTÉ in small amount of water:

1 c. eggplant
1 large clove garlic, minced
1 large onion, chopped
½ sweet pepper, chopped

SIMMER for 5 minutes and *ADD:*

6 oz. tomato paste
2½ c. canned tomatoes
½ c. sliced olives
¼ t. each oregano, sweet basil
½ t. salt

SIMMER for 5 minutes more. *SPREAD* over rolled out bread pizza dough. See recipe. *BAKE* at 425 degrees for about 20 minutes. (Also see recipe for Cashew Jack Cheese)

5 cups   553 calories
¼ c.   28 calories

LENTIL PATTIES
16%   29%   57%

1/3 c. each, chopped onion, chopped bell pepper
1¼ c. cooked lentils, mashed
1¼ c. cooked potatoes, mashed
1/3 c. walnuts, coarse, chopped
¼ t. sage
½ t. salt

MIX well and *FORM* into patties. *PLACE* on Silver Stone baking pan and brown in 400 degree oven for 15-20 minutes. *SERVE* plain or with gravy.

12-¼ c. servings   66 calories per serving

(T) TOMATO-LENTIL DELIGHT
26%   1%   74%

2 c. uncooked lentils   4 c. tomato juice
1 c. chopped onion   ¼ t. cumin
½ c. sliced celery   ¼ t. oregano
½ c. diced carrot   ¼ t. sweet basil
1 T. dried parsley   1 t. salt

COOK lentils, onion, carrot and celery together in 4 c. water for ½ hour. *ADD* other ingredients and simmer ½ hour or until lentils are cooked. (Delicious served over whole wheat toast or brown rice.)

20-½ c. servings   79 calories per serving

LENTIL ROAST
19%   33%   51%

2 c. cooked lentils   1 t. salt
1 c. cashew milk   ½ t. sage
1 c. fine bread crumbs 1 c. grated carrots
1 . chopped walnuts   1 c. chopped celery
  or pecans   1 T. food yeast

COMBINE. BAKE 350 degrees for one hour. *SERVE* with gravy or plain.

12-½ c. servings   228 calories per serving

(T) WHEAT WITH LENTILS
29%   9%   66%

1 c. lentils
1/3 c. wheat

SOAK wheat at least four hours or overnight. *COOK* one hour before adding lentils. Cook together until both are tender. *ADD* salt and seasonings that you like toward the end of the cooking period. This is a simple main dish.

6-½ c. servings   151 calories per serving

(T) BULGHUR WHEAT

3 c. boiling water
1 c. bulghur wheat

STIR until evenly moist. *COVER* and cook on low heat about 20 minutes.

1 c. chopped onions
½ t. garlic powder
Vegit seasoning

SAUTÉ in water until onions are tender.
2 c. soaked garbanzos
1 c. cold water
BLEND garbanzos with water. *MIX* all ingredients well in a large bowl. *BAKE* patties at 350° until brown. Serve with gravy.

(T) RICE WITH LENTILS
18%   3%   79%

1 c. lentils
1 c. rice

COOK the lentils with some onion and salt and season toward the end of the cooking period. **BROWN** the rice in a medium hot fry pan. It will pop and have a nice aroma. **COOL** the pan before adding 2½ c. hot water. **COVER** and gently boil until all the water has been absorbed. The rice will be fluffy. Salt should be added at the beginning of the cooking period. This may be eaten separately or in the following manner. **SPOON** rice onto the plate. **COVER** with lentils. Add a prepared salad on top which could be cabbage, carrot, onion, celery, sprouts, cucumber, tomato, avocado or your choice. Top this with a mild taco sauce, or cashew jack cheese, or croutons, or all three.

8-½ c. servings   176 calories per serving

(T) RICE ORIENTAL

4 c. cooked brown rice
1 c. diced celery
¼ t. garlic powder
½ t. onion powder
½ c. water chestnuts
3 c. frozen peas
½ c. minced onion

SAUTÉ onions and celery in water till soft and tender, **ADD** peas, water chestnuts, and seasonings. **SIMMER** 3 minutes and combine rice. This may also be used to stuff cabbage or peppers.

14-½ c. servings

MILLET-LENTIL CASSEROLE
18%   38%   49%

1 c. uncooked millet
1 c. uncooked lentils
1 onion, chopped
1 c. sunflower seeds
7 c. water
½ c. almond nuts
½ t. garlic powder
2 t. Dr. Bronner's seasoning or beef-style seasoning
½ t. salt

BLEND almonds in 1 c. water. **MIX** all ingredients. **BAKE** 350 degrees for 1-1½ hours, stirring often.

14-½ c. servings   187 calories per serving

LENTIL PATTIES OR ROAST
14%   20%   65%

2 c. cooked lentils, mashed
1 onion, chopped
2½ c. bread crumbs or
2½ c. cooked brown rice
½ c. walnuts, chopped fine
1 t. salt
¼ t. sage
1 T. soy sauce
Nut or soy milk, as needed, or tomato juice

COMBINE all ingredients, except milk and mix well. **ADD** only enough milk or juice to allow mixture to be formed into patties. **PLACE** patties on cookie sheet and bake 30 minutes at 325 degrees. May be served with a gravy, or bake in a casserole.

15-1/3 c. servings   153 calories per serving

(T) SPROUTED LENTIL CASSEROLE
26%   3%   75%

2 c. lentils, sprouted
2 c. celery and leaves. **SLICE** celery diagonally and quite thin
2 c. chopped onion
4 T. soy sauce
Dash of garlic powder
2 T. water

PLACE all ingredients in heavy fry pan. **COVER** and let steam on low heat for 10-15 minutes. **THIS MAY ALSO BE USED IN PITA BREAD AS FILLING.**

10-½ c. servings   88 calories per serving

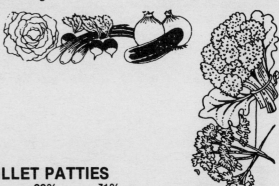

MILLET PATTIES
14%   22%   71%

1½ c. precooked millet
½ c. whole wheat flour
¼ c. soy flour
½ c. rolled oats
½ c. almonds
1 c. water, hot
½ med. onion, chopped fine
¼ t. garlic powder
1 t. salt
1 T. beef style seasoning

BLEND almonds and water. **POUR** over millet, wheat and soy flour, oats, and onion. **ADD** remaining ingredients and mix well. Form into patties and bake for 25-30 minutes at 325 degrees. Can be baked as a casserole for 45-60 minutes.

12-¼ c. servings   159 calories per serving

(T) MILLET DELIGHT

1 c. millet
2 c. cold water
1 t. seasoning of choice
¼ c. fine chopped green bell pepper
¼ c. fine chopped green onions
1 small jar pimentos

PLACE millet in kettle and bring to a boil. Immediately lower heat and **STEAM** for approximately 45 minutes or until all of the water is absorbed. Remove from heat and, using large salad fork, **STIR** in the seasoning and then "toss" in the remaining ingredients; be careful not to "mash" the millet and cause it to become lumpy. Serve with chicken-like gravy (see gravy section, page 59)

MILLET CASSEROLE
12%   45%   51%

1 c. millet
5 c. tomato juice
1 onion, blended in juice or diced
4 T. ground sesame seeds
½ c. cashew nut pieces
1 can sliced, pitted olives-green ripe are my preference
1 t. salt
½ t. sweet basil
¼ t. paprika

MIX all ingredients. Bake in covered casserole for 2 hours at 325 degrees and for 1 hour at 250 degrees.

12-½ c. servings   159 calories per serving

MILLET LOAF
12%   47%1   48%

1 c. finely diced celery
1 med. onion, chopped fine
¾ c. millet
½ c. cashews, finely chopped
½ c. sliced olives
1¼ c. water
2 c. nut, soy or sesame milk
¼ c. whole wheat flour
1 t. salt
1/8 t. sage
1 c. diced eggplant

SAUTÉ celery and onion. **PUT** millet into blender and blend to consistency of meal. In a large bowl, combine celery, onion, millet and nuts. Bring 1 c. water and the 2 c. milk to near boiling. **MIX** the flour with the remaining ¼ cup of water and stir until smooth. Add this to the hot milk, stirring continuously to prevent lumping. **ADD** the seasoning and eggplant to the sauce. **MIX** well and pour over dry ingredients. **STIR** thoroughly and add sliced olives. **POUR** into casserole and bake at 350 degrees for 1½ hours. Stir while cooking to prevent millet from staying on the bottom of the casserole and becoming too thick. If mixture is not as thick as desired, add enough bread crumbs to make desired consistency. Bake a few minutes longer and serve.

10-½ c. servings   167 calories per serving

OATMEAL PATTIES
13%   28%   61%

2 c. dry oatmeal
1 c. cooked oatmeal
½ t. salt
1 t. sage
1 small onion, chopped
¼ c. walnuts, chopped
¾ c. liquid (water, tomato juice)
1 t. soy sauce or beef-style seasoning
¼ c. rolled barley or rolled wheat

MIX and **BROWN** on teflon type skillet or griddle. **SERVE** with gravy.

10-¼ c. servings   107 calories per serving

OAT BURGERS
15%   37%   51%

9 c. water, boiling
2 large onions, diced and sautéed
1 c. walnuts, chopped or ground coarse
1 c. sunflower seeds, ground coarse
1 T. sweet basil
1 T. Italian seasoning, flakes
¼ t. oregano powder   1 c. soy sauce
9 c. oatmeal, regular   ¼ c. nutritional yeast

ADD seasonings to boiling water and all other ingredients. Gently stir in oatmeal until moist and then let it set until partially cool. Place on non-stick cookie sheets. Bake 350° ½-¾ hr. or until slightly brown. **VARIATION:** Omit sweet basil, Italian seasoning, oregano and use ½ t. each sage and thyme and ¼ t. marjoram or any other combinations which you enjoy.

48-1/3 c. servings   101 calories per serving
No nuts or seeds   11% fat, 50 calories per serving

SUNBURGERS
16%   54%   36%

2 med. carrots, grated
1 onion, chopped fine
1 t. parsley
½ c. oatmeal
1 c. sunflower seeds, ground
½ to 1 c. celery, chopped fine
½ c. tomato juice
¼ c. barley or wheat flakes
½ t. salt
1/8 t. sweet basil

FORM into patties. **BAKE** 30 minutes at 350 degrees. May need turning half way through baking time.

10-¼ c. servings   121 calories per serving

BAKED RICE AND SOYAMEAT
10%   37%   56%

1 c. rice - lightly brown in a dry fry pan - cool somewhat and add:
1 t. salt
2 c. water - **BRING TO BOIL** and cook slowly unstirred until rice is fluffy and water absorbed. **PRESS** rice into bottom of 9"x13" pan.

Make white sauce as follows:

3 c. water   3 t. onion powder
¾ c. cashew nuts   ¾ t. salt

WHIZ in blender until smooth. **HEAT** in pan until thickened. **ADD** to the white sauce: Chopped vegetables that have been sauteed in a little bit of water for five minutes—2 c. celery, 2 bunches green onions,
¼ c. green pepper.
1 jar chopped pimiento
1 c. drained water chestnuts, sliced
1 can diced soychicken (Worthington), 13 oz.
½ t. lemon juice (fresh is best)

POUR all over rice. **SPRINKLE** slivered almonds on top. **BAKE** 1 hour, 350 degrees.

12-½ c. servings   197 calories per serving

RICE ORIENTAL
9%   26%   66%

4 c. cooked brown rice   ½ c. sliced water chestnuts
1 c. diced celery   ½ c. nuts, chopped
½ c. minced onion   ½ t. salt
¾ c. cubed eggplant   1 T. soy sauce

SAUTÉ onion and celery in small amount of water until tender. Add eggplant, water chestnuts, nuts, and seasoning. Simmer for 3 minutes and combine with rice. (May be used as stuffing for cabbage, eggplant, peppers, or tomatoes).

VARIATION: Wheat or combination of rice and wheat may be used.

12-½ c. servings   125 calories per serving

POTATOES AND RICE PATTIES
11%   42%   50%

2 c. shredded raw potatoes (you may just scrub and shred)
1 c. cooked brown rice
½ c. sautéed onions
½ c. chopped brazil nuts
½ c. chopped celery
2 T. food yeast flakes
½ t. salt
1/8 t. garlic powder
2 T. soy sauce

COMBINE all ingredients and spoon onto a teflon griddle or fry pan, 350 degrees. **COVER** and cook for ten minutes. **TURN** and cook for ten or fifteen minutes longer.

12-¼ c. servings   87 calories per serving

BROWN RICE CASSEROLE
10%   30%   62%

3 c. cooked brown rice
1 c. celery, diced
1 small onion, diced
½ c. eggplant, diced
½ c. cashews, coarsely chopped
½ t. salt
2 t. chicken-like seasoning
½ t. celery salt
Nut or soy milk as needed

SAUTÉ onion and celery until clear in small amount of water. **ADD** eggplant and cook about 5-6 minutes or longer if necessary. **COMBINE** all ingredients with rice and add enough milk to moisten. **BAKE** in covered casserole for 30 minutes at 350 degrees. **REMOVE** cover and **BAKE** an additional 15 minutes. If desired, sprinkle with sesame seeds before baking.

10-½ c. servings   128 calories per serving

BAKED NUT RICE
13%   37%   52%

2 c. cooked brown rice (brown in skillet over medium heat before cooking). (Use 2 c. water for each c. of rice).
1 c. thinned peanut butter (Use about ¼ c. and 1½ c. water in blender)
2 T. finely chopped onion

BAKE in 350 degree oven for 30 minutes. This is very good served with creamed tomatoes.

10-½ c. servings   89 calories per serving

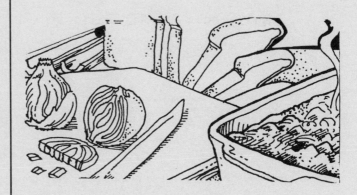

BAKED NUT RICE II
8%   58%   37%

2 c. cooked brown rice   2 T. finely chopped onion
1 c. ground filberts   1 t. sage
  or almonds   ½ t. salt
1 c. water

MIX ground nuts with 1 c. water; add rice, onion and seasoning. Mixture should be quite thin. **BAKE** in casserole at 400 degrees for 25 minutes. This is good as stuffing for green peppers. **POUR** gravy over peppers.

8-½ c. servings   166 calories per serving

RICE AND SOYAMEAT
9%   21%   70%

1 c. rice (lightly brown in a fry pan—cool somewhat and add)
1 c. celery slivered very thin diagonally
1 onion, diced
1 c. carrots, sliced thin
1 c. Soyameat Chicken Style, diced

PUT the above ingredients together in a casserole and add the following which have been blended together:
MIX gently.

2 c. water
1 t. Vegex
3 packages George Washington Broth
1 can mushroom soup

BAKE in 350 degree oven for 1 hour

10-½ c. servings   169 calories

OLIVE RICE RING
12%   26%   64%

3 c. cooked hot brown rice
1 c. ripe olives, sliced
¾ c. thinly sliced green onions
¼ c. finely chopped parsley
4 oz. jar pimiento, chopped
¾ c. finely chopped celery
½ t. salt, season salt or vegetable salt

FLUFF rice and add all other ingredients. Pack into teflon mold (ring) and **BAKE** in 350 degree oven for 30 minutes or until hot. **INVERT** over serving dish and fill center with creamed peas, carrots or your choice of vegetable.

10-½ c. servings   138 calories per serving

RICE AND TOMATO DISH
10%   16%   76%

1 c. brown rice, raw, toasted slightly
¼ c. chopped green peppers
½ c. chopped onions
¾ c. sliced olives
2 T. chopped parsley
¼ c. chopped celery
½ t. sweet basil
3 c. tomatoes in juice
Salt to taste

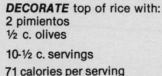

MIX all ingredients. **PLACE** in casserole. **BAKE** for one hour, 350 degrees. Keep covered. May need more tomato juice.

8-½ c. servings   131 calories per serving

SESAME RICE
9%   21%   70%

1 c. rice, toasted dry in fry pan until lightly brown
2½ c. water   1 t. salt

BRING to boil and simmer until all water is absorbed. Keep the pan covered. **ADD** chopped parsley and pack it into a ring mold. **SPRINKLE** sesame seeds, which have been toasted, on top of the mold when you have placed it on the serving dish. The center may be filled with creamed vegetables. Cashew gravy is very good as the cream sauce for most vegetables. A little chopped pimiento, if your family enjoys the flavor, along with the parsley, is a pretty addition.

5-½ c. servings   172 calories per serving

STUFFED GREEN PEPPERS (RICE)
10%   30%   63%

1 c. canned tomatoes
½ can tomato paste
3 stalks celery, chopped
3 onions, chopped

SIMMER together until fairly dry and barely tender. **ADD** the following ingredients:

1½ t. salt
½ t. sweet basil
2 t. sage
¼ t. garlic powder
1 t. thyme
1 c. coarsely chopped walnuts or
½ c. dried eggplant or 1½ cup fresh
6 c. cooked brown rice

SIMMER with above ingredients. **ADD** enough bread crumbs to make dry mixture. Unless the peppers are par-boiled, they make the mixture quite moist while baking. Put 1 T. water inbottom of baking dish to give moisture until peppers form their own. 20 Peppers. **PACK LOOSELY** into raw, stemmed and cored peppers.**BAKE** at 400 degrees for 50 minutes, covered, 10 minutes uncovered.
20-½ c. servings   165 calories each

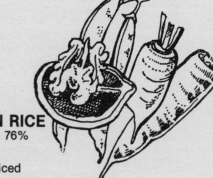

SPANISH BROWN RICE
9%   16%   76%

1 med. onion, chopped
1 small green pepper, diced
1 clove minced garlic
SAUTE in a heavy pan for just a few minutes in small amount of water
ADD
1 c. canned tomatoes or fresh
1 t. salt
2 c. brown rice, raw
4 c. water

BOIL rapidly for 5 minutes, turn down heat and simmer about 45 minutes. Turn the heat off and let stand about 10 minutes to absorb all the liquid.

DECORATE top of rice with:
2 pimientos
½ c. olives

10-½ c. servings

71 calories per serving

(T) BROWN RICE
9%   11%   12%

3 c. cooked brown rice
2 med. onions sauteed in small amount of water
1 small can crushed pineapple
1/8 c. ground cashews
¼ t. spike seasoning
¼ t. chicken-like seasoning
1 T. parsley flakes
Salt and dash of kelp (optional)

STIR lightly and place in baking dish. **BAKE** for ½ to ¾ hour and serve.

8-½ c. servings   128 calories per serving

SUNFLOWER SEED CASSEROLE
14%   48%   42%

2 c. sunflower seeds
2/3 c. cashews
¾ c. water
1 c. cubed eggplant
5 c. cooked brown rice
2½ t. chicken-like seasoning (see recipe)
1 large, or two small, onions, chopped fine
3 T. soy sauce
2 T. food yesat
1/8 t. garlic powder

GRIND sunflower seeds until fine. Blend cashews and water until smooth. **COMBINE** all ingredients and mix thoroughly. Put into large casserole and bake for 1½ hours at 325 degrees. Leave cover on casserole for first 45 minutes.

20-½ c. servings   177 calories per serving

SEVEN GRAIN PATTIES
17%   43%   50%

3 c. boiling water
¾ t. salt
1 t. thyme
2 T. soy sauce
1½ c. seven grain cereal
1 t. onion salt
¼ c. sunflower seed meal
¼ c. chopped pecans
¼ t. onion powder

ADD first 6 ingredients to 1 c. boiling water and simmer 10 minutes; then add nuts and seeds. **MIX** well, shape into patties and place on baking sheet. **BAKE** at 375 degrees for 30 minutes.

12-¼ c. servings   89 calories per serving

(T) ROMAN BEANS ON RICE
26%   3%   74%

3 c. dried split peas - add enough water to cook
2 large onions, chopped
¼ t. garlic, minced
2 carrots, grated
2/3 c. fresh parsley, chopped
2 t. each sweet basil, and flaked oregano
Salt to taste
4 large fresh tomatoes or a large can of canned tomatoes.
ADD when peas are cooked. **SIMMER** until done. **SERVE** over brown rice.

24-½ c. servings   99 calories per serving

TAMALE PIE
11%   31%   65%

1 large onion, chopped
1 large green pepper
1 cup yellow cornmeal
1 c. creamed or whole kernel corn
2 c. canned or fresh tomatoes
1 c. sesame milk or nut milk or tomato juice
1 t. salt
¼ t. cumin
¼ t. garlic powder
1 can whole pitted olives

SAUTÉ onion and peppers in a little water. **ADD** next 4 ingredients and cook until thick, stirring constantly. **ADD** other ingredients. (olives are nice left whole). **POUR** into casserole and bake for 1 hour at 350 degrees. Will be firmer if made day ahead and refrigerated. Freezes well. Just heat through to serve.

10-½ c. servings   124 calories per serving

WALNUT TOFU BALLS
20%   56%   35%

1 c. walnuts or pecans toasted on cooked sheet (200 degrees for 15 min.)
2 c. soft bread crumbs - whole grain
1 lb. tofu
2 T. whole wheat flour
3 T. dough pep or gluten flour
6 T. minced, dried onion flakes
4 T. dried parsley
¾ t. salt or to taste
1/8 t. each sage and marjoram

COMBINE. Mash or knead with hands. Roll into balls. Place on cookie sheet and bake for 30 minutes at 325 degrees.

16-¼ c. servings (2 balls)   101 calories per serving

(T) WHEAT CASSEROLE
18%   5%   79%

1 medium onion, chopped and sautéd in a little water
1 c. bulghur wheat
1 c. cooked lentils
1 c. cooked garbanzos (these may be chopped or left whole)
2½ c. liquid (juice from lentils and garbanzos)
4 t. chicken seasoning
¼ c. dried parsley

MIX all together and put in casserole dish. **BAKE** 45-60 minutes at 350 degrees.

10-½ c. servings   122 calories per serving

(T) WHOLE WHEAT SPAGHETTI WITH BROCCOLI SAUCE

8 ounces whole wheat spaghetti
4 to 8 ounces of sliced mushrooms (optional) (May use eggplant)
1 pound broccoli spears thinly sliced
3 stalks of celery, thinly sliced
4 green onions, cut fine
4 T. soy sauce or 1 T. Savorex
2 heaping T. arrowroot or cornstarch
Toasted sunflower seeds for garnish

While spaghetti is boiling in salted water, prepare the sauce. Saute broccoli, celery, onions in ½ to ¼ c. water. **ADD** mushrooms or eggplant. **DRAIN** the spaghetti and reserve the cooking liquid. **MIX** starch and two cups of the spaghetti water. **POUR** immediately over the vegetables and heat and stir until sauce is thick. **SEASON** with soy sauce. **SERVE** spaghetti on a large platter with the sauce poured over and garnished with lightly toasted sunflower seeds and serve separately.

(T) SKILLET SPAGHETTI

2 c. gluten or reconstituted Granburger
1-6 oz. can tomato paste (2/3 c.)
2 c. tomato juice
3 c. water
1-2 large onions, sliced
1/8 t. celery salt
1 t. paprika
¼-½ t. cumin powder
1 t. garlic salt
1 t. oregano or sweet basil
1 t. date sugar
1 t. salt
17 oz. package spaghetti

COMBINE all ingredients except spaghetti in skillet. **COVER** and bring to a boil, turn down and simmer 30 minutes. **ADD** spaghetti, stir to separate strands. **SIMMER** covered for 30 minutes or until spaghetti is tender. **STIR** frequently.

Yield: 4-6 servings.

MACARONI WITH PEANUTS

3 c. macaroni, cooked

BLEND ¾ c. water, ½ c. potatoes, raw, ¼ c. raw carrots, 1 t. food yeast, ½ t. salt and 3 T. lemon juice, dash of oregano, sweet basil and garlic salt. **MIX** with cooked macaroni and add ½ c. chopped peanuts and ¼ c. bread crumbs. **PUT** in ungreased baking dish and brown at 375 degrees for about 30 minutes.

CHEESE-A-RONI

2 c. macaroni, soy, whole wheat, or spinach
1 medium onion, chopped
1 recipe Cashew Pimiento Cheese Spread

COOK macaroni in salted water. **SAUTÉ** onion and add all ingredients to strained macaroni. **BAKE** in casserole at 350 degrees for 30-45 minutes.

(T) SPAGHETTI SAUCE

½ c. chopped onion
¼ c. green pepper, chopped
2-1 lb. can whole tomatoes
1-8 oz. can tomato puree
1-3 oz. can sliced mushrooms or ½ c. cubed eggplant
¼ c. chopped parsley   ¼ t. thyme
1 t. oregano   ½ c. chopped olives
½ t. cumin, ground   salt to taste
¼ t. garlic powder

SAUTÉ onion and green pepper in small amount of water. Add all remaining ingredients and simmer until sauce is thick. Stir occasionally. Add water if needed. Use over buckwheat, soy, whole wheat or spinach noodles. May be used in bean dishes or as sauce for lasagna.

VARIATION: Sweet basil, bay leaf, diced eggplant or zucchini.

(T) GARBANZOS

| 22% | 11% | 69% |

2 c. cleaned, soaked garbanzos (these also may be frozen to shorten cooking)
2 c. water
1 large onion, minced or chopped fine
1 t. salt
1 t. food yeast flakes

COOK garbanzos in water until soft. **ADD** other ingredients and **SIMMER** until juice is thickened and garbanzos have absorbed flavor. **SERVE** this over cooked bulghur wheat, brown rice, whole wheat noodles, or whole wheat toast.

10-1/3 c. servings   154 calories per serving

(T) NAVY BEAN SOUP WITH DUMPLINGS

| 24% | 4% | 74% |

1½ c. navy beans   2½ quarts of water

You may soak beans overnight, cook until tender or you may eliminate the soak time and bring to boil at once. Then turn off the burner for an hour. Bring to boil again and boil gently until tender. **ADD** 2 c. liquified tomatoes, 1 diced potato, ½ t. celery seed powder, 1 t. onion powder, 1 t. vegetable salt, ½ t. oregano leaves. Continue cooking fifteen minutes and **ADD** 2 T. soy sauce or equivalent. **DROP** dumplings into hot soup and cook gently for 20 minutes without removing the lid. (Dumplings may fall if lid is removed)

16-½ c. servings   80 calories per serving

Dumplings, page

(T) DUMPLINGS
17%   7%   82%

1¼ c. golden, unbleached white flour or whole hard wheat flour
1 T. cornmeal
1 T. soy flour
¼ t. salt

DISSOLVE ½ T. yeast in ½ c. lukewarm water. Let stand for 15 minutes then pour over the blended flours. *MIX* and let batter stand for 20 minutes. *DROP* by tablespoonfuls into hot soup and cook gently for 20 minutes without removing lid. (This should be eaten the next day reheated as foods made with yeast digest more easily after standing 24 hours.)

16 dumplings-1 T.   35 calories per serving

SUNFLOWER SEED LOAF
15%   33%   67%

1 c. sunflower seeds, ground
2 c. whole grain bread crumbs
2 c. grated raw potato
2 t. salt or less
4 c. water
¾ c. grated onion
¼ t. each garlic powder, thyme, oregano

MIX all ingredients and put in non-stick loaf pan. *BAKE* 1 hour at 350°.

20-¼ c. servings   84 calories per serving

·TOFU VEGETABLE QUICHE

½ lb. tofu
½ c. water
½ c. cashew nuts, ground fine in nut grinder
1/8 t. garlic powder
1 t. salt
2 T. arrowroot or cornstarch
1 t. sweet basil or Italian or Salad Seasoning

BLEND in blender until smooth. *SAUTÉ* the following in a small amount of water for just a few minutes:

½ c. chopped green pepper
½ c. pimientos
½ c. sliced onions
½ c. diced carrots

ADD vegetables to the creamy mixture along with ½ c. sliced olives. *MIX* and pour into an unbaked pie shell (almond-oat) and *BAKE* at 350 degrees for 35 minutes.

GRAVIES AND SAUCES

(T) BROWN OR CHICKEN-LIKE GRAVY
17%   5%   85%

SAUTÉ:
1 onion, diced
¼ c. water and 3 T. whole wheat flour
3 c. potato or green bean water
Vegix, Marmite, soy sauce or chicken-like seasoning to taste (approx. 1 T.) **BLEND** and bring to a boil. **VARIATION:** For creamy gravy add ½ c. cashews to the mixture and blend, using a little chicken-like seasoning.

12-¼ c. servings   13 calories per serving

CREAMY TOMATO GRAVY
14%   50%   42%

SAUTÉ:
½ c. water   1 large onion

BLEND AND ADD:
1 qt. canned tomatoes
½ c. nuts-almonds, cashews, or sunflower seeds
½ c. cooked rice
2 T. sesame seeds (optional)
2 T. flake yeast (optional)
Pinch of garlic powder

Bring to a boil and let cook for 5 minutes. Serve.

24-¼ c. servings   41 calories per serving

GOLDEN SAUCE
11%   32%   61%

¾ c. cooked potato   2 T. cashews
1 medium carrot, cooked   ¾ t. salt
1-1/3 c. water   1 T. lemon juice

BLEND in blender until smooth. **HEAT** and serve over vegetables such as cauliflower, broccoli, eggplant, baked potatoes, etc.

32-1 T. servings   8 calories per serving

(T) PARSLEY SAUCE
17%   5%   83%

2 T. whole wheat flour   ½ t. soy sauce
1 c. soy or *nut milk*   ¼ t. celery salt
1 t. dry parsley flakes *or*   1/8 t. salt
1 T. chopped fresh parsley

Use same method for cooking as The Thick Cream Sauce.

16-1 T. servings   8 calories per serving

THICK CREAM SAUCE
12%   73%   21%

3 T. w.w. flour
1 c. soy or nut milk
2 t. chicken-like seasoning

PUT flour into saucepan and add enough milk (approx. 1/3 c.) to blend with flour, mixing until smooth. **ADD** remaining milk and seasoning and mix thoroughly. **COOK** over low heat, stirring constantly, until sauce thickens.

16-1 T. servings   12 calories per serving

(T) GARBANZO FLOUR GRAVY
24%   12%   66%

BLEND ½ c. garbanzo flour in 2 c. water
ADD ½ t. salt, ¼ t. onion powder, 1/8 t. garlic powder, 1/8 t. celery seed, 1 t. minced onion, 3 T. soy sauce, 3 T. food yeast, 2 t. dried parsley or 2 T. fresh parsley. **COOK** on low heat until thickened. Flour may be browned before blending if desired. Potato water may be used for part of the liquid. **VARIATION:** Other flours can be used in place of garbanzo flour, such as whole wheat, barley, millet, etc. Use less or more seasoning to your taste.

32-1 T. servings   25 calories per serving

(T) SWEET AND SOUR SAUCE
11%   4%   96%

2 large tomatoes
1 small onion
5 dates
1 T. lemon juice
½ t. salt
½ t. sweet basil
½ t. celery seed

PEEL tomatoes and cut into pieces. Mince onions, Cut dates into small pieces. **COMBINE** these three ingredients and simmer until consistency of a sauce. **ADD** remaining ingredients and **COOK** slowly for 30-40 minutes. Stir frequently. **SERVE** as a relish with entrees.

16-1 T. servings   15 calories per serving

PIMIENTO-PARSLEY SAUCE
13%   60%   33%

1 c. soy milk or *nut milk*   2 T. chopped pimiento
1 T. whole wheat flour   2 T. chopped parsley
2 t. lemon juice   ½ t. salt

Heat ¾ c. of milk. Mix flour with remaining ¼ c. milk until smooth. **ADD** slowly to warm milk, stirring constantly. Bring to near boiling. **ADD** remaining ingredients. Stir well. **SERVE.**

16-1 T. servings   15 calories per serving

CASHEW GRAVY (WHITE SAUCE)
12%   63%   30%

2 c. hot water
½ c. cashews
2 t. onion powder
2 T. cornstarch or arrowroot starch
½ t. salt

BLEND until smooth. Pour in small pan and bring to boil. Use as is for white sauce. **ADD** 1 T. food yeast for gravy. **VARIATIONS:** May use soy sauce instead of food yeast and salt.

32-1 T. servings   16 calories per serving

MELTY CHEESE

4 oz. jar pimientos
2 T. arrowroot or cornstarch
½ c. cashew nuts
1 c. water
2 t. salt
¼ c. food yeast
¼ c. oat flour (finely ground rolled oats)
2 T. lemon juice
1 t. onion powder

BLEND well. **ADD** 1½ c. boiling water and cook until thick.
SERVE WARM over tacos, haystacks, corn chips, etc.

DRESSINGS AND SPREADS

NO-OIL SOY MAYONNAISE
11%   64%   29%

1½ c. water (bring to boil)

3 T. arrowroot powder or cornstarch mixed with
½ c. water
ADD to boiling water and bring to boil again. Remove from heat.

1 c. water in blender
1 c. soy milk (use ¼ c. powder and 1 c. water)
1½ to 2 c. cashew nuts
BLEND thoroughly and add

½ c. lemon juice
1 T. salt
2 t. garlic powder - blend

ADD starch mixture and mix thoroughly. Refrigerate. This makes more than a quart. **PLEASE NOTE:** In the 4th edition of this book, Sept. 1981, changes were made in this recipe as follows:

4 T. arrowroot instead of 3 T.
¼ c. quick oatmeal instead of ¼ c. soy milk powder
1 c. cashews instead of 2 c. cashews

Some didn't like the changes, but others did. This is an excellent recipe and can be adjusted to suit your needs. The reason for using the oatmeal instead of the soy milk and cutting down the cashews is to cut down on the cost and the total fat in the recipe. However, you may want to use ⅔ c. soy milk powder, ⅔ c. oatmeal, 1 c. cashews. This can be varied to suit your needs or preferences.

20-¼ c. servings   73 calories per serving
1 T. serving   18 calories

SOY MAYONNAISE
23%   36%   28%

2 c. Tofu
3 T. lemon juice
1 clove garlic or 1 t. garlic powder
½ t. celery seed (optional)
¼ t. onion powder
¼ t. onion salt
¼ t. sweet basil (optional)

BLEND all together until smooth. If too thick, add water to get desired consistency.

40-1 T. servings   27 calories per serving

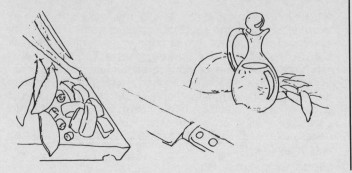

CREAMY LEMON DRESSING
16%   62%   28%

1 c. water
2 T. arrowroot or cornstarch
Blend together, simmer until thickened and put in blender when cool.

ADD ½ c. sunflower seeds
1/8 t. each ground dill seed, onion powder, garlic powder, celery seed
½ t. vegesal or ¼ t. salt
2 T. food yeast
¼ c. fresh lemon juice

BLEND until smooth.

16-1 T. serving   33 calories per serving

CASHEW SWEET BASIL DRESSING
11%   73%   22%

2 T. dehydrated onions   1 t. sweet basil
1 c. water   2 T. lemon juice
½ c. raw cashews   6 olives (optional)
½ t. salt   Dash garlic salt (optional)
1/8 t. thyme (optional)

In blender **WHIZ** all ingredients except lemon juice and olives. Then add lemon juice and olives and blend until smooth.

16-1 T. servings   28 calories per serving

CASHEW MAYONNAISE
12%   72%   23%

1 c. water
½ c. cashews
2 T. fresh lemon juice
½ t. salt
¼-½ t. onion powder (as you prefer)
Pinch garlic powder

BLEND cashews in water until smooth. **COOK** until thick. **ADD** lemon juice, salt, garlic and onion seasonings.

16-1 T. servings   29 calories per serving

GREEN ONION DRESSING
13%   56%   37%

1 c. No-oil soy mayonnaise
½ c. each, chopped, green onions, fresh parsley, green pepper
¼ t. ground dill and ¼ t. sweet basil
Few drops of lemon juice (optional)

STIR to blend flavors. Refrigerate for an hour or two to enhance flavor.

24-1T. servings   14 calories per serving

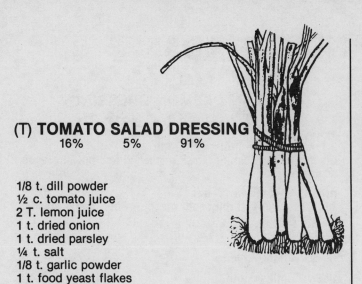

(T) TOMATO SALAD DRESSING
16%   5%   91%

1/8 t. dill powder
½ c. tomato juice
2 T. lemon juice
1 t. dried onion
1 t. dried parsley
¼ t. salt
1/8 t. garlic powder
1 t. food yeast flakes
¼ t. sweet basil

COMBINE all ingredients in jar with lid and shake well.

8-1 T. servings   7 calories per serving

(T) FRENCH-TYPE SALAD DRESSING
8%   1%   94%

¼ c. water   1 T. cornstarch

MIX and add to the following:
½ c. tomato juice   ½ t. salt
1/8 t. garlic powder   ¼ t. paprika
½ t. dried salad herbs

BRING TO BOIL and **COOK** until thick. **STIR** in lemon juice from one lemon or put in blender to combine. Fresh lemon juice is best to use in salad dressing and you may use more or less to suit your taste.

12-1 T. servings   4 calories per serving

(T) ITALIAN-TYPE SALAD DRESSING
1%   1%   98%

¼ c. water
¼ c. lemon juice, fresh
dash of garlic powder
Italian salad herbs to suit your taste
¼ t. onion salt

8-1 T. servings   2 calories per serving

MILLET MAYONNAISE

1/3 c. millet, ground   1½ c. water
Combine these two ingredients and bring to boil. Simmer five minutes, stirring all the time.

1 T. tapioca flour
2 T. soy flour
½ c. cold water

MIX together and **STIR** into millet mixture and **BOIL** one minute. Continue stirring. **ADD** ½ c. ground cashew nuts or other nuts. **POUR** all into blender while hot and whiz until smooth. Then **ADD:** ¼ t. each onion powder, celery salt, salt and 1/8 t. each paprika and garlic salt. 3 T. lemon juice and whiz again, just enough to barely mix.

40-1 T. servings   17 calories per serving

COLE SLAW DRESSING
13%   64%   31%

1 c. cashew nuts
2 cucumbers, thinly peeled if necessary
2 green onions with tops
2/3 T. onion salt
½ c. lemon juice, fresh or frozen pure lemon juice

BLEND and pour over freshly chopped cabbage. Good on any salad.

32-1 T. servings   28 calories per serving

AVOCADO DRESSING OR DIP
7%   82%   18%

1½ c. water   ¼-½ c. onion
½ c. cashew nuts   ½ t. salt
2 avocados   2 T. fresh lemon juice

BLEND cashews in water until smooth. **ADD** all other ingredients and blend.

40-1 T. servings   35 calories per serving

AVOCADO DRESSING
6%   80%   35%

½ c. orange juice   ¼ t. salt
1 T. lemon juice

ADD to a mashed avocado and beat until satiny smooth.

16-1 T. servings   34 calories per serving

(T) RUMANIAN EGGPLANT DIP

1 to 1¼ pound eggplant
½ c. cooked and drained garbanzo beans
2 T. lemon juice
2 t. parsley, finely minced
salt to taste, if permitted
1 clove garlic (optional)

PREHEAT oven to 400°. **SLICE** the eggplant in half lengthwise. Place the eggplant halves, cut side down, in an ovenproof dish. **BAKE** for 30 minutes or until eggplant is soft. Scoop out the pulp of the eggplant and puree or chop it very fine. Place the eggplant and the remaining ingredients in a mixing bowl. **MIX** well, check the seasoning and serve in a bowl or in the eggplant shells. Cashews may be used in place of the garbanzos if diet permits. Serve with raw vegetable sticks, etc. Some may think that garlic is a necessary ingredient in this dip; if so, it should be chopped extremely fine.

Serves six to eight

CREAMY MILLET SPREAD

10%   23%   75%

1 c. hot cooked millet
1/3 c. fine coconut or less
1/3 c. cooked carrots
1/3 c. warm water - may need more for right consistency
Small amount of onion and garlic powder, if you wish.

BLEND all until smooth and creamy. The millet must be hot and well-cooked.

32-1 T. servings   27 calories per serving

(T) LEGUME SPREAD

3 c. kidney beans
3 c. garbanzo beans

BLEND with just enough juice from legume to make a thick spread. *ADD:*
1 c. finely chopped celery
1 c. onion, chopped fine
1 T. dill weed
½ c. pimiento
½ c. green pepper

MIX well all ingredients.

(T) BEAN SPREAD

25%   4%   72%

2 c. cooked beans, drained
6 T. tomato paste
½ t. onion salt
1/8 t. sweet basil
1/8 t. oregano
Garlic powder to taste

BLEND beans until smooth, adding enough bean liquid to make a thick puree. *POUR* puree into top of double boiler. *ADD* remaining ingredients. (Grind the herbs into a powder before adding.) *COOK* until the mixture is thoroughly heated, stirring frequently. Chill.

32-1 T. servings   16 calories per serving

(T) GARBANZO SPREAD

1 c. garbanzos (drained)
¼ c. green onions (chopped fine)
1/8 t. garlic powder
1 t. parsley flakes
¼ c. celery
½ t. food yeast
½ t. sweet basil
½ c. green pepper, chopped fine
¼ c. pimiento

BLEND with enough water to make a thick spread.
Makes 1 cup.

HOMMUS TAHINI

18%   40%   45%

2 c. cooked garbanzos
½ c. sesame seed, ground
1 clove garlic (optional)
Salt to taste
1 T. chopped parsley (optional)
2-3 T. lemon juice

LIQUIFY beans, salt (about ½ t. if garbanzos are unsalted), garlic and seed, with barely enough bean broth to make blender turn. *SPRINKLE* with garlic powder if clove garlic is omitted. Serve over toast.

32-1 T. servings   34 calories per serving

SUNNY SPREAD

17%   75%   15%

2/3 c. sunflower seeds, ground fine
1 T. toasted peanuts, ground fine
Add 1-2 T. lemon juice and enough water to make a spreading consistency. Stir by hand. *ADD* salt to taste. May use some onion or garlic powder or soy sauce for different flavor.

8-1 T. servings   78 calories per serving

TOMATO-NUT SPREAD

14%   64%   28%

3 c. tomatoes, canned or juice
½ c. nuts, cashews, or almonds
¼ c. sunflower seeds
2 T. sesame seeds
1 T. chicken-like seasoning
1 T. cornstarch or arrowroot starch

BLEND all ingredients until smooth. Bring to a boil, stirring constantly. Boil for 3-5 minutes. *VARIATION:* 1 T. flake yeast, 2 T. onion powder, dash of garlic powder.

48-1 T. servings   19 calories per serving

SANDWICH SPREAD

11%   70%   27%

1 c. cashew nuts
2 c. water
3 T. soy milk powder (optional)
1 t. salt
4 t. onion powder
1/3-1/2 c. lemon juice
1-4 oz. jar pimientos
2 T. food yeast

BLEND. Cook and add:
1 c. chopped green pepper
4 small onions, chopped
1 can tomato sauce
2 cans sliced olives

Cook 5 minutes.

16-¼ c. servings   85 calories per serving

PIMIENTO SPREAD OR OLIVE SPREAD
10%   63%   32%

¾ c. water
1 c. cooked brown rice
¼ t. onion powder
½ c. sesame seeds, ground
3 t. food yeast
½ t. salt

1 T. lemon juice
4 oz. jar pimiento *or*
1 can chopped olives
1/8 t. garlic powder
¼ c. raw cashews

BLEND the above ingredients until smooth. **SOAK** 4 T. agar flakes in 1 c. cold water for 5 minutes. **SIMMER** until clear. **TURN** on blender and add agar to mixture while blender is running. **POUR** into a container and refrigerate. Cashews and/or sesame seeds can be omitted if desired.

32-1 T. servings   34 calories per serving

(T) RICE SPREAD

1 c. rice (or any cooked cereal)
½ t. sweet basil
½ t. onion powder
½-1 t. onion salt
garlic powder (sprinkle)
2-3 t. lemon juice
1 oz. pimiento
1 t. food yeast

BLEND well.

NUT SPREAD
13%   79%   19%

1 c. water
1 peeled lemon (remove seeds)
½ t. salt
¾ c. nuts - almonds
Onion, parsley, other herbs may be added. Blend all.

16-1 T. servings   44 calories per serving

PIZZA BUN TOPPING
11%   62%   33%

1½ c. No-Oil Soy Mayonnaise
½ chopped bell pepper
2 small onions

½ c. tomato sauce
1 can sliced olives
1 T. food yeast flakes

Cook to thicken. Make open-faced and broiled, or may be heated through at 350 degrees.

8-¼ c. servings   92 calories per serving

SAVORY SAUCE OR SPREAD
12%   59%   34%

2 c. water
3 T. raw cashews
½ t. vegetable salt
1/3 c. ground sesame seeds
3 T. arrowroot powder or cornstarch
1 t. onion powder or 1 large onion
1 T. whole wheat flour
2 T. Bronners Boullion or soy sauce

PUT above ingredients in blender and blend well. Then pour into a kettle and cook over low heat until thick. **SERVE** over cooked rice, potatoes, or toast. For a delicious spread for bread or toast, mix sauce half and half with ground cashews or other nuts. Can be frozen.

8-¼ c. servings   101 calories per serving

CASHEW PIMIENTO CHEESE SPREAD
13%   66%   28%

1 c. raw cashews
1½ c. water
1 T. food yeast
¼-1/3 c. fresh lemon juice
¾ t. salt

3 t. onion powder
4 oz. pimiento *or*
1 c. tomatoes
Pinch of garlic powder

BLEND above ingredients until smooth.
To slice - **ADD** 2 T. arrowroot or cornstarch, cook until thick, refrigerate in square container. To grate—follow directions to slice. Freeze—grate while frozen.

48-1 T. servings   20 calories per serving

PEANUT-SOY SPREAD
25%   54%   27%

1¼ c. raw peanuts
1 c. soy beans, soaked
1½ c. water
1 T. food yeast flakes
½ t. each: salt, onion salt, celery salt
¼ c. gluten flour
¼ c. whole wheat flour (100% fine)

BLEND first three ingredients until quite fine. **POUR** batter in bowl and add remaining ingredients. **FILL** tin vegetable cans with batter up to 2/3 full. **PLACE** cans in kettle with 2 inches of water. **STEAM** for 1½-2 hours. Let cool in cans. **CUT** out bottom of can and run knife around the edge to loosen and push contents out. This can be sliced for sandwiches, mixed with other ingredients, such as celery, onion, cucumbers, tomatoes, olives, no-oil soy mayonnaise—your choice.

18 servings   112 calories per serving

GUACAMOLE SPREAD
4%   75%   29%

1 hearty slice fresh tomato (may use canned tomatoes)
2 t. chopped onion
Trace garlic salt
2 avocados (ripe)

1 T. lemon juice
½ t. salt

BLEND in blender until smooth or mash avocados, add salt, garlic salt, and lemon juice. **CHOP** tomato and onion fine and combine all ingredients. **CHILL** covered to keep avocados from turning dark. **MIX** with finely chopped lettuce.

16 T.   47 calories per serving

(T) QUICK TOMATO CATSUP
16%   5%   92%

½ c. chopped onion
1 clove garlic
¼ c. lemon juice
2 c. tomato puree
1 c. tomato paste
2 dates

1 t. salt
1 t. paprika
¼ t. cumin
½ t. sweet basil
¼ c. water

BLEND onion, dates, and garlic with lemon juice and ½ c. tomato puree until smooth. COMBINE with rest of ingredients. Bring to boil and let simmer a few minutes or until desired consistency. VARIATION you can use tomato pulp without the juice for the tomato puree or tomato paste.

24-1 T. servings   12 calories per serving

(T) KETCHUP
16%   4%   92%

1-12 oz. can tomato paste
2 T. date sugar or date butter
½ t. salt

2 T. lemon juice
¼ t. onion powder
1/8 t. garlic powder

Just MIX together. Quick, easy, very tasty.

56-1 T. servings   8 calories per serving

NO OIL ARTIFICIAL CHEESE LOAF
13%   56%   38%

Place in blender:
1/3 c. lemon juice
1 c. stewed or canned tomatoes
1 t. salt
3 T. food yeast
½ t. onion powder or flakes
½ c. broken cashews
1 small cooked potato
¼ of an avocado

BLEND thoroughly until smooth texture is obtained. Put 1½ c. of warm water in pan. ADD 2½ T. agar powder or more of the flakes. Bring to boil and boil about a minute. ADD this mixture to blender with the other part and blend quickly. You may find it necessary to stop the blender to stir the mixture and then begin again. Move very quickly. As soon as this is well-mixed, and it must be quickly, POUR it into plastic refrigerator dishes and put in refrigerator to harden. It will become a loaf that can be sliced, grated or used otherwise like cheese.

16 slices   49 calories per serving

GARBANZO-PIMIENTO SPREAD
18%   34%   52%

1 c. dry garbanzos soaked for 24 hours
1/3 c. Brazil nuts-remove most of the broken husk
4-oz. jar pimientos
1 t. of salt
¼ c. lemon juice
1-1½ c. water
½ t. onion powder
¼ t. garlic powder

COMBINE all ingredients in blender until very fine. COOK 25-30 minutes in double boiler stirring occasionally. MOLD into two small bread pans which have been rinsed with cold water. CHILL. SLICE and serve. This may be grated. You may use fresh chives, sage or your choice of herbs instead of pimientos.

56 slices   19 calories per serving

MILLET BUTTER

1 c. hot millet
¼ c. cooked carrots
¼ c. cashew nuts, unroasted

1 t. salt
1½ c. water
1 t. agar flakes

COOK agar flakes in water for 2-3 minutes, stirring. Blenderize ½ of cooked agar with other ingredients until very smooth. ADD the rest of the agar blending at low speed. COOL a little and put in serving dishes to finish cooling.

CORN BUTTER

½ c. fine coconut, grind in seed grinder
2 c. cooked corn

BLEND until smooth. May have to add a little water. It thickens more when cold. May add garlic for garlic bread.

CASHEW JACK CHEESE
12%   70%   23%

1 c. water
1 c. cashews
1/8 t. garlic salt
½ t. onion salt

1 T. yeast flakes
¼ c. onion chips
2 T. lemon juice

WHIZ all ingredients until smooth. DRIZZLE over pizza, pita, burritos, tacos. USE as cheese sauce to pour over vegetables or any dishes using cheese.

24-1 T. servings   31 calories per serving

GARLIC BUTTER

½ c. cashew nuts
1 c. hot cooked/fine cornmeal
1 c. water
1 t. salt
1 T. food yeast flakes
½ c. ground sesame seeds
1 T. onion flakes
2 cloves garlic
½ t. dill weed
¼ t. marjoram

BLEND all ingredients until smooth. Good on crackers or french bread or open-faced sandwiches browned under the broiler.

SESAME SPREAD
11%   75%   20%

½ c. water
¾ c. sesame seeds (grind in Moulinex first)
1/8 t. salt
1/3 c. water
¼ c. date granules or dates

SIMMER date granules in water until soft. BLEND all ingredients together until smooth.

16-1 T. servings   90 calories per serving

DATE BUTTER

1 c. pitted dates cut in pieces   ½ c. water

BOIL for 6-8 minutes stirring constantly until smooth. You may use more water if thinner consistency is desired.

VARIATION: Use ½ c. each of apples and dates. If dates are soft, you can blend water and dates without cooking. Good with peanut butter for sandwiches.

DRIED FRUIT JAM

REHYDRATE dried apples, pears, peaches, etc., or any combination of these with just enough water to cover the fruit. Simmer until soft or soak overnight. **PUT** in blender and whiz until smooth. Store in refrigerator. Will keep at least a week. Increase sweetness by adding date granules simmered in small amount of water until soft or chopped pitted dates.

BLEND all together until smooth.

(T) APPLE JAM
2%   3%   100%

Soak 1 c. dried apples in 3 c. pineapple juice and blend.

48-1 T. servings   11 calories per serving

(T) FIG JAM
4%   1%   100%

Blend 2 c. dried figs with desired amount of orange juice.

32-1 T. servings   11 calories per serving

PRUNE JAM
8%   40%   59%

2 c. pitted prunes, 1 c. cashew nuts. Add water and blend.

40-1 T. servings   38 calories per serving

ALMOND DATE JAM

Blend almonds and dates with equal amount of water.

(T) PINEAPPLE APRICOT JAM
5%   2%   104%

1¼ c. pitted dried prunes or 1 c. pitted dates
1 c. dried apricots
½ c. crushed unsweetened pineapple

SIMMER prunes and apricots in juice or water (enough to cover fruit) until soft or soak overnight. Blend with the pineapple in blender until smooth.

32 T. Servings   27 calories per serving

(T) FRUIT SPREAD

1 #2 (20 oz.) can crushed pineapple
1 c. chopped dates
½ c. ground dried apricots
1/8 c. ground raisins
½ c. soaked dried pears

COMBINE all ingredients. To 1 cup of jam, **ADD** 1 medium sized apple blended in pineapple juice (just enough juice so it can be blended in blender).

FILBERT SPREAD
7%   81%   18%

1½ c. filberts   1-2 bananas
1¼ c. water   Pinch of salt

PUT filberts and water in blender and **BLEND** until smooth. **ADD** banana and salt and blend. Use as a spread on bread instead of butter. **NOTE:** Must be stored in refrigerator. Do not make a lot at one time as it only keeps 2-3 days.

32-1 T. servings   44 calories per serving

PEAR JAM

2 c. pineapple—coconut juice (from health food store) Thicken with tapioca and **ADD** mashed canned pears, about one cup.

This can also be made by thickening the pineapple-coconut juice with dried pears. **SOAK** the pears in the juice for an hour or so and blend, or they can be blended at once, but they will not blend as rapidly.

38-1 t. servings

(T) STRAWBERRY JAM
3%   4%   100%

1 c. dates
1 med. size can crushed pineapple
1 qt. frozen unsweetened strawberries
½ c. water

BLEND dates, pineapple, water and 1/3 of strawberries. Put all in pan and bring to boil. Add arrowroot starch or corn starch mixed with water and cook to thicken. Slice remaining berries. Add to rest of mixture and cool. May be frozen if too much for immediate use.

64-1 T. servings   14 calories per serving

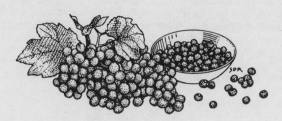

GRAPE JAM

1 large can grape and pear concentrate
2 cans water

Bring to a boil, **THICKEN** partially with 2 T. arrowroot and tapioca. Put in blender and thicken with dried apples to jam consistency. Dried apples—soak overnight in juice. **ADD** blueberries. **BLEND**-will make a grape-like jam.

APPLE-NUT SPREAD
5%   67%   35%

1 orange (blend after peeling)

ADD 2 apples, cored
1 c. nuts or less (pecans are good)

BLEND all.

48 1-T. servings   22 calories per serving

NUT OR SEED BUTTER

½ c. water in blender

ADD nuts of any kind to blender until the desired consistency of butter is reached. **ADD** a pinch of salt and flavorings if desired. Use sparingly. **ALTERNATIVE:** Grind nuts or seeds in nut grinder until fine. Pour into container and add enough water to make a thick paste. **VARIATION:** Almonds, cashews, walnuts, peanuts, hazelnuts, sesame seeds, sunflower seeds, etc. Nuts and seeds could be lightly roasted.

PEANUT PINEAPPLE JAM
16%   67%   23%

Dilute 1 c. peanut butter with 1 c. pineapple juice and add crushed pineapple.

32-1 T. servings   11 calories per serving

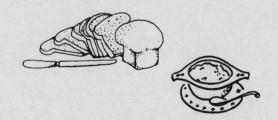

VEGETABLES

BEST METHODS FOR COOKING VEGETABLES
(They should be free from the slightest sign of decay)

1. Cook without water, if possible.

2. Cook as short a time as possible and just before serving.

3. Avoid bruising, soaking, or wilting vegetables.

4. Keep vegetables cold until ready to cook.

5. Avoid use of soda for preserving color and crispness.

6. Do not remove cover while cooking.

7. Avoid the use of utensils that are chipped, worn, have copper alloys or are made of aluminum.

8. Use plastic scouring pad or stiff brush for vegetables. A stainless steel metal mesh pad may be used but be sure to check vegetables for tiny pieces of steel that could cling to them. A stiff nylon mesh is also good for some vegetables.

9. When done, vegetables should have a crisp, tender texture. Overcooked they are mushy, strong flavored and lose attractive natural color.

10. Cook vegetables whole or in large pieces when possible. Cook with skins on to save nutrients. Be sure potatoes have all green removed and thick patches of skin.

11. Start vegetables in boiling water to conserve the greatest possible amounts of nutrients. To preserve the bright green color, cook vegetables uncovered for 1 minute **AFTER** the boiling point has been reached, cover, reduce heat promptly to lowest cooking level, and cook until done.

12. Stir as little as possible, and do not boil vigorously.

13. A small amount of lemon juice added to the cooking water will help restore the color of red cabbage and beets.

14. Serve as soon as the vegetable is cooked. Keeping vegetables warm after they are cooked causes loss of food value, particularly vitamins. If they must wait, allow to cool, then reheat.

SEASONING VEGETABLES

There are many ways to make vegetables taste well-seasoned without using too much salt and still avoid harmful substances such as vinegar, black pepper or other spices.

Herbs can be used to enhance the natural flavors of foods. There are no rules to seasoning. Experiment. If you are unfamiliar with an herb, try its effect on various foods by using a small amount at first. If the flavor needs to blend in certain foods, add the flavor at the beginning. If the flavor is to be kept distinct from the food it is used with, add just before serving. Long cooking destroys flavor. Fresh herbs are more desirable in salads. Use 3 times as much fresh than if dried.

The use of lemon juice can perk up the food. Tomato can be used in a similar way, raw and chopped, canned, as sauce or puree. Onion, green pepper, celery, parsley, or garlic will add interesting touches. The addition of chopped nuts or seeds add a delightful flavor, or try a cream sauce.

SUGGESTIONS:

Asparagus . . . . Lemon juice, Golden sauce, slivered almonds

Beets . . . . Tarragon, sweet basil, thyme, bay leaf, lemon juice

Broccoli . . . . Tarragon, marjoram, oregano, lemon juice, sesame seeds,
Cashew-Pimiento Cheese Spread

Brussel Sprouts . . . . Sweet basil, dill, savory, thyme

Carrots . . . . Sweet basil, dill, thyme, marjoram, parsley, mint, onion rings, cream sauce

Cauliflower . . . . . . Rosemary, savory, dill, Cashew-Pimiento Cheese Spread, parsley, paprika

Cabbage . . . . Caraway, celery seed, savory, dill

Corn . . . . Dill, sweet basil, pimiento, parsley, green pepper

Cucumbers . . . . Tarragon, sweet basil, savory, dill, lemon juice, paprika

Eggplant . . . . Sweet basil, thyme, oregano, sage, tomato

Beans (dried) . . . . . Sweet basil, oregano, dill, savory, cumin, garlic, parsley, bay leaf, tomato

Green Beans . . . . Sweet basil, dill, thyme, majoram, oregano, savory, tomato,
onion, garlic, almonds, mushrooms

Lima Beans . . . . Sweet basil, chives, savory

Onions . . . . Oregano, thyme, sweet basil

Peas . . . . Sweet basil, mint, savory, oregano, dill, mushrooms, parsley

Potatoes . . . . Dill, chives, sweet basil, marjoram, savory, parsley

Squash . . . . Sweet basil, dill, oregano, savory, flake yeast

Spinach . . . . Tarragon, thyme, oregano, rosemary

Tomatoes . . . . Sweet basil, oregano, dill, garlic, savory, parsley, bay leaf, lemon juice, chives

Green Salad Dressing . . . . Sweet basil, oregano, marjoram, onion, garlic, sage

Chili Substitute . . . . Spanish onions with cumin

Our mealtime should be seasoned with peace and happiness. This atmosphere makes for good eating habits and good digestion.

VEGETABLE PLATTER COMBINATIONS
1. Cauliflower in the center with small whole beets on outside or green beans and carrots.
2. Mound of cooked broccoli or brussel sprouts surrounded by carrot sticks.
3. Mound of baby carrots surrounded by green peas and small steamed onions.

(T) EGGPLANT
15%   10%   78%

PEEL large eggplant and *SLICE* in ¼ inch slices. *DIP* slices in cashew nut gravy (do not precook the gravy). Then *DIP* slices in breading meal. *PLACE* on griddle or in large flat pan to bake in oven. *BAKE* at 350 degrees until brown on underside. If on griddle, turn. If in oven you may turn slices over to brown or turn on broiler to brown. Watch carefully. Eggplant cooks rapidly and will be done when sides are browned. Garbanzo flour may be used instead of the cashew nut gravy and breading meal.

8-½ c. servings   130 calories per serving

(T) FRESH CORN SAUT'E
16%   11%   90%

4 c. fresh corn cut from cob
1 c. finely chopped onion
1 t. salt, seasoned
1 c. finely chopped pepper (green) or pimiento
Chopped parsley

MIX all together except the parsley. *ADD* small amount of water and cover. *SIMMER* about 5-10 minutes. Stir once. *ADD* parsley—serve.

10-½ c. servings   59 calories per serving

CELERY LOAF
15%   49%   40%

1-1½ c. coarse ground toast crumbs
1 c. ground celery
1 c. ground onion
1-1½ c. hot soy milk
1 c. coarse ground nuts
2 T. flax seed meal and 2 T. Do-Pep (optional)
Seasonings to taste (onion and garlic salt, soy sauce, yeast flakes) *POUR* hot milk over crumbs and soak while you grind the vegetables. *MIX* all ingredients together and *BAKE* in loaf pan at 350 degrees for 1 hour.

10-½ c. servings   145 calories per serving

CARROT ROAST
11%   14%   76%

4 c. grated carrots—½ c. chopped onion
4 c. cooked rice, brown
1 c. bread crumbs
2 T. peanut butter mixed in ½ c. water, 1/8 t. thyme, salt to taste

MIX and *BAKE* 1 hour at 350 degrees. *SERVE* with your choice of gravy.

12-½ c. servings   120 calories per serving

CREAMED CELERY
21%   17%   70%

8 large ribs celery, diagonally cut ¼" thick (about 6 cups)
½ c. water
½ t. salt
2 T. dry onion flakes
1 t. dry parsley flakes
2 t. chicken-style seasoning
2 pimiento, diced
4 oz. sliced mushrooms with 1 c. liquid (fill with water to make 1 c.) May use water chestnuts
4 t. cornstarch or arrowroot starch
4 t. sliced almonds (optional)

COOK celery in water to desired tenderness (a little on the crisp side). *ADD* all other ingredients except water and starch which should be mixed and added to all and cooked until thickened. *GARNISH* with almond slices. May be served over rice.

6-½ c. servings   29 calories per serving

(T) MACARONI AND CABBAGE DINNER
14%   3%   82%

Cashew gravy
4 c. cooked macaroni (may use whole wheat or half whole wheat or regular)
4 c. chopped cooked cabbage (do not overcook)
1 t. salt

MIX gravy, cabbage and macaroni gently. *PUT* in casserole. May break bread crumbs over top. *BAKE* 30 minutes or until hot at 350 degrees.

10-½ c. servings   147 calories per serving

GREEN BEANS ALMONDINE

WASH and cut beans in 1" pieces. *ADD* a small amount of water. Cover and cook for 8 minutes or till almost done, and *ADD* a small amount of salt and thyme. When done *ADD* 2 T. toasted almond slivers for each c. of beans. *TOSS* lightly and serve.

(T) COUNTRY POTATO PATTIES
11%   1%   89%

6 medium potatoes   1 T. chopped parsley
1 T. minced onion   2 T. flour
2 T. chopped pimiento   1 t. salt

SHRED potatoes with coarse grater. *MIX* with onion, pimiento, parsley, flour and salt. *SHAPE* into patties or mounds. *BROWN* in oven on cookie sheet sprinkled with cornmeal.

6-½ c. servings   126 calories per serving

RIBBON MACARONI WITH BROCCOLI

COOK macaroni in salted water. Cook CHOPPED broccoli to desired tenderness and combine with the macaroni. Toasted sesame seeds ground in seed grinder and sprinkled on top are nice for garnish and flavor. Also, if you cook the macaroni in a small amount of water and do not drain, this can be used as a sauce. It is especially tasty if you have cooked some whole wheat macaroni along with the ribbons.

(T) CORN AND ZUCCHINI CASSEROLE

3 c. corn
3 med. zucchini
1 onion, thinly sliced
1 clove garlic, minced
2 tomatoes, peeled, and chopped
salt as permitted

If you use fresh corn, CUT the kernels off the ears of corn with a sharp knife. SLICE the zucchini into thin rounds. Preheat the oven to 350 degrees. SAUTÉ the vegetables for ten minutes or until tender and lightly browned. ADD the onion, garlic, and zucchini. Then stir in the corn, tomatoes, and salt. Spoon the vegetables into a ovenproof dish. BAKE for 15 minutes.

Serves six.

(T) ZUCCHINI AND TOMATOES
20%   4%   87%

4 small zucchini squash
1 c. diced, canned or fresh tomatoes
1 onion, chopped
¼ c. chopped green pepper (optional)
Salt to taste

SLICE zucchini squash into a pan with a little water. ADD chopped onion, green pepper and salt and cook until zuchinni is tender. ADD tomatoes and heat through.

8-½ c. servings   28 calories per serving

(T) ZUCCHINI PATTIES
15%   8%   78%

1 diced onion
2 c. grated zucchini
1 c. bread crumbs
¾ c. garbanzo flour
2 T. chicken-like seasoning
Salt to taste

SAUTÉ onion in small amount water. MIX all ingredients. BROWN in oven on both sides. SERVE with gravy or plain
12-¼ c. servings   44 calories per serving

ESCALLOPED POTATOES
12%   33%   59%

6-8 medium potatoes (raw preferably)
¾-1 c. cashew nuts
½ T. chicken-like seasoning
2 T. flaked yeast
1 onion chopped
½ T. salt
1 bay leaf
paprika and marjoram - to decorate

PLACE the cashew nuts and seasonings except the bay leaf in the blender with 2 cups of water and blend until creamy. Add more water to make 4 c. milk or enought to cover potatoes. SLICE onions and potatoes fairly thin. PLACE in baking dish. POUR the cashew milk over all. DECORATE with bay leaf, paprika and marjoram. BAKE at 375 degrees for about 1½ hours if potatoes are raw. COVER for the first hour.

10-½ c. servings   178 calories per serving

POTATO BALLS

1 c. ground raw potatoes
2 t: soy flour
1 med. onion (chopped fine)
½ t. sage
1 c. whole wheat bread crumbs
¼ c. flour

MIX thoroughly; form into balls. BAKE 25 minutes or until brown and crisp in 350 degree oven. Serve with gravy.

POTATO - RICE CASSEROLE

3 large potatoes (sliced)
1 large onion (sliced in rings)
1 c. brown rice (uncooked)
1 T. vegit seasoning or your choice
2½-3 c. water

LAYER half of the potato slices, onion slices, and brown rice in casserole dish. Repeat. Dissolve broth in water, and POUR over layers. Water needs to cover rice so that the rice will have some water to cook in. BAKE covered at 350 degrees for 1 hour. Last 15 minutes uncover if one wishes a browned top.
5 or 6-1 c. servings.

(T) BAKED STUFFED POTATOES
11%   —   90%

SCRUB: 5 medium potatoes. BAKE at 400 degrees for 1 hour or until tender. CUT a slice from top of each lengthwise. SCOOP out insides, being careful not to break shell. MASH the potatoes in a mixing bowl and add:
1 T. parsley   ¾ c. no-oil soy mayonnaise
1 T. chives (opt.)   Salt to taste

Lightly spoon this mixture back into the potato shells. SPRINKLE top with paprika and bake for 15 minutes at 400 degrees.

5 servings - 1 potato each   115 calories per serving

(T) POTATO BOATS

3 large cleaned potatoes
2 c. rice milk
seasonings

BAKE potatoes and allow to cool. *SPOON* out inside onto large platter. Mash with fork and add rice milk until right consistency. Season as desired. Spoon mixture into potato shells and place chopped pimento or onion on top. *BAKE* at 350 degrees for 20 minutes and serve.

(T)MASHED POTATOES WITH TURNIPS

8%   1%   87%

4 c. hot mashed potatoes
4 c. hot cooked diced turnips or rutabagas

TOSS turnips with mashed potatoes and *ADD* a little seasoning salt.

16-½ c. servings   53 calories per serving

POTATOES AUGRATIN

½ recipe melty cheese (page 60)
6-8 potatoes - cook day before - slice when cold - not too thin
1 onion, chopped fine
½ green pepper, chopped fine
2-3 t. fresh parsley or 2 T dry

In 9x13 baking dish. *LAYER* potatoes and melty cheese with 1 c. water added. Make 2 layers of each. Sprinkle with paprika. *BAKE* until bubbly and crusty.

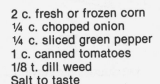

(T) CREOLE CORN

16%   10%   89%

2 c. fresh or frozen corn
¼ c. chopped onion
¼ c. sliced green pepper
1 c. canned tomatoes
1/8 t. dill weed
Salt to taste

COOK corn, onion, and green pepper over low heat until tender. Small amounts of water can be added, if necessary to prevent sticking. *ADD* remaining ingredients and *HEAT* thoroughly.

6-½ c. servings   59 calories per serving

(T) HERBED CABBAGE MEDLEY

15%   5%   91%

1 medium onion, thinly sliced
½ small head cabbage, shredded (about three cups)
3 medium carrots, shredded, 1½ c.
½ t. salt

COOK onion in a small amount of water for 5 minutes. *ADD* the cabbage and carrots and salt. *COVER;* cook over medium heat for 6-8 minutes more. *STIR* in crushed oregano.

4-½ c. servings   56 calories per serving

ENCHILADAS

Corn tortillas   Onion, chopped
Enchilada sauce, heated   Olives, chopped
Cooked pinto beans

MIX beans, olives and onions. *PLACE* one tortilla at a time in enchilada sauce and leave only until it becomes soft enough to roll (it will fall apart if left too long). *PLACE* tortilla on a plate and put about a teaspoon of sauce in center, then *SPOON* bean mixture across center, but not to edges. *ROLL* up, place in baking pan and *COVER* with more sauce. *DRIZZLE* a little Cashew-Pimiento Cheese Spread along top if desired. *BAKE* at 325 degrees for approximately 30 minutes until hot but not too dry.

SAUCE: Tomato paste watered down to sauce consistency. Add oregano, cumin, salt and garlic powder to taste.

(T) BROCCOLI ITALIAN STYLE

1 bunch broccoli   ½ c. water
1 clove garlic   1 T. chicken-like broth
salt to taste   2 oz. jar pimientos

REMOVE the leaves from the broccoli and cut off the lower part of the stalk. Cut broccoli into flowerets, rinse and drain them. *SAUTE* the garlic and broccoli for five minutes. Discard the garlic. *ADD* the broth. Salt to taste. Cover and cook over low heat for 10 to 15 minutes, or until broccoli are tender, adding a little more broth if the skillet dries out. Sprinkle with pimientos and serve. Serves four.

CHEESE BROCCOLI CASSEROLE

10%   44%   48%

1 pkg. frozen broccoli   2/3 c. each, chopped onions,
1 c. rice   celery, green pepper
1 c. water

Cheese sauce: 2 T. food yeast
1 c. raw cashews   4 ounces pimientos
2 c. water   1 2/3 t. salt
¼ c. fresh lemon juice   1/8 T. celery salt
2 T. sesame seeds   pinch of garlic powder
1 t. onion powder

BLEND all ingredients for pimiento cheese except pimientos. Add pimientos or one c. tomatoes and blend until very smooth. *MIX* all casserole ingredients together. *ADD* cheese sauce to casserole. *BAKE* in casserole dish for 1 2/3 hours at 350 degrees. If you wish to use cooked brown rice, prepare as directed, but bake only to cook broccoli—approx. 30-45 minutes.

10-2/3 c. servings   213 calories per serving

(T) SUMMER SQUASH

6 yellow squash
1 med. onion, chopped
1 med. tomato, chopped
1 c. corn
¼ c. w.w. bread crumbs

PARBOIL squash and cut in half. Scoop out center and place shells to drain thoroughly. Mix squash centers and other ingredients except the crumbs, and simmer briefly. Fill shells and top with crumbs. Bake 350 degrees until hot.

SUMMER SQUASH CASSEROLE

2 pounds yellow summer squash (about 6 cups)
¼ c. chopped onion
2 cans cream of mushroom soup or 2 c. cashew gravy
1 c. shredded carrot
18 ounce package herb season stuffing mix.

COOK sliced squash and chopped onion in small amount of water for 5 minutes. **COMBINE** soup and one can of water drained from squash, or use cashew gravy. **STIR** in shredded carrots, squash and onion. Put half of stuffing mix on bottom of 12x7x2 inch baking dish. **SPOON** vegetable mixture and sprinkle remaining stuffing over vegetables. **BAKE** in 350 degree oven for 30 minutes, or until heated through.

(T) EGGPLANT CASSEROLE
15%   8%   81%

2 c. eggplant pared and cubed
1 c. canned tomatoes
½ c. chopped green pepper
1 c. chopped onion
1 c. bread crumbs
1 t. salt

COMBINE all ingredients and **POUR** into casserole dish. **BAKE** in 350 degree oven for about one hour.

8-½ c. servings   54 calories per serving

(T) ASPARAGUS
27%   4%   81%

1 pound fresh asparagus
1 T. cold water
1 T. cornstarch
2 T. soy sauce
¼ t. salt
4 green onions
1½ c. sliced fresh mushrooms (optional)
2 tomatoes, diced

STIR FRY until crispy done.

6-½ c. servings   39 calories per serving

(T) GREEN BEANS AND TOMATOES

1 pound green beans
2 tomatoes, coarsely chopped
1 small onion, finely chopped
2 t. parsley, minced
2 t. dill, minced
salt to taste

STIR FRY the green beans in 2 T. of water and when almost done, add tomatoes and seasonings. Stir fry 1 more minute and serve hot.

PIQUANT BEANS
13%   31%   64%

1 quart beans
2 cans tomato soup (2 c. homemade)
1 medium onion diced and sautéed in water for five minutes.
PUT all in a casserole and **HEAT** thoroughly in oven. Slivered almonds may be sprinkled on top.

8-½ c. servings   99 calories per serving

ZUCCHINI RICE
19%   31%   56%

2 medium zucchini, sliced
2 T. water
1 medium onion, diced
3 c. cooked brown rice
1 T. chicken-style seasoning
½ t. sweet basil
2 t. food yeast flakes
½ c. cashew nut pieces
1 pimiento, diced

SAUTÉ onion in water, **ADD** rest of ingredients and stir-fry until hot over medium heat. May be served at once or put in casserole in refrigerator or freezer to be heated again later.

12-½ c. servings   91 calories per servings

(T) BEETS
15%   1%   92%

SHRED raw beets and just bring to temperature you wish to serve them - Hot and delicious!

6-½ c. servings   39 calories per serving

CARROT LOAF
10%   44%   45%

6 c. shredded raw carrots
2 c. bread crumbs
1 t. salt
1 onion, chopped fine
1 c. peanut butter

MIX together and **BAKE** 30-45 minutes in a 350 degree oven.

12-½ c. servings   198 calories per serving

(T) EGGPLANT CASSEROLE II
19%   6%   89%

1 medium eggplant cut in ½" cubes
1 medium onion, diced
1 small green pepper, diced
1 stalk celery, diced
1 c. tomato puree
¼ c. water
½ t. oregano
1/8 t. celery salt
½ t. onion salt
1 t. salt

MIX well and place in casserole dish. **BAKE** hour at 350 degrees.

8-½ c. servings   38 calories per serving

(T) EGGPLANT CASSEROLE DELUXE

SLICE eggplant very thin. *ROLL* slices in breading mixture of cornmeal and garlic salt. *PLACE* breaded slices on cookie sheet in very hot oven 450-500 degrees for about 15-25 minutes. *CUT* onions and bell peppers into rings. *MAKE* a sauce with tomato sauce, pimiento and oregano. Arrange eggplant slices on bottom of casserole dish, then *ADD* a layer of onions and bell pepper slices and sauce and repeat until dish is full. *BAKE* in oven at 400 degrees until done.

(T) TOFU IN PITA
17%   13%   75%

May use fresh or freeze the tofu (8 boxes). Freezing gives tofu a heavier texture. Thaw and squeeze out liquid. Save liquid. *PLACE* tofu in thin layer on baking sheets. Season with paprika, cumin, chicken-like seasoning, garlic and onion salt.
10 potatoes
6 onions
2 bunches green onions
45 pita bread (whole wheat)
Cook grated potatoes and finely chopped onion in the tofu liquid (2 c.) adding garlic and onion seasoning.

Chop green onions - add to potatoes
COMBINE all ingredients along with 2 large cans celery soup or equivalent of cashew gravy. *FILL* pita bread and arrange in pan standing up slanted. *HEAT* in 350 degree oven for 15-20 minutes or until well heated. *DECORATE* with parsley and serve hot.

45 Pita-½ c. each   65 calories per serving

(T) CABBAGE ROLLS

2 c. cooked rice
2 c. tomato sauce
SAUT'E: 1 c. chopped celery
        1 c. chopped onion
        ½ c. chopped green pepper
        ½ t. celery seed
        ½ t. sage
        ½ t. garlic powder

CORE and steam cabbage. Use ½ c. filling per cabbage leaf. Pour tomato puree over tops. (Just a little). Bake in 350 degree oven, 30-45 minutes or until well heated.

Makes 10 rolls

CREPES WITH BROCCOLI
MAKE crepes from recipe in this book. *MAKE* cashew gravy. *COOK* Broccoli crisp done. *COMBINE* gravy and broccoli and fill crepes. Place in serving dish and keep warm until served.

(T) SWEET SOUR SAUCE FOR BROWN RICE
3%   1%   98%

1½ qts. pineapple juice
2 cans pineapple chunks (20 oz.) Use juice also
½ c. dates
1 c. tomato sauce, paste or puree or 3 large fresh tomatoes

BLEND the dates in some juice along with the tomato sauce. *COMBINE* all and bring to boil. Thicken with arrowroot or cornstarch - 1 T. per cup or to the consistency you prefer.

18-½ c. servings   102 calories per serving

(T) CHINESE VEGETABLES
PREPARE BROCCOLI and CARROTS diagonally cut; ONIONS in narrow wedges, BELL PEPPERS in strips, WATER CHESTNUTS in slices, CAULIFLOWER in small flowerets, PEA PODS. If preparing for a large crowd, the vegetables may be blanched ahead of time. *MAKE* a glaze using soy sauce, Vegex, G. Washington Broth - your choice, and thicken it with arrowroot or corn starch. *HEAT* all and *SERVE* sprinkled with TOASTED, SLIVERED ALMONDS.

GARDEN VEGETABLE PIE
MAKE pie crust from recipe found in this book. *USE* Cashew Gravy Recipe also. May use package of mixed frozen vegetables or partially cooked fresh broccoli, cauliflowerets, onion, green pepper. *COMBINE* and place in unbaked pie shell. *BAKE* until bubbly and slightly brown. *LET STAND* five minutes before serving. *DECORATE* with fresh tomato wedges and parsley.

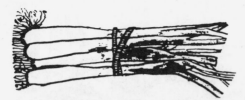

CASHEW-TOFU STIR-FRY
13%   25%   65%

½ c. boiling water
1 vegetable boullion cube (dissolve in boiling water)
2 T. soy sauce
2 t. arrowroot or cornstarch

STIR soy sauce and starch and enough water to make pouring consistency. Add to the hot water to make sauce.
2 medium carrots, thinly bias-sliced
1 head Chinese cabbage or regular cabbage cut in slices
8 ounces tofu, cubed
1 8-ounce can bamboo shoots, drained
¾ c. lighly roasted cashews

STIR-FRY carrots 3 minutes. *ADD* cabbage and stir-fry 2 minutes (use ¼ c. water in bottom of pan. *ADD* tofu, bamboo shoots, roasted cashews and stir-fry one minute more. *ADD* sauce mixture to skillet. *COOK* and stir until bubbly. *SERVE* with brown rice or in pita bread.

8-½ c. servings   308 calories per serving

SAVORY SAUCE
12%   59%   34%

This is another sauce that may be used with the Chinese Vegetables, Stir-Fry dish, or with rice.

2 c. water
3 T. cashews
1 t. Vegesal
1/3 c. ground sesame seeds
3 T. arrowroot or cornstarch
1 T. onion powder
1 T. whole wheat flour
2 T. soy sauce

BLEND all and bring to boil and simmer for a few minutes.

4-½ c. servings   148 calories per serving

(T) RICE BALLS

ANOTHER WAY to serve Brown Rice. *PRESS* soft rice into balls with hands after dipping them into salted water (1 t. per pint). *PLACE* on non-stick baking sheet and *BAKE* for 10 minutes at 450 degrees. A small piece of fruit, nut or vegetable may be enclosed in the center of each ball.

SOYBEAN CASSEROLE
29%   32%   45%

4 c. cooked soybeans
½ c. chopped celery
3 c. fresh green beans cut Italian style or 2 packages frozen, cooked
1 2-oz. jar sliced pimiento
1 c. no oil soy mayonnaise

Use 1 recipe of Cashew Gravy and add all ingredients and ½ t. dried savory. Put in 10x6x2 baking dish and sprinkle with seasoned bread crumbs. Bake uncovered in 350 degree oven for 20-25 minutes or until heated through.

20-½ c. servings   89 calories per serving

RAW VEGETABLE PLATTER COMBINATIONS

1. Arrange mounds of raw grated beets, carrots and turnips. Add favorite dressing.
2. Lettuce bed decked with radish slices, tomato wedges, cucumber and olives.
3. Combine any 2 or 3 fresh vegetables with lettuce and add cooked garbanzos. Lemon dressing goes with this very well.

(T) FRESH BROCCOLI, CAULIFLOWER SALAD
35%   5%   73%

1 bunch broccoli, washed, cut and broken into very small pieces
1 head cauliflower - washed, cut and broken into very small flowerettes
1 pkg. frozen peas
1 bunch green onions - cleaned and cut into small pieces.

ADD no-oil soy mayonnaise dressing.

20-½ c. servings   55 calories per serving

(T) GARBANZO SALAD
22%   11%   69%

2 c. garbanzos
1 stalk celery, finely chopped
¼ c. chopped parsley
¼ c. chopped pimiento
½ onion, minced
½ t. salt
½ t. savory

MIX together with no-oil soy mayonnaise. May be served on lettuce with tomato wedges.

8-¼ c. servings   122 calories per serving

(T) CABBAGE-CARROT COLE SLAW
17%   6%   90%

½ head cabbage shredded
½ c. alfalfa sprouts
1 carrot grated

MIX all vegetables together. **MIX** about ⅓ c. soy mayonnaise with 1 t. lemon juice and salt to taste. **MIX** in with vegetables just enough to moisten. You can use part green cabbage and part red cabbage for added color. **TOP** with paprika and parsley flakes. **VARIATION:** Use 1 grated turnip in place of sprouts.

4-½ c. servings   58 calories per serving

SESAME SPINACH SALAD
35%   25%   58%

1 lb. spinach   1 T. sesame seeds
½ small head lettuce   1 small handful sprouts
1 green onion, sliced

10 servings   21 calories per serving

ROSY CRUNCH SALAD
15%   45%   47%

1 c. shredded carrots   Green pepper strips
1 c. shredded beets   Endive
1 c. shredded turnips   ¼ c. sunflower seeds (opt.)

MAKE a mound of each vegetable **CLOSE** together. **DECORATE** top with alfalfa sprouts and strips of green pepper and the base with endive. **VARIATIONS:** The vegetables may be tossed with dressing.

6-½ c. servings   59 calories per serving

(T) ZUCCHINI DINNER SALAD
22%   9%   76%

1 medium zucchini
4 stalks celery
5 sprigs chopped parsley
¼ chopped green pepper
1 carrot, grated
2 tomatoes
2 green onions with tops
1 c. cooked garbanzos or green soy beans
4 lettucs cups

QUARTER zucchini lengthwise and **SLICE** thinly. Slice celery with leaves. **CUT** tomatoes into wedges. **SLICE** onions and tops. **ADD** cooked garbanzos, **TOSS** with salad dressing. Pile salad into lettuce cups and garnish with radish roses or alfalfa sprouts. The No-Oil Soy Mayonnaise is a good dressing for this.

4-½ c. servings   138 calories per serving

(T) SPROUT SALAD

1 T. sprouted lentils   ¼-½ c. alfalfa sprouts
1 T. radish sprouts

TOP with diced tomatoes, green onion, green pepper, cucumber or you choice. *SERVE* with a little onion salt and fresh lemon juice.

(T) LEBANESE SALAD (TABULI)
14%   5%   87%

1 c. bulghur wheat
½ c. scant, fresh lemon juice
4 fresh tomatoes, chopped fine
2 cucumbers, chopped fine
1 onion minced fine or
4 green onions, chopped
2 t. salt
 1 t. chicken-style seasoning (optional)
½ c. fresh parsley, chopped or 1½ T. dry parsley
¼-½ t. mint (optional) This may be dried or fresh

PLACE wheat in bowl. *ADD* seasonings and lemon juice. *ADD* enough warm water to just cover the wheat. *LET* it *SET* about one-half hour to absorb the moisture. *ADD* the other ingredients and refrigerate to blend flavors.

12-½ c. servings   70 calories per serving

(T) BARLEY SALAD
13%   4%   96%

⅓ c. barley
1 envelope G. Washington Broth
1 c. water

COOK the above for 45 minutes. All the water should be absorbed. You may have to add just a bit more. When cool, add the following:

½ c. green pepper, chopped fine
¼ t. dill weed
½ t. parsley
Juice of one lemon, more or less to taste.
1 c. thinly sliced, quartered carrots, raw
¼ t. onion salt
dash of garlic powder

MIX all ingredients and serve on a bed of chopped tomatoes.

5-½ c. servings   66 calories per serving

POTATO SALAD
10%   20%   74%

6 medium cold pre-cooked potatoes with peelings
1 c. diced celery
1 c. chopped olives
½ c. chopped pimiento
2-3 t. onion powder
1 T. dried parsley flakes
1 T. ground dill seed or dill weed
Salt to taste (approx. 2 t.)
Paprika for color

PEEL, CUBE and *MIX* potatoes with celery. *ADD* pimiento and olives. *ADD* 1 c. No-Oil Soy Mayonnaise and *MIX.* May set overnight to blend flavor.

16-½ c. servings   75 calories per serving

SPANISH BULGHUR SALAD
14%   45%   46%

¾ c. dry yellow split peas   1 t. salt
1 clove garlic, minced

RINSE peas and *ADD* 2 cups water. *BRING* to boil and *SIMMER* 25 to 30 minutes or until peas are tender. *ADD* garlic and salt. May need to add a little more water. Moisture should be absorbed—not drained off.

¾ c. bulghur
4 ounces tofu cut in small cubes
1 c. alfalfa sprouts
½ c. each chopped green pepper and green onion
¼ c. lemon juice
1 t. dried basil, crushed
2 t. chicken-like seasoning

COVER bulghur with warm water and let stand until water is absorbed. May also add the lemon juice and basil at this time, and the chicken-like seasoning. When water is absorbed, *ADD* the remaining ingredients along with the split peas. *COVER* and *CHILL.* Use a large glass plate and mound the chilled salad. Prepare tomato and avocado wedges and arrange alternately over the molded salad.

8-½ c. servings   267 calories per serving

TACO SALAD
20%   24%   63%

1 head lettuce   2 tomatoes, diced
1 large can olives, sliced   3 green onions, sliced
1 can drained kidney beans (may use pinto beans)
4 c. tortilla chips (homemade—seasoning in this book)
Dressing:
1 c. no-oil soy mayonnaise
1 large avocado
1 green onion
1 T. lemon juice
½ t. salt
1 T. chopped green pepper
BLEND until very smooth. *ADD* chips and dressing just before serving.

10 servings   143 calories per serving

(T) MARINATED ZUCCHINI-CAULIFLOWER TOSS
26%   5%   89%

1 medium head cauliflower, cut into small flowerets
4 medium zucchini, halved and sliced
1 c. cherry tomatoes, halved (may use other tomatoes)
½ c. chopped green pepper
¾ c. fresh lemon juice (blend in four med. dates)
1 T. fresh basil or 1 t. dried basil
1 t. salt

PLACE all in a covered bowl which can be turned upside down occasionally to distribute the dressing. *REFRIGERATE* overnight. Will be good for up to three days. May make ZUCCHINI-PASTA SALAD by cooking 8 ounces of noodles, whole wheat or green or soy. Rinse with cold water, drain thoroughly and add one-half of the above salad mixture.

12-½ c. servings   50 calories per serving

(T) CUCUMBER SALAD

PREPARE cucumbers in thin slices, eliminating any bitter part. ***ADD*** one-fourth as many sliced sweet onions. ***SEASON*** with onion salt, garlic salt, and Salad Seasoning or sweet basil. Add freshly-squeezed lemon juice to taste.

SOUPS

(T) GARDEN VEGETABLE SOUP
16%   3%   89%

2 medium potatoes, sliced
2 medium carrots, diced
1 c. string beans, cut small
1 medium onion, diced
2 medium summer squash, diced
2 large stalks of celery, diced
3 medium tomatoes, cut in small pieces
1/4 large green pepper, diced
2 t. salt   1/4 t. sweet basil
 t. onion salt   1/4 t. marjoram
1 T. parsley   1/8 t. dill weed
1/4 t. thyme   1/8 t. garlic salt

PUT vegetables into a large pan and cover with approximately 2½ quarts of water. **BRING** to a boil, then simmer until vegetables are nearly cooked. **ADD** cooked pearl barley, brown rice or whole wheat spaghetti and continue to cook until done. (Not included in Nutritive Values, rice, barley or spaghetti).

24-½ c. servings   23 calories per serving

(T) RICE SOUP

2 cups rice   4 cups water

STEAM COOK until soft. **ADD:**
2 carrots, chopped fine
1 small onion, chopped fine
3 stalks celery, chopped fine
1 large can pimiento
chicken-like seasoning
1 t. garlic
1 bay leaf
½ t. sweet basil
1 t. onion powder

COVER with just enough water, not more than 1" above ingredients. **SIMMER** ½ hour.

16-½ c. servings

(T) BEST BARLEY SOUP
18%   5%   82%

1/4 c. whole barley   Handful of parsley
1 c. carrots, sliced   1 T. soy sauce
½ c. celery, diced   1 t. salt
1/4 c. onions, chopped   1 t. season salt
2 c. tomatoes   1 t. onion salt
1 c. peas

COOK barley one hour in 6 c. water or more. **ADD** remainder of ingredients and simmer until tender. **ADD** chopped parsley just before serving.

20-½ c. servings   24 calories per serving

TOMATO SOUP II
14%   41%   53%

2 T. flour   4 T. water

BLEND together as for white sauce.

1 t. salt   2 c. pureed tomatoes

ADD and bring to boil. **BOIL** 1-5 minutes to cook flour. **STIR** into 2 c. HOT soy or cashew milk to avoid curdling.

8-½ c. servings   60 calories per serving

(T) ESAU'S POTTAGE
18%   4%   82%

1 c. lentils (uncooked)   2 onions, chopped fine
3 c. cold water   Salt to taste
1/3 c. raw rice   1 small clove garlic, minced
Seasonings to taste, such as savory, thyme, paprika (Spanish type), parsley, celery, salt, bay leaf.

PUT all ingredients in top of double boiler and steam for 2 or 3 hours. **OR** simmer until lentils are tender, about 1 hour, 15 minutes.

8-½ c. servings   73 calories per serving

(T) SALLIE'S NAVY BEAN SOUP
26%   6%   71%

SOAK overnight and cook until just tender (about 3 hours):

4 c. navy beans (two 12 oz. packages)

ADD:
2 large onions, chopped and sautéed
5 stalks celery, including leaves
5 t. salt
1/4 t. savory
1/4 t. marjoram
2 bay leaves

COOK until very tender and soup has thickened desirably.

OPTIONAL: Chopped parsley added at the end of cooking time, ½ c. soy flour dissolved in 1 c. water—add with sasonings.

24-½ c. servings   130 calories per serving

(T) GAZPACHO SOUP-SALAD-COLD
20%   6%   87%

3 c. tomato juice
1 cucumber, peeled and diced (¼")
2 ribs celery, diced (¼")
½ green pepper, diced (¼")
1 c. fresh tomato, diced
2 T. dry onion flakes
1 T. parsley flakes
2 t. soy sauce (optional)

PUT all ingredients in bowl several hours before serving. **STORE** in refrigerator. Serve 1 c. in each soup bowl. **DO NOT HEAT.** This Spanish salad-soup is served cold. **SHAKE** a few parsley flakes on each bowl.

10-½ c. servings   26 calories per serving

JIFFY MUSHROOM SOUP
15%   49%   41%

1-4 oz. can mushrooms with liquid
1½ c. soy or sesame milk
2 T. flour
1 T. arrowroot or cornstarch
½ t. chicken-like seasoning
½ t. basil
¼ c. chopped onion (optional)

PUT all ingredients in blender, turn on, then off; do not blend mushrooms too small, just break them up. **POUR** in small pan and cook until thickened. This soup may be used in place of canned mushroom soup.

4-½ c. servings   79 calories per serving

CORN CHOWDER I
12%   34%   61%

SIMMER until tender:

3 c. water
2 c. diced potatoes
1 small onion, chopped **or**
2 t. onion powder
½ t. celery seed **or**
½ c. chopped celery

When these vegetables are tender, **ADD:**

2 c. of whole kernel corn

BLEND:

2 c. water
½ c. cashews
2 T. arrowroot or cornstarch

ADD this blended mixture to the above and heat thoroughly or until it thickens.

18-½ c. servings   59 calories per serving

(T) CREAM OF POTATO SOUP
13%   2%   90%

CHOP up: 2 medium size onions
8 sticks of celery
½ c. fresh parsley

PUT in a pan with ½ c. water and steam 5-8 minutes. **ADD:**

5 c. water   1 t. sweet basil
5 potatoes, cubed   ½ t. thyme
2 t. salt   ¼ t. oregano

BOIL until potatoes are soft. **BLEND** ½ c. cashew nuts and 1 c. water. **ADD** to soup and simmer.

20-½ c. servings   38 calories per serving

(T) LENTIL SOUP
27%   3%   73%

1 large, or 2 medium chopped onions
4 cloves minced garlic
3 c. lentils (1#) cleaned and washed
2 quarts water
1 quart tomatoes or tomato juice
2 t. salt
½ t. dill seed
2 bay leaves

COOK lentils, onions and garlic in water for 40 minutes. **ADD** tomatoes, salt and seasoning. **COOK** 20-40 minutes more. This soup tastes even better when made ahead!

24-½ c. servings   93 calories per serving

(T) SPLIT PEA SOUP
25%   2%   74%

2 c. green split peas
2 quarts water
1 stalk celery, chopped
1 c. diced potatoes
1 large chopped carrot (may be grated)
1 chopped onion
¼ t. thyme or marjoram
1 bay leaf (optional)
½ t. salt
1 clove garlic
½ t. sweet basil (optional)

COOK peas in the 2 qts. water for 20-30 minutes. **ADD** vegetables—cook until ingredients are done. **ADD** seasonings. **SIMMER** a few minutes.

20-½ c. servings   81 calories per serving

YELLOW SPLIT PEA SOUP

2 c. yellow split peas   ¼ c. dried onion
6 c. water   1 clove garlic, minced
½ c. diced celery   ½ t. basil
¾ c. shredded carrots   1 bay leaf

START the split peas cooking while preparing the vegetables and seasonings. **COOK** until tender and mostly pureed. Can be blended in blender or served as is.

16-½ c. servings

—80—

BROCCOLI SOUP

Recipe for Cashew Gravy, page 59, double the recipe. Cook 1# bag of broccoli in a small amount of water. Blend and add to the gravy. If a little too thick, add a bit more water. Season with 1 T. chicken-like seasoning.

(T) ZUCCHINI VEGETABLE STEW
19%   3%   89%

2 large onions and 2 cloves garlic, diced
8 small zucchini, sliced
3 medium carrots, cut in small carrot sticks
¼-½ green pepper, diced
¼ c. fresh chopped parsley, less if dried
2 large stalks celery, diced
1 c. tomato sauce
1 c. water
Pinch each of sweet basil and oregano

PLACE all ingredients in a large sauce pot. *MIX* gently with a wooden spoon. *SIMMER* 20-30 minutes, stirring occasionally. May be cooked in a little water and served as a vegetable.

16-½ c. servings   36 calories per serving

CUCUMBER SOUP—COLD
14%   38%   54%

3 c. cucumber, cut up
3 c. water
1 T. beef-like seasoning or G. Washington broth
3 T. whole grain flour (barley or millet)
½ c. chopped onion
1 c. cashew nut milk
1 T. chopped green onion
1 T. minced parsley or a sprinkle of dried parsley

COOK cucumbers for about 10 minutes with the broth and flour. *ADD* the nut milk and bring to boiling. Do not boil. *ADD* parsley and onion. *BLEND*, chill and serve with chopped green onion for garnish. This may be served hot or chilled.

12-½ c. servings   38 calories per serving

SQUASH SOUP
15%   52%   48%

1 quart squash soup base
Cashew milk made of 2 c. water and ½ c. cashew nuts

Blend together and heat. Do not boil. May want to add onion salt, garlic salt or plain salt to suit your taste.

12-½ c. servings   54 calories per serving

(T) **SOUP BASE:** When zucchini, patty pan, or yellow summer squash are plentiful, make soup base for use at once or for winter. *COOK* squash in water, filling pan with cutup squash and ¼ full of water. *COOK* until squash is done. *COOL* slightly and *BLEND,* adding 1 t. beef-like seasoning and ½ t. salt for each quart of squash, or other seasonings such as onion and garlic. This may be frozen for future use.

(T) GARBANZO SOUP
21%   10%   72%

4 c. pureed garbanzos (use enough water to make soupy consistency)
2 minced onions
2 buds garlic
½ t. cumin, 1 t. oregano, salt as needed
½ c. tomato sauce

SIMMER to blend flavors and serve. (May puree only half of the garbanzos and leave the others whole if you prefer).

10-½ c. servings   112 calories per serving

(T) FRIDAY STEW
20%   3%   80%

1 c. navy beans, washed, soaked and cooked-water to cover
2 c. potatoes, diced
2 c. carrots, diced
2 big onions, diced

ADD these to the cooked beans. When almost done, add the following seasonings and simmer in just enough water to keep from sticking.

1 c. chopped parsley (¼ c. dried)
2 heaping t. chicken-like seasoning and ¼ t. garlic powder

14-½ c. servings   89 calories per serving

(T) BARLEY AND PINTO BEAN SOUP
18%   3%   82%

1 c. pinto beans, cleaned and soaked overnight, drain
4 c. water
1 c. barley, cooked in 2½ c. water
1 c. tomato sauce
½ medium onion, finely chopped
2 carrots, finely chopped
½ c. parsley flakes
3 c. water
Salt, garlic salt, onion salt to taste

BRING beans to boil in 4 c. water. Turn off heat and let stand for one hour. Cook until beans are nearly tender. **ADD** all other ingredients and simmer until all are cooked and flavors well-blended.

20-½ c. servings   77 calories per serving

(T) BEAN-CORN CHOWDER
19%   16%   72%

1 c. chopped green onion, saut'eed in 3 T. water
3 c. cream-style corn
3 c. green soybeans or baby limas
1 c. stewed tomatoes
1 t. salt
2 c. cashew milk or sesame milk

SIMMER all ingredients for a few minutes except the milk. **ADD** the milk just before serving. May add a few herbs and serve with corn bread if desired.

20-½ c. servings   73 calories per serving

(T) FRESH GARDEN VEGETABLE SOUP

1 c. sliced onions
½ c. fresh peas (may use frozen)
1 c. fresh-cut corn, cut from cob
4 c. water

COOK together until onion is crispy done. Add 2-3 t. chicken-like seasoning, onion and garlic to taste and ½-¼ t. sweet basil flakes. Good warmed over.

12-½ c. servings

(T) CREAM OF CELERY SOUP

½ c. chopped onions
2 c. chopped celery
½ c. diced turnips
1 c. diced potatoes
2 qts. warm water
3 T. unbleached white flour
½ c. cold water
¼ c. chopped parsley
½ t. sweet basil
Vegit seasoning to taste
1½ c. rice or soy milk
2 cloves garlic
¼ c. chopped parsley

PUT onions, celery, turnips, potatoes in 2 qts. warm water and boil for 25 minutes over low flame. **MIX** the flour with cold water. Slowly add to the boiling soup and simmer 2 minutes. **REMOVE** from fire. Put 2 cups of soup in blender. Add ¼ c. parsley, 2 cloves garlic, and sweet basil. **BLEND** until smooth. Pour into the soup and mix with the other ¼ cup of parsley, vegit seasoning and milk. Serve hot.

12 cups

(T) VEGETABLE BEAN SOUP

3 c. cooked whole wheat noodles
2 c. cooked soy beans (1 c. uncooked)
1 diced onion
1 c. diced celery
2 diced carrots
1 diced potato
½ c. frozen corn
½ c. chopped, canned, tomatoes
¼ c. flour
3 c. soybean stock (cooking water from soybeans and noodles
½ t. sage
½ t. sweet basil
½ t. garlic powder
¼ c. minced parsley
2 t. Vegit seasoning

COOK soybeans early in day. Cook noodles and retain liquid. Prepare all vegetables. Cook in soybean stock and noodle water until vegetables are soft. Mix flour with cold water and stir in slowly. **ADD** soybeans and noodles. Heat through. Sprinkle with parsley and serve.

Makes 10 cups

(T) TOMATO SOUP

2 c. tomato puree
2 c. diced tomatoes
1/8 c. dehydrated onions
1/8 t. garlic powder
¾ c. corn, blended till smooth
1 c. rice, blended till smooth

ADD enough water to make seven cups of soup.

7 cups

(T) GARDEN SOUP

2½ c. frozen peas
3 c. sliced zucchini
1 c. diced onions
1/3 c. diced green pepper
6 c. water
1/3 c. barley
2½ c. chopped celery and leaves
2½ c. finely shredded green cabbage

COOK barley with 6 c. of water. **ADD** the vegetables and cook until done.

10 cups

(T) NAVY BEAN SOUP

8 c. water
2 c. dry navy beans
¾ c. diced carrots
¾ c. diced celery
¼ c. chopped parsley
1/3 c. diced turnip
¾ c. diced potatoes
1 clove garlic
Vegit seasoning

SOAK beans in 8 c. water overnight. Next day, **COOK** until tender with the chopped onions. **ADD** the other vegetables. **COOK**. Take out part of the beans and vegetables and blend. **ADD** back to soup. Heat and serve.

10 cups

(T) VEGETABLE CHOWDER

6 medium potatoes
2 large carrots
1 medium onion
1-4 oz. jar pimientos
½ c. finely chopped celery
½ c. finely chopped bell pepper
1 pint frozen corn, whole kernel
1 qt. water
2 c. rice milk
1 t. chicken-like seasoning
1 t. sage powder
1 t. onion powder
¼ t. garlic powder
½ t. sweet basil
¼ t. ground bay leaf
salt as permitted

CUT potatoes in about 1 inch cubes, dice carrots in small pieces (not fine) and place in pan with ½ of the water. *BRING* to full boil and then lower heat and cook until well done. *BLEND* the onion with the balance of the water and add to the chowder. Now add the corn, all of the seasoning, the balance of the water, the pimientos and let *SIMMER* for ½ hour, adding the bell pepper and celery the last 5 minutes. Serve.

14 cups

CORN CHOWDER II

3 c. water
2 c. diced potatoes
2/3 c. onion (chopped)
2 T. onion powder

2/3 c. chopped celery
2 c. whole kernel corn
4 c. cooked corn
2 c. water

BLEND the 4 c. cooked corn, 2 c. water, and *ADD* to rest of soup when cooked.

24-½ c. servings

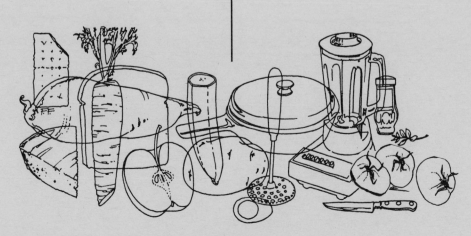

NATURAL SWEETS

(T) APPLE PIE FILLING
2%   6%   102%

8 apples
2 T. arrowroot powder, dissolved in ¼ c. water
½ c. raisins
½ c. dates chopped
½ T. coriander
½ t. anise
Pinch of salt

CORE and SLICE apples. COOK with raisins and dates until tender. ADD other ingredients. STIR and COOK until clear. POUR into baked pie shell.

8 servings   170 calories per serving

CAROB PIE FILLING OR PUDDING
7%   38%   61%

BLEND:
1 c. water   1 t. vanilla
½ c. cashews   ¼ t. salt

ADD AND BLEND:
1 c. water
15 dates, a few at a time
3 T. arrowroot powder

PUT the above mixture in a pan and bring to a boil to thicken. REMOVE from heat and ADD 3 T. carob mixed with a little water. POUR into baked pie shell.

8 servings   109 calories per serving

CASHEW BANANA CREAM PIE
7%   37%   64%

¾ c. cashews
2½ c. water
18 dates
3 bananas
1½ t. vanilla
½ t. salt
4 T. arrowroot or cornstarch
Coconut

BLEND all ingredients, except bananas, until smooth. ADD one more cup of water and blend thoroughly. COOK over low heat until mixture thickens. COOL. SLICE bananas and place one layer on coconut pie crust, cover with half of the cooked filling. Add another layer of bananas and the rest of the filling. SPRINKLE with coconut. Chill.

8 servings   244 calories per serving

(T) FRESH FRUIT PIE
3%   4%   96%

2 c. fresh or frozen pitted cherries or strawberries
2 c. fruit juice
3 T. arrowroot or cornstarch, dissolved in ¼ c. water or fruit juice

FILL baked pie shell with fruit mixture. In a saucepan, bring juice to boil. Thicken with cornstarch mixed with water or juice. COOK five minutes. COOL. POUR over fruit. Serve with cashew cream or plain.

8 servings   60 calories per serving

PUMPKIN PIE OR PUDDING
9%   21%   78%

SIMMER:
1¾ c. dates with 1 c. water

BLEND date mixture with
3 c. milk, soy or cashew
10 c. cooked pumpkin
½ c. whole wheat flour
½ c. cornstarch
1½ t. salt
3 T. vanilla
1½ T. coriander
1/8 t. cardamon
2 T. finely ground orange rind
7-8 drops lemon extract

MAKES 2-2 qt. pyrex bowls quite full of pudding or 3-4 pies. BAKE for 1 hour at 350 degrees.

24-½ c. servings, pudding   90 calories per serving

32 servings, pie   67 calories per serving
                                 (crust not included)

(T) LEMON PIE FILLING
35%   7%   94%

1 c. pineapple juice
1 c. fresh orange juice
4 T. fresh lemon juice
10 dates
¼ c. water
1/3 c. and 1 T. arrowroot or cornstarch
¼ t. salt
1 T. cashews

PLACE all ingredients in blender and blend until smooth. COOK on low heat, stirring constantly until mixture thickens. Let COOL and POUR into baked pie crust. If stronger lemon flavor is desired, use ¾ c. orange juice, and ½ c. lemon juice. Ground lemon peel can also be added (1-2 T.)

ALTERNATE: Put 1 c. pineapple juice in kettle and add 1 T. powdered agar. SOAK 5 minutes. SIMMER until dissolved. Put rest of ingredients in blender. BLEND until very smooth. ADD agar mixture while blender is running. POUR into baked pie shell.

8 servings   96 calories per serving

(T) LEMON PIE
2%   1%   100%

1½ c. pineapple chunks with juice
¾ c. dates
½ c. (scant) cornstarch or arrowroot

WHIZ smooth. **COOK** to thicken. **ADD** finely grated rind of 1 lemon and 2 T. juice of fresh lemon.

8 servings   100 calories per serving

SQUASH OR PUMPKIN PIE
8%   28%   69%

BLEND:
1½ c. water with
½ c. nuts
½ c. cooked rice

POUR into bowl and add:

3¼ c. cooked squash or pumpkin
¼ c. arrowroot powder
2/3 c. dates
1 T. vanilla
1 T. ground coriander
½ t. salt

BLEND all ingredients together and **POUR** into 9" pie shell and **BAKE** at 425 degrees for 15 minutes. Continue baking at 350 degrees for 30-45 minutes.

ALTERNATE pie crust: **ROLL OUT** bread dough very thin to use as pie crust. Let it rise somewhat around filling before baking.

VARIATION: May add 1-2 t. orange rind and 2 drops pure lemon extract.

16 servings 2-9" pies   67 calories per serving

(T) APPLE PIE
2%   8%   99%

4 c. shredded or thinly sliced apples
1 6-oz. can frozen apple juice concentrate
1 T. cornstarch, tapioca or flour
1 t. vanilla, coriander or fennel or combination

BRING apple juice concentrate to a boil and stir in the thickening which has been blended with a little water. **ADD** the apples to the mixture and stir well. Put all into 9" pastry shell. If you are going to put on a top crust, moisten the edge of crust and seal together to prevent juice from leaking out. **BAKE** for 45 minutes at 350 degrees. May use Crumb Crust. See index.

8 servings - 9" pie   35 calories per serving

(T) FRUIT PIE FILLING
2%   2%   98%

6 c. fruit juice   ½ c. cornstarch
½ c. tapioca   6 c. cherries

BRING all to a boil, **COOL** and **ADD** 4-6 cups fresh or frozen fruit. **POUR** into baked pie crust.

32 servings (4-9" pies)   59 calories per serving

NO OIL PIE CRUST
13%   50%   43%

1 c. cashew nuts
½ t. salt
½ c. water
1 c. whole wheat flour, oatmeal flour, or ½ of each.

GRIND cashews in nut grinder. Mix with flour and salt. **ADD** water to make soft dough. **MIX** very gently, only to blend. **PRESS** into pie pan or may roll between wax paper. Bake at 375 degrees until slightly brown.

8 servings   148 calories per serving

OATMEAL PIE CRUST
14%   45%   44%

3 c. rolled oats
2/3 c. cashews or other nuts
2/3 c. water
½ t. salt
½ c. sunflower seeds

BLEND oats to flower consistency. **GRIND** nuts. **MIX** together with salt and **ADD** water to make a dough to **ROLL OUT** between two sheets of wax paper. **ADD** more water if dough is too stiff. Bake at 375 degrees until slightly brown.

16 servings   116 calories per serving

ALMOND-SESAME PIE CRUST
22%   38%   46%

1/3 c. almonds, ground
1/3 c. sesame seeds, ground
½ c. whole wheat flour
½ c. barley flour (or may use 1 cup of the whole wheat)
1/3 c. soy flour
½ t. salt

BLEND the dry ingredients with fork and **ADD** ½ c. water. Dough should not be sticky. If it is, add a little more flour. **ROLL** between wax paper until very thin (about 1/16"). **PRICK** with fork. Bake at 375 degrees until golden brown. Walnuts or pecans can be substituted for almonds.

8 servings   136 calories per serving

FROZEN PIE CRUST

Barely **COVER** 1. c. dates with water and **BLEND** to make a very thick paste. **ADD** ½ c. coconut and t. lemon or orange rind and blend, or stir. Spoon and spread into pie pan. Make crust thin. Press chopped walnuts all over and freeze.

FILLING: Slice peaches, strawberries, or other berries into coconut cream (see recipe page 37). Put into frozen pie crust and serve.

(T) (INDIVIDUAL) STRAWBERRY ICE CREAM PIE
6%   6%   98%

Strawberry ice cream - 3 c. frozen strawberries, 1½ c. frozen bananas, ½ c. orange juice or pineapple juice.

BLEND at high speed until smooth and keep frozen until serving time. **MAKE** pie crust from one of the following recipes. **FORM** individual pie shells over the bottom of muffin tins. **BAKE.** When ready to serve, spoon ice cream into shells and garnish with coconut, whole strawberries or serve plain. Pie Crusts will be of good texture if rice flour is used to replace some of the whole wheat flour and equally as much nuts or seeds as flour is used.

8-½ c. servings each   58 calories per serving

CRUMB CRUST
12%   30%   62%

2½ c. quick oats
½ c. whole wheat pastry flour
¼ t. salt
1/3 c. date sugar
1/3 to ½ c. chopped nuts
¾ t. coriander, ground

MIX thoroughly and place mixture on apples, patting lightly. Enough for two pies. Also good as a topping for homemade ice cream.

16 servings   100 calories per serving

ALMOND-WHOLE WHEAT PIE CRUST
12%   58%   12%

1½ c. ground almonds
2 T. whole wheat flour (preferably whole wheat pastry flour)
¼ t. salt
2 T. water

MIX first three ingredients and then **ADD** water. **MIX** lightly and **PRESS** into pie pan. **BAKE** at 275 degrees for about 15 minutes. **WATCH** so the crust does not turn brown.

8 servings   201 calories per serving

OATMEAL-ALMOND PIE CRUST
26%   39%   40%

1½ c. oatmeal, ground to flour
¾ c. ground almonds
¼ c. ground sesame seeds
¼ t. salt
1/3-½ c. water for soft dough

MIX first four ingredients and then **ADD** water. **MIX** lightly and **DUST** with oatmeal flour. **ROLL** out 2 crusts and put in pie pans. **BAKE** at 375 degrees for 10-15 minutes, watching carefully. It should be slightly brown. **COOL** before adding the cooled filling. *Fruit Pie Filling* is delicious in this.

16 servings   86 calories per serving

PIE CRUST
14%   44%   47%

1 c. cashews, ground   ¾ c. water, more if needed
1 c. oatmeal, ground   ½ t. salt
1 c. whole wheat pastry flour

(May add coconut to make enough for 2 double pie crusts). **BAKE** at 375 degrees until light brown.

16 servings   97 calories per serving

COCONUT PIE SHELL
5%   84%   17%

1 c. coconut
1 T. whole wheat pastry flour
Enough nut milk or water to hold it together

PRESS thin in 9" pie plate. **BAKE** at 375 degrees for 10 minutes or light golden brown. **WATCH** carefully. Burns easily.

8 servings   65 calories per serving

MILLET OR RICE PUDDING
11%   20%   78%

MIX together:
4 c. cooked rice or millet   1 c. raisins

PUT into baking pan and sprinkle with ½ c. slivered almonds and a little grated orange rind. Over this, pour cashew milk and bake for ¾ hour.

MILK:
1 c. cashews or almonds   1 t. vanilla
4 c. water   Pinch of salt
½ c. dates

BLEND till smooth

20-½ c. servings   214 calories per serving

(T) MILLET PUDDING
11%   7%   90%

1 c. millet   2 c. pineapple with juice
4 c. water   1 c. cherries, frozen, pitted or fresh
½ t. salt

BLEND until smooth while still hot, using juice from pineapple. Then **ADD** vanilla, pineapple and fresh or frozen fruit. (Cherries and mandarin oranges may be added instead; coconut may be added also).

14-½ c. servings   217 calories per serving

BREAD PUDDING
9%   17%   76%

1 qt. bread crumbs or cubes from whole grain bread
2 c. water
¼ c. cashew nuts or other nuts
½ t. salt   1 c. raisins
½ c. dates   2 c. diced apple
1 t. vanilla   ¼ c. coconut

BLEND all except fruit and bread. **PUT** fruit and bread in baking dish and **POUR** liquid ingredients over all. Bake 20 minutes at 350 or until well heated. **SERVE** with fruit sauce. (Fruit juice thickened with added fruit. Grape juice with frozen blueberries added after thickening the juice, grape juice with boysenberries, etc.)

16-½ servings   170 calories per serving

EAST INDIAN RICE PUDDING
7%   41%   58%

1/3 c. almonds, slivered or ground
1/4 c. coconut
1/2 c. raisins
1/4 c. date sugar

1/4 c. rice
1 c. nut milk
1/4 t. salt

PUT in baking dish, stir well. *BAKE* at 300 degrees until rice is cooked. *STIR* occasionally. *USE* covered dish.

4-1/2 c. servings   316 calories per serving

(T) MILLET PUDDING OR CEREAL
9%   10%   89%

1 qt. apricot juice
1 c. millet

1/4 c. coconut
1/2 c. chopped dates

COOK one hour or until done. *ADD* one small can pineapple. *SERVE* with bananas and cashew cream.

8-1/2 c. servings   464 calories per serving

(T) PEACHY CRUMB CAKE

5½ c. whole wheat bread crumbs
1-16 oz. can unsweetened peaches
½ c. fresh orange juice
1/8 t. almond extract
1½ t. vanilla
1 c. raisins
4 large bananas

TEAR 2 slices whole wheat bread in pieces and whiz in dry blender to make crumbs. *REPEAT* to make 5½ cups. *WHIZ* peaches, 2 bananas, juice, 1/3 c. raisins, almond extract, and vanilla. *LAYER,* using 1/3 crumbs, ½ of liquid, 1 sliced banana, and ½ of raisins. *REPEAT* procedure, ending with last 1/3 of crumbs. *BAKE* at 325 degrees for 40 minutes.

OPTION: Use equal amount of mango, papaya, or other fruit.

APPLE CRISP
8%   23%   77%

1½ c. rolled oats
½ cup cashew cream
1½ c. whole wheat flour
½ c. chopped dates
½ t. salt
½ c. chopped nuts

10 apples, sliced
20 oz. can pineapple
2 T. arrowroot powder
1/4 t. ground coriander
1/4 t. ground sweet anise

BLEND pineapple and set aside. *COMBINE* dry ingredients and add cashew cream and ½ c. blended pineapple. *HEAT* apples and dates and stir in coriander, anise, and arrowroot powder blended in remainder of pineapple. *POUR* apples in baking dish and drop topping in chunks on top and pat down. *BAKE* at 350 degrees until apples bubble and top is brown.

24 servings   134 calories per serving

APPLE CRISP II

8-10 apples, peeled and sliced
3-4 T. apple juice concentrate

TOPPING:
1 c. oatmeal, fine
1 c. nuts (walnuts)
3 T. apple juice concentrate
Pinch salt

MIX and put over apples. *BAKE.*

(T) APPLE RICE BETTY
5%   14%   84%

½ c. brown rice (uncooked)
1 c. apple juice
1 c. water
1/8 t. salt
2 T. chopped dates or raisins (add raisins with apple)
1 c. diced fresh apples
2 T. coarsely chopped nuts

COMBINE apple juice, water, salt and dates and bring to a boil. *ADD* rice, cover and simmer at low heat for 40-50 minutes. Then add apples and stir in thoroughly. *COOK* ten minutes longer and add nuts. *SERVE* warm or chilled, plain or with soy or nut cream.

8 servings   100 calories per serving

APPLE-RICE DESSERT
6%   40%   57%

1 c. uncooked rice
1/4 t. salt
3 c. apple juice

COOK until rice is done. Then cool and add:
2 c. fresh grated apple
1 t. vanilla
1 t. almond extract

Then *ADD* to rice
1 c. nut cream
1 c. coconut

STIR in gently. Chill.

18-1/3 c. servings

125 calories per serving

(T) APPLE BURRITOS

6 large Delicious Apples
½ c. water
1/4 c. raisins
1/4 t. cardamon (optional)

WHIZ raisins with water until partially broken up. *ADD* apples, cored and chopped. *COOK* until almost tender, season with cardamon. Let simmer with lid off, or thicken with arrowroot. Place 1/4 to 1/3 c. apple slices in the center of a tortilla. *ROLL* and place seam side down in a sprayed baking dish. When all burritos are in place, cover with apple sauce. *BAKE* for 20-30 minutes in a 350 degree oven. Total recipe equals 977 calories. Page   - Tortilla recipe.

6 servings   166 calories per serving

FRESH APPLE DESSERT
4%   26%   79%

½ c. unsweetened pineapple juice
2 large unpeeled, cored Golden Delicious apples
  or your choice
5 medium sized dates
1/8 t. salt
3 T. finely cut walnuts

BLEND all ingredients, except the walnuts. *STIR* in walnuts. *SERVE* soon.

2 servings   295 calories per serving

(T) APPLE BREAD PUDDING

qt. apples, cut up or other fruit
3 c. cubed bread
2 c. pineapple juice
1/8 c. lemon juice
4 T. arrowroot or cornstarch

PLACE apples or other fruit in baking dish. Cover with the bread cubes. **BLEND** pineapple juice, lemon juice and cornstarch and cook to thicken. **POUR** over fruit and bread. May sprinkle raisins on top. **BAKE** 350 degrees for 30-40 minutes.

16-½ c. servings

BANANA LOGS
6%   28%   76%

2 ripe bananas
10-12 soft pitted dates
4 T. unsweetened pineapple juice
1/3 c. crushed walnuts, coconut or other nuts

HEAT dates in juice over very low flame, stirring constantly until a smooth paste is formed. **PEEL** bananas and cut in half crosswise. **COMPLETELY COVER** the banana with date paste and **ROLL** in nuts. Freeze. Remove from freezer a few minutes before serving as a delightful dessert.

VARIATIONS: Use water and few drops of lemon juice instead of pineapple juice. Place coated banana on popsicle stick, then freeze for children's treat.

4-½ banana   213 calories per serving

(T) ICE CREAM

1¼ c. water
3-5 soft dates
1-2 frozen bananas
2 c. frozen strawberries or other fruit

BLEND dates and water until smooth. **ADD** bananas and fruit. Blend and serve. This should be thick as soft ice cream.

5-½ c. servings   84 calories per serving

CAROB ICE CREAM
10%   56%   45%

(like chocolate)

5 dates   ½ c. cashews
¾ c. water   2 T. carob powder
¼ t. salt   1½ t. vanilla

BLEND together and slowly add four large frozen ripe bananas. Don't overload the blender. Pour into container and freeze or eat immediately as soft ice cream.

8-½ c. servings   122 calories per serving

(T) HOT FUDGE SUNDAE
4%   2%   100%

2 c. dates   2 t. vanilla
2 c. water   Frozen sliced bananas
¾ c. carob   10 large

HEAT dates in water and liquify. **ADD** carob to make dark fudge color. **ADD** vanilla. **POUR** over frozen sliced bananas and sprinkle with nuts. **NOTE:** This can be made by blending the dates in water without heating if the dates are soft. Try adding ½ c. carob and continue adding to taste. You may like less than ¾ c. carob.

12 servings   195 calories per serving

(T) PINEAPPLE SLUSH
4%   2%   100%

2½ c. crushed pinepple
3 frozen bananas
1 T. orange juice concentrate
2½ c. unsweetened grapefruit sections (fresh or canned). Do not include section membrane, it is bitter. **BLEND** and **SERVE.**

14-½ c. servings   62 calories per serving

(T) SHERBERT

1 pint berries, frozen
½ c. pineapple juice
1 banana, frozen

BLEND until smooth. Serve.

4-½ c. servings

(T) ORANGE ICE CREAM

2 ripe, frozen bananas
2 oranges, peeled, sectioned, frozen
1 c. orange juice
1 c. crushed pineapple with own juice

BLEND all until smooth. Serve or store in freezer until ready to serve. Those not on therapeutic plan may add ¼ c. cashew nuts or almonds for a richer consistency. Be sure the nuts are blended smooth before adding the frozen ingredients.

6-½ c. servings

PINEAPPLE ICE CREAM

7%	42%	62%

¼ c. water
¼ c. cashew nuts
1 20-oz. can pineapple chunks (frozen in can-may use any pineapple canned in its own juice
¼ t. fresh lemon juice
1 T. fine, unsweetened coconut (the quantities of all these ingredients may be adjusted to suit your individual taste)
½ t. vanilla

BLEND water and cashews. **ADD** flavorings and frozen pineapple with juice. **BLEND** and serve at once. This may be made ahead and kept in freezer for 30 to 45 minutes and it will retain its soft consistency.

VARIATION: Raspberry Ice Cream. Put through sieve to remove seeds. Use raspberries in place of pineapple. Add ½ c. dates and blend all.

5-½ c. servings   84 calories per serving

BLENDER STRAWBERRY ICE CREAM

8%	28%	74%

4-5 ripe bananas, frozen
6 oz. frozen apple juice concentrate
10 oz. frozen strawberries (without sugar)
½-¾ c. raw cashews (these may be omitted for less rich product)

PUT apple juice in blender with cashews. **BLEND. ADD** water to the 2½ c. mark. **ADD** strawberries. **BLEND. ADD** frozen banana pieces a few at a time until the mixture is as thick as soft ice cream and it won't blend any thicker. Good served right away or stored in freezer for a later time. If frozen for a few days, it should be taken out of freezer about ½ hour before serving to thaw a little.

10-½ c. servings   111 calories per serving

(T) DATE-BANANA BLENDER ICE CREAM

½ c. rice milk
½ c. dates
1-3 bananas, frozen

BLEND milk and dates. **ADD** bananas until consistency of soft ice cream. All of the blender ice creams may be put in freezer until serving time. They will usually hold the soft texture for an hour or two.

3½ c. servings

BANANA-PUMPKIN ICE CREAM

8%	54%	45%

2 bananas (frozen)   ½ c. walnuts
2 c. pumpkin or squash   1 c. water

BLEND. SEASON with pumpkin pie flavorings.

8-½ c. servings   80 calories per serving

MAPLE PECAN ICE CREAM

4%	85%	16%

5 c. coconut
4 c. water, hot

BLEND and **STRAIN. ADD** ½ c. dates and 2 T. maple syrup or natural flavor to 2 c. of the coconut milk and blend well **ADD** ½ c. chopped nuts (almonds or pecans) and rest of milk. Do not blend. **FREEZE** in ice cream freezer.

8-½ c. serrvings   375 calories per serving

FRUIT SHAKES

Frozen chunk bananas   Crushed pineapple
Frozen berries or fruit

BLEND in blender. Coconut milk may be used. Also, frozen persimmons. Experiment with various fruits to find your favorite. Bananas can be used for thickness. Carob and dates may also be used. Cashew nut milk may be used as the base.

BANANA ICE CREAM

5%	2%	104%

BLEND frozen bananas with just enough nut milk to make the blender go. **ADD** vanilla flavoring. Frozen bananas can also be made into soft ice cream by putting them through a **CHAMPION JUICER** or if your mixer is strong, bananas slightly thawed will whip up for a soft dessert or a whipped topping for other fruit desserts. Top your soft banana ice cream with carob or fruit sauce and spinkle with nuts for a healthful sundae.

1 c.   191 calories

FROZEN BANANA LOGS

10%	46%	56%

6-8 bananas, cut in ½ or 1/3
chopped peanuts or
macaroon coconut

FREEZE bananas—they will be much easier to handle. Coating·for bananas:
1 c. apple sauce   ¼ c. peanut butter
¾ t. Postum   1/3 c. carob powder

COMBINE thoroughly in a bowl; **ROLL** frozen bananas in coating and then in chopped peanuts or macaroon coconut. Put at once in freezer on cookie sheet and **FREEZE**. Transfer to covered pan or plastic to store. Serve slightly thawed.

16-½ banana servings   195 calories per serving

FAVORITE DESSERTS

PEEL and *SLICE* two very ripe bananas. Freeze in plastic bag. *PUT* bananas in a blender with a small amount of soy milk (about 1/3 c.). This will be a thick mixture like whipped cream. It may be eaten with fresh or frozen fruit such as blueberries, strawberries, or as a parfait. Serve instantly. Delicious just plain or use at once as whipped cream. To make a banana shake, just add more milk when blending. May also use nut milk.

(T) CALIFORNIA FRUIT SOUP
5%   3%   100%

1 c. water
1½ c. apricot nectar
3 T. minute tapioca
Dried apricots and 1 raw apple
4 bananas or 1 c. whole strawberries
4 c. canned peaches with juice

2½ c. pineapple juice
2 T. lemon juice

COOK friut juice and tapioca until thick. *ADD* fruit. *POUR* over toast. *SLICE* bananas on top. This is a great breakfast treat. May also be served in a bowl omitting toast and used for lunch or dessert.

20-½ c. servings   90 calories per serving

(T) FRUIT SOUPS

Dried fruits—apples, prunes, apricots, peaches, pears, raisins, etc. Liquid—regular or reconstituted apple juice, apricot juice or pineapple juice and 1/3 part of water. *PUT* fruits (according to amounts and kinds desired) into saucepan with enough liquid to cover. Simmer over low heat until fruit is plump and tender. Thicken slightly with small amount of arrowroot or cornstarch dissolved in cold water. May also use minute tapioca to thicken. If too sweet, add more water and less fruit juice.

(T) CALIFORNIA FRUIT SOUP II

2 c. canned apricots, blended
3 c. pineapple juice
¼ c. tapioca
¾ c. water
COOK above ingredients until thick. *ADD:*

5 c. canned peaches
1 c. canned apricots
1 c. diced apples

24-½ c. servings

(T) DARK FRUIT SOUP

½ c. raisins
1 c. pitted prunes
1/5 c. crushed pineapple and its juice
¼ c. tapioca
1 sliced banana

COOK prunes, raisins, and tapioca in 5 c. water until fruit is cooked and thickened. (More or less water may be added according to desired thickness.). *ADD* the crushed pineapple and sliced banana. Good served warm or cold. Garnish with orange twist.

14-½ c. servings

(T) GOLDEN FRUIT SOUP

4 c. unsweetened pineapple juice
4 c. orange juice
½ c. tapioca
½ c. dried apricots
STIR over low heat until thickened. *ADD:*

½ c. seedless green grapes (optional)
1 c. fresh or frozen peaches
1 c. pineapple chunks
1 c. diced apples or strawberries (optional)
1 sliced banana

You can add fresh or frozen unsweetened fruits of your choice.

24-½ c. servings

(T) PAT'S FRUIT SOUP
4%   4%   98%

¼ c. tapioca (quick cooking)
2 quarts water
2 c. small pitted prunes
2 large apples, diced
½ each dried raisins, apricots, peaches, pears
2 bananas
Juice of 1 lemon
1 c. cherries if you have frozen or canned
2 c. fruit juice (1 c. orange and 1 c. grape or 1 c. pineapple)
Pinch of salt

COOK tapioca in 2 quarts of water until half done. *ADD* fruit and fruit juice. Add salt. *COOK* until tapioca is done and fruits are soft. *SERVE* hot or cold.

32-½ c. servings   122 calories per serving

(T) FRUIT SOUP
3%   1%   98%

6 c. fruit juice   2 T. cornstarch
¼ c. tapioca

BRING to a boil, *COOL* and *ADD* 4 cups fresh sliced strawberries or frozen fruit. This could be served warm if you prefer.

20-½ c. servings   61 calories per serving

SESAME BARS
10%   64%   32%

½ c. water
1 c. dates
COOK to soften dates.

½ c. unsweetened shredded coconut
½ c. sunflower seeds
1 c. sesame seeds, grind ½ in nut grinder
½ c. cashews, grind in nut grinder. Add 3 T. water to make nut butter.

MIX all ingredients well and **ROLL OUT** on non-stick cookie sheet putting dough directly on sheet and covering with wax paper to roll out. **ROLL THIN** and **BAKE** 350 degrees for 15 to 20 minutes watching carefully. Bake crisp but not too brown.

24 servings   124 calories per serving

BANANA NUT COOKIES
11%   37%   57%

1 c. thick cashew milk   3 c. rolled oats
6 mashed bananas   2 t. vanilla
1¼ c. chopped nuts   1 t. salt
1½ c. whole wheat flour

MIX flour and oats. **ADD** remaining ingredients and mix well. Drop by spoonful on teflon sheet and bake 325 degrees until light brown. (This is a heavy, moist cookie.)

36 servings   94 calories per serving

CAROB FRUIT BARS
7%   30%   72%

1 T. yeast
¼ c. warm water
1½ c. cooked, pitted prunes
1 c. each, pitted, chopped dates, raisins
1 c. whole wheat pastry flour
3 T. carob powder
½ c. chopped nuts

DISSOLVE yeast in water and add to fruit. **LET RISE** until bubbly. **ADD** rest of ingredients. **MIX** well. **PUT** in teflon pan and spread out evenly one inch thick. **LET RISE** 30 minutes. Bake at 350 degrees for 35-40 minutes. Cool and cut into 16 bars.

32 servings   102 calories per serving

COOKIE HAYSTACKS
6%   51%   51%

4 c. unsweetened shredded coconut
¾ c. whole wheat flour
1/3 c. rolled oats, old fashioned
3 c. dates
1/3 t. salt
1/8 c. water
1½ c. raisins
1 2/3 c. chopped walnuts
½ c. orange or pineapple juice

BLEND water, juice, dates, raisins, until smooth. **ADD** dry ingredients. **MIX LIGHTLY. SCOOP** onto ungreased cookie sheet with small ice cream scoop. **BAKE** until browned, 20-30 minutes at 350 degrees. May add peanut butter. May use 2 c. dates and 3 c. coconut.

48 servings   120 calories per serving

FIG WALNUT BARS
6%   46%   55%

1 c. dried figs
1 c. raisins
1 c. walnuts

GRIND or chop fine all ingredients. **PRESS** in thin layers and cut in 4" by 1" strips and wrap in waxed paper and **CHILL.** May be rolled in balls, then in coconut or chopped nuts.

16 servings   93 calories per serving

POLYNESIAN BARS
7%   29%   72%

2 c. chopped pitted dates
1 20-oz. can unsweetened crushed pineapple (about 2¼ c)

MIX together in saucepan and cook until consistency that can be spread.

3 c. oatmeal
1 c. millet flour
1 c. unsweetened coconut (optional)
½ c. chopped nuts
1 c. orange juice
1 t. salt

MIX flour, oatmeal, coconut, nuts and salt together. **ADD** orange juice and moisten thoroughly. **COVER** a 9 by 12 inch pyrex baking dish with half of the oatmeal mixture and pat down. **SPREAD FILLING** on this and put the rest of the oatmeal mixture on top and pat down. **BAKE** at 350 degrees for 30 minutes or until lightly browned.

32 servings   100 calories per serving

DATE BARS
13%   33%   61%

Filling:
1½-2 c. dates
½ c. orange juice or more
½ c. walnuts

Crust:
¾ c. almonds, ground
¼ c. sesame seeds, ground
1½ c. oatmeal, ground to oat flour
¼ t. salt
1/3-½ c. water for soft dough

COOK dates with enough orange juice to make thick paste. **ADD** chopped walnuts. The rest of the ingredients will be the crust. **MIX,** divide dough, dust with more ground oat flour and roll between clear wrap into an 8x8 square. **PLACE** on bottom of square pan. **SPREAD** with date mixture. **SPRINKLE** with walnuts. **ADD** the top 8x8 square dough, **PRICK** with fork and **BAKE** 375 degrees for 20-25 minutes.

24 servings   98 calories per serving

GOLDEN MACAROONS
7%   60%   40%

3 c. grated carrot
3 c. dates, pureed in water
6 c. coconut
¾ c. soy flour

¾ c. whole wheat flour
1½ t. salt
3 t. pure almond flavoring
1½ c. chopped walnuts

STIR lightly. Place on non-stick cookie sheets. Bake 350-375 degrees about ten minutes or until slightly brown.

60 servings   105 calories per serving

BANANA OATMEAL BARS

COVER teflon cookie sheet with a thin layer of oatmeal (quick cooking). BLEND OR MASH four medium bananas with 3 T. apple juice concentrate. DRIZZLE mixture over oatmeal and BAKE 250 degrees until leathery—about one hour. Remove from pan, cut while warm. If not crisp, return to oven and continue baking at 200 degrees until crisp.

CHIP-OATMEAL COOKIES
9%   30%   19%

2 c. date sugar
2 c. carob-date chips
1 t. salt
6 c. oatmeal
2 c. whole wheat flour, barley or millet (or part golden wheat contains wheat germ and some bran)
2 c. walnut pieces, fine
1 t. vanilla
½ t. corriander
Water to hold dough together. DO NOT STIR more than necessary. DROP on Te-Fal cookie pans and press out thin with fork. BAKE 10-15 minutes at 350 degrees until light brown.

48 servings   111 calories per serving

FRUIT CRISPS
11%   21%   72%

1½ c. whole wheat pastry flour
½ c. whole wheat flour
½ t. salt
3 T. date sugar
½ c. ground coconut (use nut grinder)

MIX dry ingredients and ADD just enough water to moisten. ROLL half of dough on a non-stick cookie sheet. SPREAD with the following ingredients: Wash 2 cups of raisins in hot water. DRAIN. Let stand 5 to 10 minutes. PUT through grinder. SPREAD raisins on dough and sprinkle with ½ cup chopped walnuts. ROLL the other half of dough out between wax paper to fit the tops of crisps. PUT on top of filling. CUT into squares using plastic knife. PRICK with plastic fork. Bake 350 for 10 minutes and 325 for 20-25 minutes until golden brown and kind of crispy.

32 servings   67 calories per serving

(T) FRUIT BARS

4 c. granola
1 c. raisins
1 c. chopped dates
2 c. cooked brown rice
½ c. whole wheat flour

2 c. water
1 t. salt
2 t. lemon extract
1 t. vanilla
1 banana

BLEND brown rice in as small amount of the water as possible. Blend in the banana then ADD the raisins and dates and BLEND until smooth adding the balance of the water as you BLEND. Do not add more water, but stop blender and push mixture with spoon until it will blend. POUR into large bowl and add all of the ingredients except the granola. Place granola in plastic bag and roll with rolling pin until medium coarse then add to mixture. POUR into large glass cake dish which has been sprayed and then dusted lightly with whole wheat flour, and bake at 400 degrees for 15 minutes or until fork comes out clean.

FRUIT CHEWS
7%   48%   54%

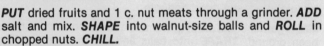

1 c. dried figs
1 c. dried apricots
1 c. pitted dates
1 c. nut meats
½ c. shredded coconut
1/8 t. salt
½ c. chopped nuts

PUT dried fruits and 1 c. nut meats through a grinder. ADD salt and mix. SHAPE into walnut-size balls and ROLL in chopped nuts. CHILL.

VARIATION: Dried pears, raisins, prunes.

24 servings   110 calories per serving

(T) FRUIT BRAID SPREAD

1 c. prunes, pitted
1 c. raisins
½ c. crushed pineapple

HEAT the three ingredients until soft and tender. BLEND it all to a thick paste. Use as a filling in "Fruit Braids" or "Sweet Rolls." You can use any dried fruit in place of prunes and raisins—like apricots, pears, apples, figs.

NO-COOK FIG SWEET
9%   61%   35%

¾ c. dried figs
1 t. grated lemon rind
1 t. fresh lemon juice

PUT figs through food grinder adding lemon rind and juice as it grinds. ADD ½ c. chopped nuts. FORM into one inch balls and roll in fine coconut.

5 servings   110 calories per serving

CAROB FUDGE
10%   62%   40%

½ c. water
½ c. carob
1 c. peanut butter (peanuts ground very fine)
1 c. date butter
½ c. coconut
1 c. walnuts, chopped

BOIL the carob in water, stirring, for 5 minutes until a smooth paste. **MIX** all ingredients and press into square pan. Refrigerate.

40 servings   58 calories per serving

APRICOT TREATS
5%   34%   70%

½ pound dried apricots (soak 30 minutes in hot water)
½ pound pitted dates
1½ c. coconut, unsweetened

GRIND using coarse blade in food grinder. **MIX** with coconut. **FORM** into balls or put into square pan, **SPRINKLE** with coconut or roll balls in coconut.

16 servings   116 calories per serving

APRICOT WALNUT TREATS
8%   52%   49%

Raw walnuts
Unsulphured, sun dried apricots

MIX together equal parts of walnuts and apricots which have been ground. **SHAPE** into balls and roll in coconut. The variety of natural sweets which you can put together is unlimited. Combine different nuts and dried fruits, ground sprouted wheat, orange and lemon rind, various natural flavorings, using the nuts and fruits that your family likes best.

12 servings   148 calories per serving

SPROUT TREATS
18%   26%   67%

1 c. sprouted tricale or wheat
1 c. raisins
1 c. nuts (walnuts, pecans, almonds or mixed)
Salt and grated coconut

GRIND raisins, nuts and sprouts. **ADD** a dash of salt and mix well. **FORM** into little balls and **ROLL** in grated coconut. **STORE** covered in refrigerator or may be frozen.

16 servings   128 calories per serving

DRIED FRUIT BALLS
6%   33%   67%

1 c. dried apricots
½ c. each: raisins, pitted prunes, pitted dates, coconut, nuts
Juice from one orange and grated orange rind (optional)

GRIND first four ingredients in food grinder. **ADD** rest and mix well. **FORM** into balls and **ROLL** in finely chopped nuts or coconut. **REFRIGERATE.**

16 servings   148 calories per serving

CAROB SNOWBALLS
8%   55%   48%

5 T. nut butter (peanut, hazelnut, almond or mixed)
1 c. dates (cooked to softened in ½ c water)
1 c. raisins
2 c. chopped hazel nuts
¾ c. sunflower seeds
¾ c. carob chips
2 t. each lemon or orange peel, pero, carob powder
½ c. dried pineapple bits
1 t. salt and 1 T. vanilla
1 c. grape nuts—add last

MIX well, **ROLL** into balls and **ROLL** balls in coconut.

35 servings   130 calories per serving

WHIPPED TOPPING
9%   55%   43%

2 yellow delicious apples, cored but *not* peeled. Cube, put in blender.
¼-½ c. apple juice—just enough to get blender working
1 t. lemon juice, add to blender

WHEN PUREED, gradually **ADD** one cup ground raw cashew nuts and continue to blend until smooth. Good wherever whipped cream is suggested. Great on fruit salads, fruit pie, etc. Can be combined with thickened fruit juices for an elegant parfait.

16-2 T. servings   72 calories per serving
(Real Cream Whipped—106 calories per 2 T.)

CASHEW TOPPING
11%   70%   24%

2 c. warm water
1 c. cashew nuts
1 T. arrowroot starch or cornstarch
Dash of salt

BLEND and **COOK** until thick, stirring constantly. **COOL** and add vanilla. Good on crepes or any dessert where a topping is desired.

16-2 T. servings   54 calories per serving

(T) FRUIT TOPPING
5%   3%   97%

2 c. orange juice
3½ t. fresh lemon juice and ½ t. lemon rind
6 dates
1 T. cashew nuts
¼ c. arrowroot or cornstarch
¼ t. salt

BLEND all, **COOK** to thicken, **COOL.**

16-2 T. servings   22 calories per serving

COCONUT CREAM TOPPING
16%   46%   51%

3 c. fine, unsweetened coconut
2½ c. hot water

BLEND coconut until very fine. **ADD** hot water. Continue blending. **STRAIN** through nylon/chiffon cloth and chill thoroughly. Before using, blend to thicken. Try on strawberry pie!

16-2 T. servings   93 calories per serving

BANANA-NUT CAKE
8%   21%   78%

6 ripe bananas
1 c. chopped dates
1 c. raisins
¼-½ c. pineapple juice
1 t. salt
1 t. coriander
4 c. oatmeal
½ c. chopped nuts
½ c. unsweetened coconut (optional)

MASH bananas leaving some pieces. **ADD** nuts, raisins, dates. Then **ADD** salt, coriander and oatmeal. **MIX** in pineapple juice. **MIX** very lightly—**DO NOT PACK** in pan. It cannot rise. Use 9x12 pan or similar. **BAKE** at 350 degrees until done.

48 servings   79 calories per serving

TOFU CHEESE CAKE
18%   36%   51%

BLEND in blender
2 c. tofu
1 T. lemon juice
1 T. vanilla
1 can crushed pineapple - 20 oz.
2 T. cornstarch or arrowroot starch
1 banana

MIX together for crust:
1 c. rolled oats
1 c. rolled barley
½ c. ground sunflower seeds
½ t. salt
1/3 c. chopped walnuts
1/3 c. ground almonds
1/3 c. or more water

MIX gently and put in 8x8 pan. **PRESS** to cover the bottom of the pan. **POUR** the blended ingredients on top and spread evenly. **BAKE** at 350 degrees for 20 minutes or until just brown on the sides. May serve with strawberries on top.

16 servings   149 calories per serving

FRUIT CAKE
6%   31%   71%

1 lb. dried pineapple
1 c. raisins
2 c. chopped dates
½ c. each pears and apricots (dried)
1 T. fresh lemon peel
1/8 t. cardamon and ¼-½ t. coriander
1 t. vanilla
2 T. soy flour
3 T. frozen orange juice concentrate
4 T. pineapple juice
1½ c. whole wheat flour
1 lb. whole pecans
½ c. water (or enough to moisten all dry ingredients)

PUT bran in the bottom of the pan to prevent sticking. **PACK** into small loaf pans rounding top; this does not rise. **BAKE** at 325-350 degrees and 45 minutes to an hour.

45 servings   107 calories per serving

(T) MELON BALL RAINBOW

Using the melon ball maker—**PREPARE** the balls from cantaloupe, Crenshaw, Persian melon, casaba, watermelon, etc. Serve one kind or a combination in any fruit juice. Always have melon balls and juice chilled. Garnish simply with a mint sprig.

FRESH FRUIT SALAD

Peel and slice several peaches
Peel and slice 1 cantaloupe
Add about 1 cup of watermelon balls
Add 1 cup of blueberries
Mix about ½ can orange juice concentrate over all.

(T) FRUIT PLATE

Fresh or frozen strawberries
Mandarin or fresh oranges
Apple slices
Pineapple chunks

Serve with thick strawberry cream for dip or dressing.

CREAMY COCONUT FRUIT SALAD

1 c. of each of the following: orange cubes, pineapple, green grapes, shredded coconut
¾ c. cashew nut cream (see recipe)
2 bananas, sliced

HAVE all ingredients chilled. **PLACE** together in bowl, **ADDING** shredded coconut and cream last. **COMBINE** gently. **CHILL** thoroughly.

(T) FRUIT LEATHER

BLEND any very ripe fruit with a very small amount of water or fruit juice. A ripe banana may be added if fruits are very tart. Line a flat pan with plastic wrap (saran). **POUR** fruit on pan and spread to ¼" thickness or thinner. **PLACE** in warm oven at 125 degrees, with oven door slightly ajar. If sun is hot, may place in sun for two or three days. When you pick it up and remove it from the plastic easily, it is dry enough. Approximately 12 hours. May be cut in squares or rolled. Children enjoy tearing off a piece for a wholesome dessert. If you have a food dryer, blended fruit is easily dried for fruit leather.

(T) APRICOT KUCHEN

	16%	5%	85%

1 c. water	1 t. salt
2 dates, chopped	2½ c. whole wheat flour
1 T. dry yeast	

COOK dates in water to soften or just blend if using soft dates. Add yeast to the lukewarm mixture and let stand for 15-20 minutes. **ADD** remaining ingredients and blend with hands. Add more flour if necessary to have mixture the consistency of bread dough. **TURN** on to a lightly floured board and knead. Place in bowl and cover with damp cloth. Let rise until double in bulk. Punch down and roll out to approximately ¼" thick and place in a 9x13 inch baking dish. Have the dough extend up the sides of the dish. Let rise for 15-20 inutes. **NOTE:** the bottom of the pan should be sprinkled with cornmeal or bran to prevent sticking.

12 servings   88 calories per serving

FILLING:
	7%	29%	73%

3½ c. canned unsweetened apricots with juice (#2½ can)
8-10 dates
2½ T. arrowroot powder or cornstarch
Chopped walnuts or almonds, as desired

12 servings   102 calories per serving

PLACE apricots, dates, and cornstarch in blender and blend well. **PLACE** in saucepan and cook until thick, stirring constantly. (Should be very thick). Let **COOL** slightly. **POUR** over dough, **SPRINKLE** with nuts and **BAKE** at 350 degrees for 30-40 minutes or until shell is light brown. Let **COOl. CUT** into squares. **RE-HEAT** the following day or later.

KUCHEN

Use a yeast dough you use for sweet rolls. May use recipe for Dough for Cobbler in this book. Roll a ball of dough in a circle to fit a 9 or 10 inch pie plate. It should be no thicker than ¼ inch.

Filling: Use recipe for banana cream pie, but *do not cook it.* **DON'T** use bananas. The filling is enough for 2-3 kuchen. **PUT** some fruit on top of the dough in the pie plate (soaked raisins, cooked pitted prunes, sliced, fresh, frozen or canned peaches). **POUR** cream filling on top. **BAKE** 350 degrees for 25 to 35 minutes or until crust is browned nicely and filling set. Freezes well—just reheat after freezing.

SUGGESTION Serve strawberry cream with sliced fresh strawberries mixed in or make peach cream, using the same recipe and slice fresh peaches into it. Delicious on waffles or for crepes or for shortcake.

(T) FRUIT PUNCH

16 oz. orange juice concentrate, frozen plus water as directed
1 small can crushed pineapple
3 bananas
1 pt. strawberries
BLEND all.

SIMPLE DESSERTS

COCONUT— Select a coconut with the heavy outer covering. If this has been removed, the coconut water has been removed and replaced with ordinary water. After removing the outer covering, make a hole in the soft eye and drain out the liquid. This can be used in ice cream, fruit soup, or anything that would call for fruit juice. The coconut shell may be removed by cracking it with a hammer or by placing in a 300 degree oven until the shell cracks. Remove the shell and peel the brown part away from the white coconut. Fresh coconut cut up in small pieces may be served on a pretty plate.

DATES— Remove the pit and fill with a walnut or pecan. Roll in coconut. Serve.

(T) **CHERRIES—** Frozen cherries (beautiful, big, dark cherries) are lovely when they are just beginning to thaw. Pass around a bowl full.

(T) **PERSIMMONS—** This is a lovely fruit in season. Cut in wedges and pass around to your family or guests. You may also want to serve a more common fruit as some may be unacquainted with this.

DRIED FRUIT— A plate containing several dried fruits, apples, bananas, apricots, prunes, strawberries, along with a bowl of mixed nuts to be shelled while eating, is a fun way to finish a noon meal.

(T)**PUDDING—** A fruit pudding, using just pure, unsweetened juice or with an addition of fresh fruit, or canned or frozen fruit layered in a glass dish with cashew nut cream is delicious as well as pretty. (The fruit juice would be thickened with cornstarch or arrowroot powder).

BANANA DATE ICE CREAM— 2½ c. nut milk, 1 c. fresh dates, enough frozen bananas to thicken for a soft ice cream.

(T) FROZEN STRAWBERRIES

When strawberries are in season, freeze a few pints or quarts using white grape juice for sweetening. It does not take much—less than ½ cup per quart of berries. Slice or mash the berries a little. Serve as sauce or use for your fruit blender desserts, or on waffles.

(T) FROZEN PEACHES

Peaches can be prepared and used very similarly to the strawberries. However, peaches taste better when frozen in orange juice concentrate. I spoon it directly from the frozen can to the bowl in which I cut up the peaches. This preserves the color and also sweetens the peaches. The amounts to use will be according to your taste, but remember, you want the fruit flavor to be predominent rather than the juice in which you are preserving the fruit.

TOASTED COCONUT CHIPS
4%   88%   14%

1 coconut   Salt to taste

May use coconut flakes, unsweetened, natural, from the health food store. Follow instructions for toasting.

TO PREPARE coconut, **PIERCE** soft eye in end of coconut and **DRAIN** liquid. **ROAST** coconut in shallow pan in preheated 350 degree oven 20 to 30 minutes, or until shell cracks in several places. **REMOVE** from oven and pound with hammer to crack coconut open. Remove meat in fairly large chunks when possible and run potato peeler down edges to make strips. Spread half in pan; sprinkle with salt and toast in 300 degree oven 20 to 25 minutes, stirring occasionally. Repeat with second batch. Cool. Makes about 2 quarts.

32-¼ c. servings   16 calories per serving

(T) PUMPKIN POCKETS
4%   2%   99%

2 c. pumpkin
2 T. arrowroot
1 t. salt
½ t. vanilla
½ t. coriander
2 c. dates (add 1 c. water) Cook to thicken

Use Dough for Cobbler. **ROLL OUT** the crust and **CUT** in rounds. **PLACE** filling in center and **FOLD** over, sealing the edges. **PRICK** top. **PLACE** on cookie sheet and bake at 375 degrees until slightly brown. Good served warm.

32 servings   34 calories per serving

(T) APPLE POCKETS

2 c. apple sauce
1 c. chopped apple
2 c. raisins
Chopped walnuts

(T) CREPES
15%   18%   70%

1½ c. whole wheat flour (try all whole wheat pastry)
1½ c. rolled oats
¾ t. salt.

MIX AND ADD
4-1/3 c. soy milk (4 c. water to 1 c. soy powder)
1 T. date sugar or date equivalent

Let stand 5 minutes. **BLEND** until smooth. 25 crepes. **SERVE** as a main dish using spinach or asparagus and cashew gravy with parsley or as a dessert with thickened fruit and cashew cream or vanilla pudding as topping. (Cashew or coconut topping).

25 Crepes   58 calories per crepe

BLUEBERRY DESSERT

Crust:
1 c. oatmeal, ground
1 c. almonds, ground
1/8 t. salt
2 T. water (Add enough water to moisten)

ROLL OUT between two sheets of wax paper or plastic wrap. **PUT** in pie dish and **BAKE** for 15 minutes or until light brown, at 325 degrees.
Filling: Make 1½ times the cashew banana pie filling without the bananas. **Topping:** 12 oz. unsweetened grapejuice and 1 can water. **BRING TO BOIL** juice and water. **ADD** 3 T. cornstarch or arrowroot starch dissolved in ½ c. water. **ADD** this to the boiling juice and cook to thicken. **ADD** 2-3 c. fresh or frozen blueberries. **COOL** and put filling in crust and add topping.

CAROB MILLET PUDDING
OR PIE FILLING

¾ c. water   1 T. peanut butter
½ c. dates, chopped   ½ t. vanilla
2 T. carob powder

BLEND in blender until smooth. **ADD** 1 c. hot cooked millet. **WHIZ** in blender until creamy smooth. **CHILL** and serve with garnish of coconut or granola.

OATMEAL CAROB BARS

6 c. oatmeal
1 c. each raisins, nuts, seeds
1½-1¾ c. peanut butter
2 c. dates, cooked in 2 c. water

MIX WELL and divide between 2 - 9x12 glass baking dishes. **MELT** 2 c. carob chips with ½ c. water for frosting. **SPREAD** over bars. Bake at 350 degrees for ½ hour.

Serves 72

CRUMBLY CRUST

¾ c. grapenuts   3 T. chopped almonds
¾ c. quick oatmeal   1/8 t. salt

MOISTEN with enough date paste (dates blended with water) to make it hold together. Press into 9x12 pan. May be evened out by placing plastic wrap over the top and using a small can to roll it out. **BAKE** at 325 degrees until slightly brown, if to be used with a cooked filling. If used for a pumpkin pie or one that will be baked, do not pre-bake.

VANILLA FREEZER ICE CREAM

2/3 c. cashew nuts
3½ c. water
1½ c. cooked rice, soft
¾ c. dates or more to suit your taste
2 t. vanilla
¼ t. salt

BLEND well and **FREEZE** in ice cream freezer or may be frozen in pans and put through the Champion Juicer as for other frozen desserts. May add 2 T. carob for carob ice cream. May add nuts and cherries (chop in small pieces)

FRESH FRUIT PIE II

Make crust (almond-oatmeal) Use pyrex glass or pretty pie dish. *COOL.*

MAKE Banana Cream Pie filling omitting bananas. Cool. Put in crust.

ARRANGE fresh fruit using three or four different kinds (apricots or peaches or nectarines—green or red seedless grapes—cherries—and then sprinkle with blueberries and raspberries). *BEAUTIFUL AND TASTY!*

CAROB-NUT-FRUIT BARS

2 c. freshly ground peanut butter
2 c. date butter
½ c. ground sesame seeds
¼ c. whole sesame seeds
1 c. sunflower seeds
1 c. raisins
1½ c. carob chips
1½ c. coconut

MIX together and *PRESS* in pan. May *FROST* with thin layer of melted carob. *REFRIGERATE.*

CAROB FUDGE II

1 c. chunk peanut butter
½ c. date paste
1½ c. unsweetened carob chips

MELT in microwave or oven. *ADD:*
1 c. raisins
1 c. unsweetened coconut

MIX well. *PRESS* into pan and *REFRIGERATE.*

MISCELLANEOUS

SAUT'EING VEGETABLES WITHOUT FAT (OR OIL)

Place a little water in bottom of skillet. Add chopped vegetables and cook on low or medium heat until tender. Stir as needed. A little extra water may be added if vegetables become too dry during cooking process.

PREPARATION OF RAW CASHEWS

Raw cashews are sometimes dirty. If so, they should be washed well in lukewarm water and rinsed several times. If they are to be used in a cooked food, it is not necessary to toast them. If they are not to be cooked, as in milk, etc., they should be washed and spread out onto a cookie sheet and put in the oven at 200 degrees or less for 2-3 hours — *DO NOT BROWN.*

SOYBEAN BASE

To be used for milk, mayonnaise, etc.
Soak 1 c. soybeans in 2 c. water overnight. Drain and rinse beans and place in pan with 3-4 c. water. Bring to boil slowly, but *DO NOT BOIL.* Taste the beans when almost boiling to determine flavor. Bean taste should be gone and a nutty flavor appear. When this takes place, put 1 c. beans in blender. Blend until very smooth. Repeat until all are blended. For serving, dilute to consistency you wish. May add salt, vanilla, and dates when used for cereals.

SOY MILK

Bring 8 c. water to boil
Blend 1 c. dry soybeans until smooth without water. Then add enough boiling water to cover beans and blend until smooth again. Keep adding boiling water until blender is full. Pour mixture into the remaining water and cook for 40 minutes in a double-boiler, stirring occasionally. Cook milk in water-bath until warm and pour through a fine strainer. Can then be put through cheese cloth (optional). Blend ¼ c. dates in 1 c. warm water (optional). Add to milk concentrate. Add 1 T. vanilla (optional) and 1 t. salt. Then double the milk concentrate with warm water. Cool. Increase or decrease the water for desired milk consistency.

SOY CHEESE

Proportions: 3 c. water to 1 c. soy flour.
Sift full fat soy flour into bowl. Bring water to rolling boil. With wire whip, whip in the soy flour. Watch heat carefully as it boils over easily. Let it cook 10 minutes stirring occasionally. Turn off heat and add scant t. citric acid or small amount lemon juice (add lemon juice very slowly until it curdles and the liquid looks like whey). Stir as little as possible when adding citric acid or lemon juice. The less agitation, the larger the curd remains. Drain through fine sieve or cheese cloth.

TOFU

Recipe yields approximately 2 lbs. curd
1. Wash 2 c. dry soy beans and soak overnight.
2. Rinse well. Liquify beans until very smooth: 1 part beans to 2-3 parts of water.
3. Separate residue from milk (squeeze in nylon hose or nylon chiffon material).
4. Bring milk to boiling point. Stir constantly as milk scorches easily or place non-scorch pad under pan and stir occasionally.
5. Add 1 heaping T. Epsom salts (dissolved in ¼ c. warm water) to milk stirring slowly while adding. Stir gently, not too much.
6. Wait 3-6 minutes until milk curdles well. Gently lift curd into nylon cloth. Run water through to rinse out salts. Leave in cloth and press into mold. May put weight on top to press out water. Let drain well.
7. Put curd in container and store in refrigerator for use within a week.

DEXTRINIZED CEREALS

Heat until very light brown, in frying pan or in oven, uncooked grains such as rye, oats, cornmeal, cracked wheat, rice, before cooking. It shortens the cooking time and improves the flavor.

CHILI POWDER SUBSTITUTE

2 T. paprika
1 T. parsley flakes
1 t. ground oregano
1 T. dried bell pepper (green or red)
½ t. ground dill or 1 t. dill seed
½ t. savory
¼ t. garlic powder
2 bay leaves
1 T. cumin
1 T. sweet basil
1 t. onion powder

Put all ingredients together and grind to fine powder in Moulinex grinder. Good for flavoring beans.

CINNAMON SUBSTITUTE

Coriander seed or
1 part coriander seed and 1 part sweet anise seed or
3 parts coriander seed and 1 part cardamon or
2 parts coriander seed and 1 part cardamon

GRIND together. Use in recipes calling for cinnamon.

CHICKEN-LIKE SEASONING

1/3 c. flaked food yeast
½ t. sweet pepper flakes powder
1 t. onion powder
¾ t. salt
½ t. sage
½ t. celery salt
½ t. thyme
½ t. garlic powder
¼ T. marajoram

BLEND all together in seed mill. Can add dried parsley.

VEGETABLE BROTH POWDER

1 T. dried parsley
2 T. dried green bell pepper
1 T. dried red bell pepper
1 T. celery seed
4 T. onion powder
1 c. food yeast

MIX together and WHIZ up in Moulinex grinder. Other dried vegetables can be added to this to get different flavors. Experiment, using dried summer squash, tomatoes, spinach, peas, etc. Dry your own or purchase in health food stores, or sporting goods shops.

PARCHED WHEAT

Clean and cook wheat. Drain and spread on cookie sheet. Season with salt, onion salt, garlic salt or other seasoning of your choice. Then place under broiler for 10 minutes until the wheat starts to pop. Set the oven on bake and continue baking at 350 degrees for 20 minutes or until crisp. You may use sprouted wheat.

POPPED CORN

Corn popped in an air popper or in a kettle without oil can be seasoned with salt, food yeast flakes, or whatever seasoning you wish. Make a heavy brine solution of water and salt. Put it into a bottle with a very fine sprayer. As the corn pops, spray lightly with salt solution and sprinkle with other seasoning. If corn is too wet, it can be dried in the oven, but do not spray heavy.

COMMUNION BREAD

2 c. 100% whole wheat flour, pastry or other whole grains
½ t. salt
1 c. almonds, ground fine. Mix thoroughly into flour and salt. Then add:
½ c. water or just enough to wet dough as for pie crust.

Mix gently. Roll out *very* thin. Mark in squares with a knife. Bake in 350 degree oven until light brown. Watch carefully. Use teflon cookie sheet. Should be crisp. (Don't over mix as that develops the gluten and makes the cracker tough). This is a very good pie crust also.

FRENCH FRIED POTATOES
(without oil)

Scrub potatoes with a stainless steel sponge to remove some of the outer brown covering. Clean well. Cut in strips for french fries. Place on silverstone pan and season with vegetable salt, onion and garlic salt, savor salt or your choice. The potatoes should be only one layer so they will bake evenly.

Scrubbed potatoes may be shredded and baked in the waffle iron. The thinner the layer, the crisper the potatoes will be. There is a non-aerosol PAM spray available which can be used before using the waffle iron the first time, either for the potatoes or for waffles. Usually you do not need to spray it for the second baking.

—99—

The silver stone or T-Fal pans are very good for browning fresh cut potatoes. Just add a little water to the bottom of the pan along with seasonings. Waffle iron or fry pan may be covered with thin layer of ground sesame or sunflower seed. Brown-crisp and tasty!

SESAME SEASONING

In a dry skillet, on medium heat, toast ½ c. sesame seeds for 5-10 minutes, stirring constantly, until they turn slightly brown and they begin to pop. Grind in seed grinder when cool. This can be used as seasoning for vegetables with a little salt and is especially tasty on brown rice. Just sprinkle it over your bowl of rice—as much or little as you prefer. Stir it in and enjoy!

CRANBERRY RELISH

GRIND 2 c. cranberries, 1 orange with small amount of the peel, several sweet apples. ADD some chopped walnuts and sweeten with a little orange or apple juice concentrate if too tart. Dates may also be cut fine or blended to sweeten.

SPROUTED WHEAT WAFER

2 c. washed wheat, soaked overnight
SPROUT wheat for five days. Grind fine in food grinder. Spread thin in rounds on cookie sheet and bake in 350 degree oven until brown and crisp. Surprisingly sweet and good.

MINTY PEAS

Put a Peppermint Tea bag in the water when cooking peas.

SAUER KRAUT

For every 5 pounds of shredded cabbage, add 3 T. canning salt. Mix and pack in jars until juice forms and covers the cabbage. Set aside on trays. Ideal temperature about 70-75 degrees. Cover tops of jars with lid, but do not seal. Some liquid may bubble over the top of the jars. In three days—no more and no less, wipe the top of the jars and put lids on tight. In a few days the kraut will be ready to use. This is a very mild sauer kraut.

SIMPLE PICKLES

1 c. salt
1 gallon water
BRING these two ingredients to boiling;
PRICK the cleaned cucumbers a few times with a fork. Cut carrots in strips to fill in the spaces between cucumbers. Cut onions may be put in for flavor and to eat as pickled onions. In clean half gallon jars, place grape leaves, then ADD prepared cucumbers, carrots and sliced onions, 1 t. garlic powder, dill, and FILL the jar with the brine which is boiling. PUT on the lids and SEAL tight. These pickles are very tasty. Use after two weeks.

LEMON JUICE PICKLES

In clean, hot jars, pack chopped dill and grape leaves and garlic. Pack with cleaned cucumbers and put some more dill on top, plus 2 T. salt to one-half gallon jar or 1 T. per quart. Pour this mixture over the cucumbers filling the jars to almost full. 3 c. water and 1 c. lemon juice—boiling. Seal the jars and place in a canner which has hot water in it. Bring just to a boil. Water should be up to lids in canner. Set aside to cool in the water and when cool, remove and put away. I believe this should be a healthful way to preserve cucumbers for the winter months, and the pickles are exceptionally good.

GARBANZO NUTS

Soak garbanzos overnight. *DRAIN. ADD* water and cook gently until tender. *ADD* salt the last 10 minutes of cooking time. *DRAIN* (Liquid may be used in soup or gravy). *PLACE* garbanzos on teflon cookie sheet. *BAKE* 375-400 degrees shaking the pan now and then so all surfaces are exposed from time to time. *BAKE* until a bit brown and quite dry—about 30 minutes.

SPROUTING

ADVANTAGES OF SPROUTING

Seeds can be kept dry for many months or even years, and are still suitable for sprouting. The sprouting process accomplishes biologically what grinding does through the use of physical means, and heating does through chemical changes. The chemical bondages for long term storage of nutrients are broken through the sprouting process, making them more easily available for use by the body. Additionally, there is the development of vitamins C, A, and B, and the development of chlorophyl. Sprouting is said to increase the content of vitamins B-1 and B-2, niacin, pantothenic acid, pyridoxine, biotin, and folic acid.

SEEDS TO BE SPROUTED

Any seed that will grow can be sprouted in a jar, and used in meal preparation. A special favorite is alfalfa. Radish seeds, all the legumes, including lentils, soybeans, and mung beans, are suitable for sprouting. Lettuce, radishes, and similar plants that "go to seed" furnish good seeds for sprouting.

You can sprout almost any whole natural seed: alfalfa, lentils, mung beans, soy beans, garbanzos, peas, sunflower seeds, wheat, rye, corn, oats, etc. Be sure to buy untreated seeds and grains. These can be obtained in the health food stores. Radish seeds, sprouted, add a zesty flavor to salads.

USES FOR SPROUTS

In winter, when greens are in short supply and are expensive in the market, sprouts can be prepared in the kitchen for use at a very inexpensive price. One can do one's own organic gardening in the kitchen. This kind of gardening requires no weed killing and no mulching. With judicious planning, sprouts can always be ready for use.

Sprouts can be used separately with a little salad dressing such as mayonnaise, or used with other greens, tomatoes, celery, bell pepper, etc., as a tossed salad. Sprouts may be added to soups at the moment of serving. A favorite way to serve a thick vegetable stew is to float a large handful of sprouts on the top, and drop a dollop of mayonnaise on the mound. Sprouts may be liquified in tomato juice or nut milk in the blender to make a delicious and nutritious beverage, using a sprinkle of salt to prevent flatness. Sprouts may be sprinkled on potato or pumpkin pie for an unusual and crispy dessert. The use of sour soy cream or soyonnaise on top of the dessert makes a delightful blend of the sweet and sour. Sprouted wheat and sunflower seeds are good with fruits. Sprouts may be mixed in breads, using them whole or ground. Bean sprouts used as a main dish are very good with chow mein, burgers, or as cooked lentil or garbanzo sprouts. Soy bean sprouts are especially good cooked as a main dish. The cooking time is greatly reduced (to about 30 minutes) for difficult to cook beans such as garbanzos and soy beans.

METHOD:

The simplest method for preparing sprouts is by using a half-gallon jar with a jar ring and a screen wire or piece of nylon stocking or chiffon cloth. Three tablespoons of whole, unsprayed seeds are placed in the half gallon jar with a generous quantity of water to soak overnight. The next morning the seeds are rinsed well through the wire screen or nylon. The jar is turned upside down to drain for a few seconds and then left with the kitchen towel covering the jar to make a dark place. The seeds should be rinsed twice daily through the screen wire (more frequently in summer to prevent developments of undesirable acids). Gently distribute the seeds around the sides of the jar wall. Sprouts are ready for use when ¼ to ⅔ inch long. Alfalfa seeds can be allowed to develop up to 1-2 inches. After 2 more days, place the jar in the sun to develop the chlorophyl and other nutrients. Rinse in water to eliminate unfertile seeds and hulls.

Soy and other large beans and lentils, and grains are best used when the sprouts are short—about ¼" long. Alfalfa and radish seeds can have longer sprouts.

1 T. alfalfa seed will fill a quart jar full of sprouts. Use 2 T. seeds when using radish seeds. Use ⅔ c. of mung beans, wheat, or rye, etc. Use 1 c. soy or other beans or lentils.

"Soybeans and soybean sprouts need to be cooked as they contain toxins which inhibit growth and proper digestion." **Discovering Natural Foods,** *Roy Bruder, Ph.D.*

SPROUTING SUNFLOWER SEEDS

(These are really special...tasty)

Use an old sheet cake pan. Fill with an inch of garden or potting soil and soak cups of unhulled sunflower seeds 8-12 hours. Scatter one layer thick and press them down firmly on the soil with your hand. Sprinkle with water—must be kept very moist. Cover with a brown paper and spray to dampen. Keep damp. In about four days the plants should be pushing the paper up several inches. Pick the seed hulls off the leaves only after the small plants begin to stand up. Remove paper and allow plants to green in the sun. Cut harvest with scissors when the first two leaves are open and green. Cut above the soil. Rinse and shake dry. Eat in sandwiches, pita bread, salads, etc. Store rest in refrigerator. The soil will not be reuseable.

ROASTED CHESTNUTS

Nothing can substitute for fresh chestnuts to roast and eat warm right out of their shiny brown shells. Take advantage of their short season and serve them as elegantly simple party appetizers. They are good served with steamed brown rice and may also be used in dressing.

To cook with vegetables or as an accompaniment for meals, there is a more convenient way to begin. Dried chestnuts come with the difficult shell already peeled off. They are available year-round in Italian and Chinese markets and delicatessens and are usually less expensive than fresh chestnuts. After soaking, they become interchangeable with fresh shelled nuts for all kinds of dishes.

HOW TO PREPARE CHESTNUTS FOR ROASTING: Wash chestnuts. Use a small, sharp knife to make a deep slash in the top of the nut, or crossed slashes in one side of each chestnut. Spread in a single layer in a shallow pan. Roast in a 450-500 degree oven for 15 minutes. Roast only as many chestnuts at a time a you will peel and eat while warm. If, however, you have roasted too many, peel while warm and store in refrigerator for future use. Unlike other nuts, chestnuts are low in fat and protein and high in complex carbohydrate and may be used often.

PROPER USE OF WATER

How could one live without water! Water is one of heaven's most marvelous life-savers. Have you enjoyed the restfulness of the pounding ocean waves, the rippling stream, a quiet lake or pond? Even a bath!

The main function of water in people, houses, streams, and oceans is to clean. Ocean waves remove harbor pollution. Streams flow briskly letting fresh air and sunlight purify its contents (unless completely overloaded by man's carelessness). Every homemaker constantly uses water for cleaning the family's food, dishes, clothing, and surroundings. Everybody has a daily bath!

Unfortunately not everyone realizes that water is the single most important part of proper diet. Water should be used between meals. Upon rising, flush out the system with two glasses of water, preferably warm. Then between breakfast and noon meal, at least one-half hour before dinner, drink two glasses of water. In the afternoon, drink two more glasses of water. This will take care of the body needs and keep you from being thirsty at meal time. Water should not be taken with the meals. The body's need for water is second only to its need for fresh air. Body weight is over half water. You could lose all reserve carbohydrates and fat and about half the body protein without any real danger. To lose as little as ten percent of body water is serious and about twenty percent loss is fatal.[1]

OUTSIDE THE BODY, hot and cold water is well known to relieve pain and to prevent infection and skin diseases. When you bathe, you breathe more easily. Bathing makes the muscles more flexible. It invigorates the body and mind, making you livelier. It soothes your nerves.[5]

A bath helps you perspire. It stirs up your blood, giving new life to your digestive and excretory organs. It actually strengthens them.[5] A properly taken bath fortifies against taking cold because it improves circulation.

Within your house, water along with sunlight and fresh air can be heaven's cleaning agents. The proper use of sunlight, and fresh air will keep your house scrupulously clean. Germs and pests that invite disease cannot live where it is clean.

INSIDE THE BODY, water is a universal solvent. Without water there is no growth or healing. Food must be in solution to pass through the walls of the intestine into the blood stream. Blood is about ninety percent water and carries nutrients to cells and waste products away from them.[4]

Water aids in regulating body temperature. It equalizes temperature by evaporation and by transporting heat from one part to another through circulating fluids. A physically fit person sweats more. Dreadful? No, sweat is an important defense against dangerous rises in temperature which may result in heat exhaustion and heat stroke.[3] Water, along with vitamins and minerals, regulates body processes.[4] Most body water is held within each cell (sixty percent).[1] Other water bathes each cell, allowing food and wastes to be exchanged.

Water is tremendously important to the kidneys, the body's filters. The kidneys primed with fluids helps them wash out wastes instead of letting it accumulate in some part. Any waste soluble in water is removed by the kidneys including drugs taken when ill. Wastes stagnating in the kidney for lack of water foreshadow cystitis and bladder cancer.[2]

To be effective, water must pass through the body, not remain in any one place. As the bladder fills, blood pressure rises. During urination, blood pressure drops immediately. Sitting on a full bladder is not only uncomfortable but bad for the blood pressure.[3] So when the body signals an urge to pass the water on through, comply immediately!

Along with wastes, the kidneys remove both sugar and water, then take sugar and water out as needed according to your activity or condition (For instance sleeping, eating, traveling in hot dryness, troubled with diarrhea, make different demands on body sugar and water[2]). When chilled, the tubules don't work as well. This leaves your urine paler in color. In cold country you can see why it is important to health (waste removal and circulation) to dress warmly.[2][5] Diuretics increase the flow of urine by over-activating the tubules. Common diuretics are tea, coffee, or cocoa. Their use creates a cycle of thirst and satisfaction by their use which to a varying extent is habit-forming.[2][5]

Everyday loss of water must be made up by fluids taken and by water contained in solid foods (About a pint of water a day is produced in the body itself during the metabolic processes). Since the body normally excretes through breath, perspiration, and urine, two to two and one-half quarts of water a day, about eight glasses of water is needed to keep the system balanced.[1] Water is the best liquid possible to clean the tissues.[5] Common constipation, backache, and headache can all be relieved by drinking enough water at regular times. Attempting to lose weight through losing water such as during a steam bath or by using a diuretic is not only ineffective but may be dangerous. To lose weight, lose fat![3]

[1] Boger, L. Jean, *Nutrition and Physical Fitness* (1966, W. B. Saunders)
[5] White, Ellen G., *Life at Its Best* (1964, Pacific Press Pub. Assoc.)
[2] Gomex, Dr. Joan, *How Not to Die Young* (1972, Stein and Day)
[3] Guild, Warren R., M.D., *How to Keep Fit and Enjoy It* (1962, Harper)
[4] Peyton, Alice B., *Practical Nutrition* (1962, J.B. Lippincott)

WHAT EXERCISE CAN DO FOR YOU

1. It increases the efficiency of your lungs, conditioning them to process more air with less effort.

2. It increases the efficiency of your heart in several ways. It grows stronger and pumps more blood with each stroke, reducing the number of strokes necessary.

3. It increases the number and size of your blood vessels as well as your total blood volume, thus saturating the tissue throughout the body with energy-producing oxygen.

4. It increases your body's maximal oxygen consumption by increasing the efficiency of the mean supply and delivery. In doing so, it improves the overall condition of your body, especially its most important parts, the lungs, the heart, the blood vessels and the body tissue, giving you protection against many forms of illness and disease.

5. It improves the tone of your muscles and blood vessels, changing them from weak and flabby tissue to strong and firm tissue, often reducing blood pressure in the process.

6. It slows down your aging process and physical deterioration as it restores your zest for life and youthful activity.

7. It may change your whole outlook on life. You learn to relax, develop a better self-image, and tolerate the stress of daily living. You will sleep better and get more work done with less fatigue.

NOTE:

Dr. Cooper suggests that some of the best exercises for building cardiovascular endurance are running, swimming, cycling, walking, stationary running, handball, basketball and squash. He also points out that exercise must be regular, vigorous, and sufficiently prolonged, if it is to be of any appreciable benefit.

From *The New Aerobics* by Kenneth Cooper, M.D., and *Physical Fitness and Dynamic Health* by Thomas Cureton, Ph D.

Let men and women work in field and orchard and garden. This will bring health and strength to nerve and muscle. If those who are sick would exercise their muscles daily, women as well as men, in outdoor work, using brain, bone and muscle proportionately, weakness and languor would disappear. Health would take the place of disease, and strength the place of feebleness. "Ye are God's building." God made nerve and muscle in order that they might be used. It is the inaction of the human machinery that brings suffering and disease.

From *Healthful Living* and *Medical Ministry* by E. G. White

TOTAL FITNESS comes not only from exercise but by proper diet, water, rest, sunlight, fresh air, temperance, and trust in Divine Power.

AIR

THE BREATH OF LIFE

Often when we start on a good health program, we emphasize diet, and we do not consider various other activities. The air we breathe is approximately 21% oxygen. Many scientific studies are now showing that a lack of oxygen in the system may be the root cause of hardening of the arteries.

Dr. Robertson,[1] of the Cleveland Clinic Foundation, did some of the early work and concluded that a lack of oxygen in the artery wall played and important part in accelerating the process of hardening of the arteries. From this basic conclusion, that a lack of oxygen in the system was one of the causes for hardening of the arteries, much research has been done showing that increasing the oxygen in the tissues will prevent hardening of the arteries from taking place.

Dr. Kjeldsen[2] found that he could not only prevent hardening of the arteries, but he could also lower the cholesterol and the fat or triglycerides in the blood by slightly increasing the oxygen that his experimental animals breathed. The real exciting part of his study shows that *hardening of the arteries can be reversed* by increasing the amount of oxygen that his experimental animals breathed.

Dr. Vesselinovitch[3] repeated the studies a few years later and confirmed the fact that hardening of the arteries is reversible by increasing the oxygen in the air that the experimental animals breathed. Dr. Vesselinovitch found that by combining a low fat diet with the increase in oxygen that the best results were obtained.

Dr. Joyner[4] showed that as the fat content of the diet was increased, the amount of oxygen in the tissues decreased. This information will help us in understanding how the diet that is high in fat can contribute towards hardening of the arteries.

Dr. Josephson,[5] in his book, "Breathe Deeply and Avoid Colds", feels very strongly that colds and upper respiratory infections can be prevented by deep breathing. He also feel that headaches and fatigue are improved, that tension and stress are relieved, and that relaxation is the natural result of deep breathing.

Many of the chronic degenerative diseases can be traced to a lack of oxygen in the tissues. Stomach and duodenal ulcers that are caused by stress can be caused from a lack of oxygen in the tissues.

It is important to breathe pure fresh air. Sometimes we complain about the smog, and then enclose ourselves in our houses with no ventilation. The air can become unfit to breathe especially with the use of aerosols, cooking, and heating of our homes. We need to keep a good fresh supply of air which contains vital oxygen into our homes continually, as it is being continually used up as we breathe. Also, the air acts as a natural purifying agent and can protect against the growth of mold, fungus, and bacteria. Airing our bedding out everyday is important.

Proper breathing should be slow with a slight pause at the end of inhaling and exhaling. It should be nasal breathing and should bring into action all the muscles of the abdomen, diaphram, chest, shoulder, girdle, and neck. Tight clothing should not be worn as it will tend to inhibit proper breathing. Tensions and pressures of modern life seem to cause shallow breathing.

Deep breathing is almost a lost art and will take some persistence to redevelop. The first few days that you try it, it may be fatiguing because the muscles have not been used for years. But after six to eight weeks, it will become an unconscious natural habit to you.

If you become slightly dizzy when you first start breathing deeply, don't become alarmed. This is normal and will gradually become less of a problem as you persist in your breathing exercises.

1. Robertson, A. Lazzorini, *Oxygen Requirement of the Human Arterial Intima in Atherogenesis.* Progr. biochem. Pharmacol. 4:305, 1968.
2. Kjeldsen, K.P. Astrup and J. Wanstrup. *Reversal of Rabbit Atheromatosis by Hyperoxia. Journal of Atherosclerosis Research* 10:173, 1969.
3. Vesselinovitch, Dragoslava, Robert W. Wissler, Katti Fisher-Dzoga, et al. *Regression of Atherosclerosis in Rabbits. Atherosclerosis* 19:259, 1974.
4. Joyner, Claude R. Jr., Orville Horwitz, Phyllis G. Williams. *The Effect of Lipemia Upon Tissue Oxygen Tension in Man. Circulation* 22:901, 1960.
5. Josephson, Emmanuel M., *Breath Deeply and Avoid Colds.* Chedney Press, New York, NY 1957.

TEMPERANCE - ABSTEMIOUSNESS

Indulging in eating too frequently and in too large quantities, overtaxes the diegestive organs and produces a feverish state of the system. The blood becomes impure and then diseases of various kinds occur. The sufferers should commence to relieve nature of the load they have forced upon her. Fast a short time and give the stomach chance for rest. Reduce the feverish state of the system by a careful and understanding application of water. These efforts will help nature in her struggles to free the system of impurities.

Intemperate eating is often the cause of sickness and what nature most needs is to be relieved of the undue burden that has been placed upon her. In many cases of sickness, the very best remedy is for the patient to fast a meal or two that the overworked organs of digestion may have an opportunity to rest. A fruit diet for a few days has often brought great relief to brain workers. An abstemious diet for a month or two would convince many sufferers that the path of self-denial is the path to health. *Food should be prepared by one who realized that he occupies a most important position, inasmuch as good food is required to make good blood.*

Abstemiousness in diet is rewarded with mental and moral vigor; it also aids in the control of the passions. Overeating is especially harmful to those who are sluggish in temperament; these should eat sparingly and take plenty of physical exercise. There are men and women of excellent natural ability who do not accomplish half what they might if they would exercise self-control in the denial of appetite.

Those upon who rest important responsibilities, those, above all, who are guardians of spiritual interests, should be men of keen feeling and quick perception. More than others, they need to be temperate in eating. Rich and luxurious food should have no place upon their tables.

Every day men in positions of trust have decisions to make upon which depend results of great importance. Often they have to think rapidly, and this can be done successfully by those only who practice strict temperance.

We cannot be too often reminded that health does not depend on chance. It is a result of obedience to law. Those foods should be chosen that best supply the elements needed for building up the body. In this choice, appetite is not a safe guide. Through wrong habits of eating, the appetite has become perverted. Often it demands food that impairs health and causes weakness instead of strength. The disease and suffering that everywhere prevail are largely due to popular errors in regard to diet.

The true fasting which should be recommended to all, is abstinence from every stimulating kind of food, and the proper use of wholesome, simple food, which God has provided in abundance.

From *The Ministry of Healing* and *Counsel on Diet and Foods* by E. G. White

NATURAL FOODS

PROPER DIET

Proper diet means eating intelligently. It doesn't mean eating only certain few foods, avoiding others, or starving to become thin.

Proper diet means eating a wide variety of all fresh and properly cooked available natural foods. It means moderation in kind and amount.

Proper diet means choosing food according to the season, the climate in which we live, the occupation we follow. Some foods suitable for people doing hard physical work are not suitable for those with sedentary habits.

TOO MUCH

For too many Americans, the best food is less food![5] In any age group, overweight is one of our most pressing health problems. Great health hazards accompany obesity. A fifty year old man, fifty pounds overweight, needn't plan for retirement. He has only half the life expectancy of a man of normal weight.[4] Fat deposits are what you see of an unseen killer. Various diseases often accompany or are triggered by overweight.

More than ninety percent of overweight people are fast eaters, stand-up eaters, plate cleaners.[3] Part of the solution is learning a new way of eating. Parents should train the appetites of their children. Eat slowly, chew thoroughly. Eat small portions or serve food on smaller plates.[3]

A clogged stomach means a clogged brain. Your all-gone feeling is not hunger, but tired digestive organs. Nothing should be eaten between meals: no confectionary, nuts, fruits, or food of any kind.[7] Eating before going to bed is also a bad habit. When you go to bed for rest, your stomach should be able to rest.

Part of the solution to overweight is exercise, preferably in fresh air. Man, like and over-ripe banana, has become soft.[5] Exercise is not so important in losing weight as it is in improving your total well-being. Without exercise, even plain food should be eaten sparingly.

However, don't stage a strenuous workout just before or after eating. A feeling of fullness, belching, and cramps are a sign of interrupted digestion.[6] Walking in moderation is beneficial because it aids circulation.

TOO LITTLE

Proper diet has much to do with healthy teeth and gums. If the diet is deficient, it is most likely deficient in unabsorbable bulk needed for a healthy colon.[4] Bulk, or indigestible fiber, stimulates blood circulation in the gums (by chewing fibrous foods). It shortens the time that waste remains in the colon. Bulk can soften the stool; it lowers pressure inside the colon while it pushes waste along.[4]

More than one in four adults have no natural teeth either above or below or both. More women than men lose all their teeth.[1] Perhaps this is because of snacking or childbearing demands not met by additional foods or activities. (Like eating calcium and phosphorous rich food during pregnancy and getting enough sunshine to use the food that is eaten.) For everything there is a cause. Fiber is best gotten from fruits, vegetables and thoroughly cooked whole-grain foods.[1] These supply bulk and valuable minerals and vitamins.

Most refined foods contain little or no fiber and all have markedly fewer vitamins and minerals. About 20 known nutrients of whole wheat are lost in refinement and only four are added to "enriched flour".

Sugar is another highly refined food. Used excessively, it causes problems. It may irritate stomach lining or ferment in the intestine. As little as 24 teaspoons, the amount in a banana split, lessens the ability of a white blood cell to destroy bacteria from 14 to 1. This is like sending a soldier to war with no ammunition!

Excessive sugar clogs the system. When fluids inside the teeth don't move, the teeth aren't nourished and they begin to die or decay. With the average American eating about one-fourth pound of sugar a day in commercial and homemade products, is it any wonder it is a contributing factor in causing tooth decay, overweight and diabetes?

Getting fiber as well as minerals and vitamins from unrefined foods is to our advantage. They are in natural foods for our health and healing.

[1] The American Assembly, *The Health of Americans* (1970, Prentice-Hall)
[2] Bogert, Briggs, & Calloway. *Nutrition and Physical Fitness* (1966, W.B. Saunders)
[3] Glenn, Morton B., M.D., *How to Get Thinner Once and For All* (1965, E.P. Dutton)
[4] Gomes, Dr. Joan, *How Not to Die Young* (1972, Stein and Day)
[5] Graham, M. F., M.D., *Prescription for Life* (1966, David McKay Co.)
[6] Guild, Warren R., M.D., *How to Keep Fit and Enjoy It* (1962, Harper)
[7] White, Ellen G. *Life at its Best* (1964, Pacific Press Pub. Assoc.)

VEGETARIAN FOOD

For several reasons a growing number of people choose foods from the plant kingdom alone. Cost, health, religious, and personal reasons predominate. The earth supports plants in a variety and abundance. All animal food has been nourished from plants. When you eat animal foods, you are merely getting plants secondhand. It is no wonder the cost is higher for flesh foods.

Nutritious pure vegetarian food of a wide variety, unrefined, eliminates added cholesterol and will promote health.

The editor of the *"Journal of the American Medical Association"* stated that certain studies show "A vegetarian diet can prevent 97 percent of our coronary occlusions" (heart attacks). *J.A.M.A.* June 3, 1961, p. 806.

No known diseases can be transmitted from unhealthy plants to people, but more and more experiments show that diseases can be transmitted from animal to man. The experimental scientist does not have enough volunteers to see how diseases from animals are given to man.

However, experiments do show that extra liberal amounts of protein decrease the life span of experimental animals. The reasons are not all in, but you can read in Genesis 9:29, 11:10-26, 32 how life span took a marked drop after the introduction of flesh foods. (The original diet included only fruits, nuts, grains, and after sin vegetables were added.)

VARIETY

With abundance of different foods, it is a pity that we do not use more of them.

Have you noticed the variety of color the Creator made: green, red, white, brown, yellow, orange, blue, and purple? Have you tried the various textures and tastes: dry, juicy, limp, crispy, sweet, sour, soft, hard, squishy, stringy? Mixing varieties of texture, tastes, and color from meal to meal makes our food interesting, pretty, tasty, healthful, and reasonable in cost.

However, too much variety at any one meal encourages overeating and causes indigestion.

REST

"As a man rests, so also does he run." Rest is a re-charger. It can come from a change of pace, from active work to quiet enjoyment, from a desk job to vigorous exercises enjoyed in fresh air.

Rest means relax, and one way to relax is to exercise vigorously![4] During exercise you mentally and physically concentrate on work or play. Afterward you are physically tired and mentally relaxed.

When your large muscles exercise, your digestive tract rests.[4] [5]Why? Because the blood is serving your skeletal muscles. (This is one reason you should not exercise vigorously just before and after eating. A moderate walk, however, is beneficial.[5])

Your kidneys, deprived of blood going to muscles, also rest while you exercise. So does your brain.[4] During study, the brain is on the alert. Perhaps for many people the brain rests too often!

Your body rests when you bathe, too. Bathing improves circulation and that strengthens all your insides![5] It even makes you livelier!

Rest is sleep. "Sleep causes a fall in blood pressure"[4] Sometimes this pressure is raised long enough to cause trouble.[4] Exercise releases these tensions and brings sounder sleep.

The body was designed for activity. Excessive sleep or rest can be harmful. Normal men over 50 who sleep nine hours a night double their death rate chances from cardio-vascular causes. Sleeping ten hours a night makes four times the risk.[5]

You see, more people rust out than wear out.[4] Most people rest their large muscles, their skeletal muscles, too much.[1] Have you left your feet in favor of your seat?[3]

The body as a whole does need rest: Physical, spiritual, social, and emotional rest, but most of the rest should be a change, not a chair!

1. Cooper, Kenneth, M.D., *Aerobics* (1968, N. Evans & Co.)
2. Gomez, Dr. Joan, *How Not to Die Young* (1972, Stein & Day)
3. Graham, M.F., M.D. *Prescription for Life* (1966, David McKay Co.)
4. Guild, Warren R., M.D., *How to Keep Fit and Enjoy It (1962, Harper)*
5. *White, Ellen G., Life at Its Best* (1964, Pacific Press Pub. Assoc.)

SUNLIGHT

SUNLIGHT is a seldom appreciated lifesaver known since creation. All life, including that in the deep darkness of the ocean requires it. Sunlight along with fresh air, exercise, and scrupulous cleanliness promotes mental and physical health and healing. [2]

Though its blessings are not fully understood, it is known that some of sunlights' values can be passed from creature to creature.[1] This includes ocean creatures nearly never surfacing but that eat smaller creatures that eat smaller creatures, etc. that receive sunlight.

Only the ultraviolet rays seem to produce the changes in the body oils that become Vitamin D. These rays can be screened by glass, clothing, smog, shade, or indoor life.[1]

"Nature's plan seems to have been that man should generate most of his supply of Vitamin D by sunlight, for it is contained more sparsely in foods than is any other vitamin."[1]

You can see then, that regardless of what natural foods you eat, you need sunlight to promote health.

When exposed to sunlight, oily material on the skin of animals and man absorbs sunshine and becomes Vitamin D. This helps bones to grown in several different ways, all related to vitamins and minerals, carbohydrates, proteins, and fats.[1] Any excess can be stored in the body for later use.

In other words, though sunlight's exact use is not understood, enough is known to realize its importance within the body.

Sunshine contains many different rays. Some of these penetrate glass. You know how a window lets in heat when the sun shines. Germ-killing rays also enter. Dust, smoke, and smog are far less harmful than a dirty house. Germs settle in poorly ventilated dark areas.

Don't allow heavy curtains, drapes, blinds, vines, or trees to shut out the sunshine. Sunlight is a powerful disinfectant,[1] and combined with fresh air is capable of stirring up and killing a tremendous amount of potential troublemakers. "Truly the light is sweet" Ecclesiastes 11:7.

Finally, who doesn't feel more relaxed, yet invigorated, after pleasant exercise in fresh air, congenial surroundings, and sunlight. Surely some mental and emotional benefits cannot be measured.

[1] Bogert, L. Jean, *Nutrition and Physical Fitness* (1966, W.B. Saunders)
[2] White, Ellen G., *Life at Its Best* (1964, Pacific Press Pub. Assoc.)
[3] Cooper, Kenneth H., M.D. *Aerobics* (1968, H. Evans [Co.)
[4] Gomez, Dr. Joan, *How Not to Die Young* (1972, Stein & Day)
[5] Graham, M.F., M.D., *Prescription for Life* (1966, David McKay Co.)
[6] Guild, Warren R., M.D., *How to Keep Fit and Enjoy It* (1962) Harper)
[7] White, Ellen G., *Life at Its Best* (1964, Pacific Press Pub. Assoc.)

TRUST IN DIVINE POWER

The same power that Christ exercised when He walked visibly among men is in His word. It was by His word that Jesus healed disease and cast out demons; by His word He stilled the sea, and raised the dead; and the people bore witness that His word was with power. He spoke the word of God, as He had spoken to all the prophets and teachers of the Old Testament. The whole Bible is a manifestation of Christ.

The Scriptures are to be received as God's word to us, not written merely, but spoken. When the afflicted ones came to Christ, He beheld not only those who asked for help, but all who throughout the ages should come to Him in like need and with like faith. When He said to the paralytic, "Son, be of good cheer; they sins be forgiven thee," (Matt. 9:2) when He said to the woman of Capernaum, "Daughter, be of good comfort; thy faith hath made thee whole; go in peace," (Luke 8:48) He spoke to other afflicted, sin-burdened ones who should seek His help. So with all the promises of God's word. In them He is speaking to us individually, speaking as directly as if we could listen to His voice. It is in these promises that Christ communicates to us His grace and power. They are leaves from that tree which is "for the healing of the nations." (Rev. 22:2) Received, assimilated, they are to be the strength of the character, the inspiration and sustenancy of the life. Nothing else can have such healing power. Nothing besides can impart the courage and faith, which give vital energy to the whole being.

"Fear not; for I have redeemed thee, I have called thee by thy name; thou art Mine. When thou passest through the waters, I will be with thee; and through the rivers, they shall not overflow thee; when thou walkest through the fire, thou shalt not be burned; neither shall the flame kindle upon thee. For I am the Lord thy God, the Holy One of Israel, thy Saviour....Since thou wast precious in My sight, thou hast been honorable, and I have loved thee." "I, even I, am He that blotteth out thy transgressions for Mine own sake, and will not remember they sins." "Fear not; for I am with thee." (Isa. 431-4, 25, 5)

"Like as a father pitieth his children, so the Lord pitieth them that fear Him. For He knoweth our frame; He remembereth that we are dust." (Ps. 103:13, 14). "Only acknowledge thine iniquity that thou has transgressed against the Lord thy God." "If we confess our sins, He is faithful and just to forgive us our sins, and to cleanse us from all unrighteousness." (Jer. 3:13; 1 John 1:9). "I have blotted out, as a thick cloud, thy transgressions, and, as a cloud, thy sins; return to Me; for I have redeemed thee." (Isa. 44:22)

"Come now, and let us reason together, saith the Lord: Though your sins be as scarlet, they shall be as white as snow; though they be red like crimson, they shall be as wool. If ye be willing and obedient, ye shall eat the good of the land." (Isa. 1:18)

"I have loved thee with an everlasting love: therefore with loving-kindness have I drawn thee." "I hid My face from thee for a moment; but with everlasting kindness will I have mercy on thee." (Jer. 31:3, Isa. 54:8)

"Let not your heart be troubled." "Peace I leave with you, My peace I give unto you; not as the world giveth, give I unto you. Let not your heart be troubled, neither let it be afraid." (John 14:1, 27)

"A Man shall be as an hiding-place from the wind, and a covert from the tempest; as rivers of water in a dry place, as the shadow of a great rock in a weary land." (Isa. 32:2)

"When the poor and needy seek water, and there is none, and their tongue faileth for thirst, I the Lord will hear them, I the God of Israel will not forsake them." (Isa. 41:17)

"Thus saith the Lord that made thee: "I will pour water upon him that is thirsty, and floods upon the dry ground: I will pour My Spirit upon thy seed, and My blessing upon thine offspring." (Isa. 44:2, 3)

"Look unto Me, and be ye saved, all the ends of the earth." (Isa. 45:22). "Himself took our infirmities, and bare our sicknesses." "He was wounded for our transgressions, He was bruised for our iniquities; the chastisement of our peace was upon Him; and with His stripes we are healed." (Matt. 8:17; Isa. 53:5).

"If any of you lack wisdom, let him ask of God, who giveth to all men liberally, and upbraideth not; and it shall be given him." (James 1:5). "For we have not an high priest which cannot be touched with the feeling of our infirmities; but was in all points tempted like as we are, yet without sin." (Heb. 4:15)

"Great peace have they which love thy law; and nothing shall offend them." (Ps. 119:165)

"Jesus said unto him, If thou canst believe, all things are possible to him that believeth." (Mark 9:23)

"And whatsoever ye shall ask in my name, that will I do, that the Father may be glorified in the Son." (John 14:13)

Our heavenly Father has a thousand ways to provide for us of which we know nothing. Those who accept the one principle of making the service of God supreme, will find perplexities vanish, and a plain path before their feet. (MH 481)

From *Steps to Christ* by E. G. White

Dear Friends,

We hope that you are enjoying or will enjoy this new, healthier life style. Our bodies are made of what we eat and drink; therefore, it is important that we follow right living habits. Many deaths in this country are caused by diseases which could be prevented if people would care for their bodies in the right manner.

In the Bible, God has given us the message that we are to present ourselves to Him in a healthy and happy condition. We need to be physically, mentally and spiritually whole. A thorough knowledge of right living habits will keep our physical being well, if we put them into practice. If a thorough knowledge of the Bible and what God wants us to be is a part of our life, we will be kept in mental and spiritual health and work as a harmonious whole.

There are a number of excellent sources from which you might secure additional information for health which will lead you into a clearer understanding of God's way for all people.

The Quiet Hour, Redlands, CA 92373 (radio)

Faith for Today, P.O. Box 1000, Thousand Oaks, CA 91360 (TV)

It is Written, Box O, Thousand Oakes, CA 91360 (TV)

Amazing Facts, P.O. BOx 3194, Baltimore, MD 21228 (radio)

Voice of Prophecy, Box 55, Los Angeles, CA 90053 (radio)

Please check your local paper for time and stations.

If we may be of service to you in any way in your search for more abundant health and a better understanding of combining physical, mental and spiritual growth, feel free to call or write to us.

Sincerely,

Melvin E. Beltz, M.D.
Black Hills Health & Education Center
Box 1
Hermosa, SD 57744

P.S. Please *study* the materials in this cookbook, **Cooking With Natural Foods** as well as the supplementary materials that you may have received at the Better Living Seminars. Remember that the true remedies are sunshine, fresh air, and use of water, proper diet, exercise, rest, temperance in all things and most of all, trust in Divine Power.

The staff at the Black Hills Health & Education Center is dedicated to helping all who want to be in health. Contact us for more information.

B.H.H.E.C., Box 1, Hermosa, SD 57744, Telephone - 605-255-4579, 255-4101 or 255-4789.

GLOSSARY

AFLOTOXINS, mushrooms - have been found to contain aflotoxins, (toxic substances that are highly carcinogenic - cancer forming - and seem to be the product of a mold formation). They are the fleshy fruiting body of a fungus. A fungus is any of a major group of saprophytic and parasitic lower plants that lack chlorophyll, and includes molds, rusts, mildews, smuts and mushrooms. However, these same toxins are found in fruits and vegetables which have spoiled spots on them. This is why we are discouraged in using fruits or vegetables that have the slightest sign of decay. Commercially canned or frozen juices have a strong possibility of spoiled fruit or vegetables being used in their production. The aflotoxins also exist in grains, peanuts and other products as a result of improper storage which has allowed molds to form. This problem can be avoided in most cases by care in regard to storage or being careful to use good quality fruits and vegetables. With mushrooms it may not be as easy to detect just which ones might be afflicted with this problem. These toxins are not destroyed by heat.

MUSHROOMS - have been replaced in some recipes by using eggplant. Peel and dice and use in recipes such as Spaghetti Sauce, Lasagna Sauce, Pizza Sauce and also in casserole dishes.

AGAR AGAR - is a vegetable gelatin obtained from seaweed. It comes in large flakes, fine flakes, and powder. The amounts called for in these recipes are for the large flakes. If the small flakes are used, cut the amount to half. If the powder is used, cut the amount to one fourth.

ARROWROOT - is a powder made by grinding the root of the arrowroot plant and is used like cornstarch. It is preferable due to the fact that it is not a derivitive and has considerably better nutritive value because of its high mineral content of calcium, potassium, and magnesium. It can be obtained in most health food stores and used in place of cornstarch in any recipe and in the same amount called for. Use this in lemon pie filling if possible.

BIOLOGIC - Digestibility

BLEND - In most instances this means blend in a blender

BREAD - fresh is not healthful and should be used 2-3 days after baking. To serve, reheat by placing in a covered pan, 250 degree oven until heated thoroughly. This bread will taste as good or better than freshly baked bread.

BREAKFAST IDEAS - Fruit toast, fruit soup, scrambled tofu, tomato soup, whole grain waffles made previously and frozen, hot soupy beans on toast, etc. **DINNER TYPE MEAL FOR BREAKFAST** - is enjoyed by many making it possible for the evening meal to be light, or eliminated.

COMPLEX CARBOHYDRATES - the perfect nutrient entirely utilized. The whole grains, unrefined cereals, bread from whole grains without adding fat or oil, whole grain pasta, vegetables, fresh fruits, and a few nuts and seeds.

CARBOHYDRATES - Refined - when whole wheat flour is processed into white flour, brown rice into polished white rice, sugar beets into refined sugar making them deficient in important nutrients and fiber. Calories usually remain about the same. Refined carbohydrates are too quickly digested which leads to snacking and obesity.

CAROB POWDER - is made from the locust pod (St. John's Bread). It is high in natural sugars. The fat content is about 7% (chocolate has 52%). Carob is high in calcium, and a good source of phosphorus, potassium, iron, magnesium and other important minerals and vitamins. Carob has its own vitamin B (needed to digest sugar). Three level tablespoons carob powder plus two tablespoons soy milk, nut milk or water equals one square of chocolate.

COOKING WATER - is loaded with minerals and vitamins and is good in soups and gravy. Better yet, thicken it for a glaze effect on "crispy cooked vegetables". Use a very small amount of water for vegetables and many times the water will all be gone when the food is cooked.

DATE GRANULES or **DATE SUGAR** - can often be used in place of whole dates. They are interchangeable, but there may be a little difference in flavor. Spreads are best made with fresh dates. Approximate proportions would be 1 C whole dates, or ½ C granules, or ⅓ C date sugar.

DEXTRINIZE - In a dry fry pan, lightly brown dry grain such as millet, rice, oatmeal, etc. Cook as recipe indicates.

DIASTATIC MALT - A natural food for yeast in place of sugar, molasses, honey, etc. This could be made with sprouted barley, but wheat may be used. The quantitiy to be used can be increased beneficially to 2 t. diastatic malt to 2 T dry yeast. Diastatic malt is made by sprouting the wheat or barley. Dry in food dryer or dry naturally. Grind in nut grinder or blender to fine powder.

DINNER AFTER CHURCH - Casseroles prepared the day before and stored in the refrigerator over night may be placed in the oven at 225 degrees at 9:00 or so and will be just right when you return home. You may wish to turn up the oven when you get home to 350 degrees for a few minutes. The LASAGNA is very good baked this way.

DRIED FRUIT - should be rehydrated by covering it with water and soaking several hours or simmering a few minutes on low heat.

FRUITS AND VEGETABLES - nicely prepared will be beneficial if they are the best quality, not showing the slightest sign of decay, but are sound and unaffected by disease or decay. We have no idea how many die from eating decayed fruit and decayed vegetables which ferment in the stomach and result in blood poisoning (CDF 309). Please read about aflotoxins under the paragraph on mushrooms.

MALT - is made from the sprouted and dried barley. Be sure when purchasing it that you get pure malt. It may be difficult to find, but some health food stores have it. Any purchased in a grocery store will usually contain sugar.

MILK - Try the nut milk recipe, using ½ of the amount of nuts and adding dried pears, or bananas. Other dried fruit could be used. The amount should be in proportion to the consistency and flavor desired. This makes a good cream or beverage.

MOULINEX GRINDER - This is an electric nut and seed grinder which is almost indispensible. There are other brand name grinders which are comparable and can be used instead.

NATURAL FOODS - Whole, unprocessed food containing all or most all of the nutrients of the original source. No artificial substances, a food that is best for humans giving health to the body. Reduces chance of disease, especially the degenerative diseases, increases life expectancy and improves quality of life.

NUTS OR SEEDS - GROUND - The ingredient should be measured first and then ground in the nut grinder unless otherwise stated.

OILS AND LECITHIN - Lecithin is a refined soybean fat. All oils are refined food and it would be better to eliminate them from the diet. 2 T. corn oil equals 252 calories equals 28 grams of fat. To get the same amount of oil by eating fresh corn, you would have to eat 28 ears of corn with calories amounting to around 2324.

PERO - is a cereal drink obtainable at most health food stores. If equal parts of Pero and carob are combined, a flavor very much like chocolate is obtained. You may wish to use a little less of Pero to suit your tastes. Some prefer this to the plain "carob" flavor.

PREPARATION OF BAKING PANS - If you have regular baking dishes and pans rather than the T-Fal or Silver Stone, you may prepare these pans by rubbing liquid lecithin over the pan, then wiping it off with a paper towel. This will leave an invisible film which will release baked items but not put grease or oil in the baked product.

PROTEIN - If you eat whole, unrefined foods you will have sufficient protein providing you eat enough calories to maintain your proper body weight.

SALT - The use of too much salt is of much concern. The recommended daily allowance is 3 gm. (less than ½ t.) per day. The average American is using about 18 gm. per day (over 3 tsp.). You might wish to try VEGESAL which is a vegetable seasoning salt which does not contain any harmful spices.

SAUTÉE IT IN WATER - Use your non-stick skillet or fry pan and add a little water - just a tablespoon or two, cover and simmer over a low to medium heat. Done in minutes - no added unhealthful calories!

SEASONINGS - Almost all prepared seasonings such as Chicken Seasoning, Rich Brown Broth, etc. have some objectionable ingredient such as white pepper. Therefore, we recommend that you make up your own. Recipes are given in **Cooking With Natural Foods** miscellaneous section. By experimenting with herbs and dried vegetables, you may be able to develop some exciting new ones. Give it a try!! Or perhaps we should try to educate our tastes to enjoy simple fruits, vegetables, nuts and grains rather than the flavoring of the seasonings. What is palatable to a person used to highly seasoned foods would not be enjoyed by a person with a properly educated appetite.

SERVINGS - HOW MANY PEOPLE WILL THIS RECIPE SERVE? A common question with many answers. An ample serving for most foods would be one-half cup per person. However, much depends on how many other foods are being served and the appetite of the guests. If soup were the main course along with bread, crackers, etc., you probably should plan for at least one cup each. Desserts can serve many or few depending a lot on the hostess. Information in this book on number of servings is approximate.

SOYBEAN SPROUTS - **should not be eaten raw** as they contain a protein-inhibiting enzyme which heat destroys. Steam for a least five minutes.

SOY FLOUR, FULL FAT - is the regular soy flour that has not had the fat removed. Whole foods are more desireable than refined. The label on the flour should indicate if it is defatted. Soy flour can also be purchased raw or toasted. The raw is preferable for making the soy cheese and the toasted is preferable for most everything else.

SOY SAUCE - is usually a fermented product and has been found to be a source of aflotoxins, which are very harmful. It is preferable to use Dr. Bronner's Bullion or Chef Bonneau's Aminotone or Savorex which have similar flavor and are available at health food stores. Another product "Natural Vegetable Seasoning & Instant Gravy" is marketed by Bernard Jensen Products.

T-FAL, SILVER STONE, TEFLON - usually need no added preparation when used in baking or browning food products. In some of the recipes in this book, the baking instructions will call for a TEFLON pan or griddle. Some feel that the T-FAL or SILVER STONE are more acceptable. When using non-stick utensils, DO NOT use metal. Spoons, turners, knives, etc., are available made from materials which will not harm the utensil.

THERAPEUTIC DIET - For those needing a regression diet, there are many Therapeutic Recipes in **each section** of this cookbook as well as **Therapeutic Menu Suggestions.** Therapeutic recipes will be marked (T) and are recipes which approximate 10% protein, 10% fat and 80% complex carbohydrate. This will aid in dietary management for anyone with a degenerative disease.

The **Therapeutic Recipes** are marked with a T- in the Index.

TOFU - is a high protein food made from soybeans and is not a Natural Food, but a refined, concentrated food. Use it sparingly...occasionally.

It should be understood that any ingredient called for is **"unsweetened"** or **"unrefined"** even though it may not be indicated by the receipe, such as *"unsweetened coconut"*, *"unsweetened crushed pineapple,"* *"unpolished brown rice"*, *"unbleached flour"*; the explanatory word may be eliminated to conserve space.

VACATION - AWAY - Many things from your refrigerator should be put in your freezer. Some things, such as salad dressings, nut milks, etc., may need to be re-blended.

YEAST - is a yellowish surface froth or sediment that promotes alcohol fermentation . It consists largely of cells of a fungus and is used in making alcoholic beverages and as a leaven in baking by producing fermentation in the dough. It produces carbon dioxide which leavens the product.

FOOD YEAST is used to indicate any of the many brand names of Nutritional Yeast such as Food Yeast, Brewer's Yeast, Torumel, etc. The amounts in these recipes are proportional for flake yeasts rather than powdered, which is more concentrated. **BREWER'S YEAST,** which is not an active yeast and will not cause fermentation or leavening activity, is the product of a mold and is derived from the brewing industry. Because of its origin, it is felt by some that the other **FOOD YEASTS** (which are grown on molasses especially for food) would be more desirable. We do not recommend the use of food yeast in large quantities as a food supplement, but as a seasoning to be used in small quantities. We know that it is not objectionable to use active yeast in leavening baked products and since yeast consist largely of cells of a fungus, it would seem logical to conclude that all fungus is not objectionable. The process of fermentation is also not necessarily undesirable. In body metabolism, it is an essential chemical process that occurs in the breakdown of foodstuffs. Fermentation, however, can sometimes have end products that are undesirable such as the production of alcohol, depending upon the variable factors involved. For example, the combination of milk and sugar causes a fermentation in the stomach with end products that do harm the body.

INDEX

BREAKFAST
Cooking Whole Grains

Boiling Method 26
Crock-Pot Method 26
Thermos Method 26

MAIN DISHES

T Baked Oatmeal 27
  Baked Oatmeal 27
T Breakfast Beans 30
  Brown Rice Cereal 26
  Cashew French Toast Batter 28
T Cherries on Toast 30
  Coconut-Millet Waffles 28
T Cornmeal Delight 27
T Cornmeal with Corn 28
T Cottage Fries 30
  Crunchy Granola 29
T Delicious Millet 26
  Delicious Millet 27
T Early Morning Pancakes 35
  Fruit Nut Granola 29
T Fruit Toast 30
T Golden Breakfast Potatoes 30
T Granola 29
  Granola 29
T Ground Grain Type Cereal 27
T Hash Brown Potatoes 30
  Millet Breakfast Dish 27
T Multi-Grain Waffle 29
  Museli 28
  Onion French Toast Batter 27
T Oatmeal 27
  Oatmeal Gems 33
T Rice Breakfast Patties 30
T Rolled Four Grain Cereal 26
T Rolled Wheat and Oats 26
  Scrambled Soy Cheese 29
  Scrambled Tofu 30
  Southern Pancakes 35
  Soy-Oat Waffle with Topping 28
  Tomato Soup 30
T Triticale 27
  Waffle Perfect 28
T Wheat Berries 27
T Whole Barley Cereal 27
T Whole Millet Cereal 27
T Whole Oats, Barley, Rice 26
T Whole Rye Cereal 26
T Whole Wheat Cereal 26
T Yummy Granola 29

CRACKERS, MUFFINS, ETC.
(without yeast)

  Apple-Oatmeal Muffins 33
  Apple Sauce Muffin 33
T Burritos or Wheat Lefse 33
  Coconut or Sesame Sticks 32
  Corn Bread 34
T Corn Crackers 32
  Corn Crisps 34
  Corn Dodgers 34
  Cornmeal Rice Cakes 34
  Crackers 32
  Crispy Cornbread 34
  Crispy Corn Chips 35
T Date Muffins 18
  Fresh Fruit Muffins 33
T Indian Corn Crackers or Corn Chips 32
  Jean's Crackers 32
  Natural Corn Chips 34
  Oatmeal Gems 31
T Onion Crisps 33
  Quick Corn Bread 34
T Rice Crackers 31
  Sesame Crackers 32
  Sesame Crisps 32
T Sprouted Wheat Bread 33
T Taco Chip Seasoning 33
T Tortillas 34

SAUCES AND SYRUPS

T Apricot-Pineapple Sauce 31
T Blueberry Syrup 31
T Cranberry Fruit Sauce 30
T Currant Delight 31
T Lemon Sauce 31
T Orange Date Sauce 31
T Peach-Berry Sauce 31
T Pineapple-Orange Sauce 31
T Spicy-Apple Syrup 31
T Strawberry-Pineapple-Banana Sauce 31
T Strawberry Sauce 31
T Topping for Waffles 28

MILKS AND CREAMS

T Basic Rice Milk 36
  Cashew Cream 37
  Cashew Nut Cream 36
  Coconut Cream 37
  Coconut Milk 36
  Fruit Milk 37

Nut Milks-Almond, Cashew 36
T Oatmeal Milk 36
  Rice Milk 36
  Sesame Milk 36
  Sesame Milk for Cooking 36
  Strawberry Cream 37
  Sunflower Seed Milk 36

BREAD (with yeast)

T Apple Bread 39
T Brown Bread 40
T Brown Bread Muffins 43
T Corn Bread 40
  Corn Bread II 43
T Corn Oat Muffins 43
T Cracked Wheat Bread . . . . · 40
  Date Muffins 43
T Date Rolls 42
T Dough for Cobbler 42
T Fast Whole Wheat Bread 40
T Fruit Pockets 42
T Garlic French Bread 40
  Herb Bread 39
T Multi-Grain Bread 39
  No Knead Bread 43
T Oatmeal Crackers 42
  Oatmeal Raisin Bread 41
  Onion Bread 43
T Pear Bread 41
T Peasant Bread 40
T Pita 42
  Pita Filling 42
  Scottish Oat Crisps 42
T Swedish Limpe Bread 39
  Wheat Oat Muffins 43
T Whole Grain Bread 38
T Whole Wheat Bread 38
  Whole Wheat Bread II 39
T Whole Wheat Bread III 41
  Whole Wheat English Muffins 41

MAIN DISHES

T Baked Beans 48
  Baked Nut Rice 54
  Baked Nut Rice II 54
  Baked Rice and Soymeat 54
T Barley Casserole 49
T Barley Garbanzo Patties 49
T Barley Patties 49
T Bean Burgers 47
  Bean Oat Patties 47
  Brazil Nut Casserole 49
T Bread Dressing 49
T Brown Rice 56
  Brown Rice Casserole 54
T Bulghur Wheat 51

T Bushnell Beans 46
T Cabbage Rolls 74
T Carrot Bean Croquettes 48
  Cheese-A-Roni 57
T Chili 46
T Chili Beans 48
T Dried Lima Beans and Rice 46
T Dumplings 57
T Garbanzo Burgers 49
T Garbanzo Noodle Casserole 49
T Garbanzo Pot Pie 50
T Garbanzo Roast 45
T Garbanzos 57
T Garbanzo Sauce 50
T Green and White Beans 48
T Haystacks 50
  How to Cook Dry Beans 45
  Lasagna 50
  Lentil Patties 51
  Lentil Patties or Roast 52
  Lentil Roast 51
T Lima Bean-Tomato Casserole 46
  Macaroni with Peanuts 57
  Millet Casserole 53
T Millet Delight 52
  Millet Lentil Casserole 52
  Millet Loaf 53
  Millet Patties 52
T Navy Bean Soup-Dumplings 57, 58
  Oat Burgers 53
  Oatmeal Patties 53
T Olive Rice Ring 55
T Pizza 51
  Pizza Sauce 51
  Potatoes and Rice Patties 54
  Potatoes Au Gratin 72
T Quick Pinto Beans 45
T Refried Beans I 48
T Refried Beans II 48
T Rice and Lentils 52
  Rice and Soymeat 55
T Rice Oriental 52
  Rice Oriental 54
T Rice and Tomato Dish 55
T Roman Beans on Rice 56
  Sesame Rice 55
  Seven Grain Patties 56
T Skillet Spaghetti 57
  Soybean Loaf 46
  Soybean Loaf II 47
  Soybean Omelette 47
T Soybean Patties 47
  Soybeans 46
  Soybean Souffle 46
  Soy Oat Patties and Tomato Sauce 47, 48
  Soyteena 47
T Spaghetti Sauce 57
T Spanish Brown Rice 55
T Sprouted Lentil Casserole 52

Stuffed Green Peppers 55
Sunburgers 53
Sunflower Seed Casserole 56
Sunflower Seed Loaf 58
T Tamale Pie 56
Tofu Vegetable Quiche 58
T Tomato-Lentil Delight 51
Tomato Sauce 48
Tostada with Beans 48
Walnut Tofu Balls 56
T **Wheat Casserole** **56**
T **Wheat with Lentils** **51**
T **Whole Wheat Spaghetti with Broccoli Sauce** **57**

GRAVIES and SAUCES

T Brown Chicken-like Gravy 59
Cashew Gravy (White Sauce) 59
Creamy Tomato Gravy 59
T Garbanzo Flour Gravy (Browned Flour) 59
T Golden Sauce 59
Melty Cheese 60
T Parsley Sauce 59
Pimiento-Parsley Sauce 59
Sweet and Sour Sauce 59
Thick Cream Sauce 59

DRESSINGS AND SPREADS

Almond-Date Jam 66
T Apple Jam 66
Apple-Nut Spread 66
Avocado Dressing 62
Avocado Dressing and Dip 62
T Bean Spread 63
Cashew Jack Cheese 65
Cashew Mayonnaise 61
Cashew Pimiento Cheese 64
Cashew Sweet Basil Dressing 61
Cole Slaw Dressing 62
Corn Butter 65
Creamy Lemon Dressing 61
Creamy Millet Spread 63
T Date Butter 65
T Dried Fruit Jam 66
Fig Jam 66
Filbert Spread 66
T French-Type Salad Dressing 62
T Fruit Spread 66
T Garbanzo Spread 63
Garbanzo-Pimiento Spread 65
T Garlic Butter 65
T Grape Jam 66
Green Onion Dressing 61
Guacamole pread 64
Hommus Tahini (Garbanzo) 63
T Italian Type Dressing 62

T Ketchup 65
T Legume Spread 63
Melty Cheese **60**
Millet Butter 65
Millet Mayonnaise 62
No Oil Artificial Cheese 65
No Oil Soy Mayonnaise 61
Nut or Seed Butter 67
Nut Spread 64
Peanut-Pineapple Jam 67
Peanut Soy Spread 64
T Pear Jam 66
Pimiento Spread or Olive Spread 64
T Pineapple-Apricot Jam 66
Pizza Bun Topping 64
Prune Jam 66
T Quick Tomato Catsup 65
T Rice Spread 64
T Rumanian Eggplant Dip 62
Sandwich Spread 63
Savory Sauce or Spread 64
Sesame Spread 65
Soy Mayonnaise 61
T Strawberry Jam 66
Sunny Spread 63
Tomato-Nut Spread 63
T Tomato Salad Dressing 62

VEGETABLES

T Asparagus 73
T Baked Stuffed Potatoes 71
T Beets 73
T Broccoli Italian Style 72
Carrot Loaf 73
T Carrot Roast 70
T Cashew-Tofu Stir Fry 75
Celery Loaf 70
Cheese-Broccoli Casserole 72
T Chinese Vegetables 74
T Corn and Zucchini Casserole 71
T Country Potato Patties 70
T Creamed Celery 70
T Creole Corn 72
T Crepes with Broccoli 74
T Eggplant 70
T Eggplant Casserole 73
T Eggplant Casserole II 73
T Eggplant Casserole Deluxe 74
Enchiladas 72
Escalloped Potatoes 71
T Fresh Corn Sauté 70
Garden Vegetable Pie 74
Green Beans Almondine 70
T Green Beans and Tomato 73
T Herbed Cabbage Medley 72
T Macaroni and Cabbage Dinner 70

Mashed Potatoes and Turnips 72
Piquant Beans 73
Potatoes Au Gratin 72
T Potato Balls 71
T Potato Boats 72
T Potato Rice Casserole 71
T Ribbon Macaroni and Broccoli 71
T Rice Balls 75
Savory Sauce 75
Soybean Casserole 75
T Summer Squash 72
Summer Squash Casserole 73
Sunflower Seed Loaf 58
T Sweet Sour Sauce for Brown Rice 74
T Tofu in Pita Bread 74
T Zucchini Patties 71
Zucchini Rice 73
T Zucchini and Tomatoes 71

SALADS

T Barley Salad 77
T Cabbage-Carrot Cole Slaw 76
T Cucumber Salad 78
T Fresh Broccoli, Cauliflower Salad 76
T Garbanzo Salad 76
T Lebanese Salad (Tabouli) 77
T Marinated Zucchini-Cauliflower 77
Potato Salad 77
Rosy Crunch Salad 76
Sesame Spinach Salad 76
Spanish Bulghur Salad 77
T Sprout Salad 77
Taco Salad 77
T Zucchini Dinner Salad 76

SOUPS

T Barley and Pinto Beans 82
T Bean-Corn Chowder 82
T Best Barley Soup 79
Broccoli Soup 81
Corn Chowder 80
T Corn Chowder II 83
T Cream of Celery Soup 82
Cream of Potato Soup 80
Cucumber Soup 81
Esau's Pottage 79
T Fresh Garden Vegetable Soup 82
T Friday Stew 81

T Garbanzo Soup 81
T Garden Soup 82
T Garden Vegetable Soup 79
T Gazpacho Soup-Salad 80
Jiffy Mushroom Soup 80
T Lentil Soup 80
T Navy Bean Soup 82

T Rice Soup 79
Sallie's Navy Bean Soup 79
Split Pea Soup 80
Squash Soup 81
T Tomato Soup 82
Tomato Soup II 79
T Vegetable Bean Soup 82
T Vegetable Chowder 83
T Yellow Split Pea Soup 80
T Zucchini Vegetable Stew 81

NATURAL SWEETS

Almond-Sesame Pie Crust 85
Almond Whole Wheat Pie Crust 86
T Apple Bread Pudding 88
T Apple Burritos 87
Apple Crisp 87
Apple Crisp II 87
T Apple Pie 85
T Apple Pie Filling 84
T Apple Pockets 96
T Apple Rice Betty 87
Apple Rice Dessert 87
Apricot Kuchen 95
Apricot Treats 93
Apricot Walnut Treats 93
T Banana Ice Cream 89
Banana Logs 88
Banana Nut Cake 94
Banana Nut Cookies 91
Banana Oatmeal Bars 92
Banana-Pumpkin Ice Cream 89
Blender Strawberry Ice Cream 89
Blueberry Dessert 96
Bread Pudding 86
T California Fruit Soup 90
T California Fruit Soup II 90
Carob Fruit Bars 91
Carob Fudge 93
Carob Fudge II 97
Carob Ice Cream 88
Carob Millet Pudding Pie Filling 96
Carob-Nut-Fruit Bars 97
Carob Pie Filling, Pudding 84
Carob Snowballs 93
Cashew Banana Cream Pie 84
Cashew Topping 93
Chip-Oatmeal Cookies 92
Coconut Cream Topping 94
Coconut Pie Shell 86
Cookie Haystacks 91
Creamy Coconut Fruit Salad 94
T Crepes 96
Crumb Crust 86
Crumbly Crust 96
T Dark Fruit Soup 90

T Date Banana Blender Ice Cream 89
  Date Bars 91
  Dried Fruit Balls 93
  East Indian Rice Pudding 87
  Favorite Desserts 90
  Fig Walnut Bars 91
  Fresh Apple Desserts 84
T Fresh Fruit Pie 84
  Fresh Fruit Pie II 97
T Fresh Fruit Salad 94
  Frozen Banana Logs 89
T Frozen Peaches 96
  Frozen Pie Crust 85
T Frozen Strawberries 95
T Fruit Bars 92
T Fruit Braid Spread 92
  Fruit Cake 94
  Fruit Chews 92
  Fruit Crisps 92
T Fruit Leather 95
T Fruit Pie Filling 85
T Fruit Plate 94
T Fruit Punch 95
  Fruit Shakes 89
T Fruit Soup 90
T Fruit Soups 90
  Fruit Topping 93
  Garbanzo Nuts 101
T Golden Fruit Soup 90
  Golden Macaroons 92
T Hot Fudge Sundae 88
T Ice Cream 88
  Individual Strawberry Ice Cream Pie 86
  Kuchen 95
T Lemon Pie Filling 84
T Lemon Pie 85
  Maple Pecan Ice Cream 89
T Melon Ball Rainbow 94
T Millet Pudding 86
T Millet or Rice Pudding 86
  Millet Pudding or Cereal 87
  No-Cook Fig Sweet 92
  No Oil Pie Crust 85
  Oatmeal-Almond Pie Crust 86
  Oatmeal Carob Bars 96
  Oatmeal Pie Crust 85
T Orange Ice Cream 88
T Pat's Fruit Soup 90
  Peachy Crumb Cake 87
T Pie Crust 86
  Pineapple Ice Cream 89
T Pineapple Slush 88
  Polynesian Bars 91
  Pumpkin Pie or Custard 84
T Pumpkin Pockets 96
  Sesame Bars 91
T Sherbet 88
T Simple Desserts 95

  Sprout Treats 93
  Squash or Pumpkin Pie 85
  Strawberry Ice Cream Pie 86
  Toasted Coconut Chips 96
  Tofu Cheese Cake 94
  Vanilla Freezer Ice Cream 96
  Whipped Topping 93

MISCELLANEOUS

Chicken-like Seasoning 99
Chili Powder Substitute 99
Cinnamon Substitute 99
Communion Bread 99
Cranberry Relish 100
Dextrinizing Cereals 98
French Fried Potatoes 99
Garbanzo Nuts 101
Lemon Juice Pickles 100
Minty Peas 100
Parched Wheat 99
Popped Corn 99
Preparation of Raw Cashews 98
Roasted Chestnuts 103
Sauer Kraut 100
Sauteing Vegetables Without Oil 98
Sesame Seasoning 100
Simple Pickles 100
Soy Bean Base 98
Soy Cheese 98
Soy Milk 98
Sprouted Wheat Wafers 100
Sprouting 102
Sprouting Sunflower Seeds 103
Tofu 98
Vegetable Broth Powder 99

ALPHABETICAL INDEX

Almond-Date Jam 66
Almond-Sesame Pie Crust 85
Almond-Whole Wheat Pie Crust 86
T Apple Bread 39
T Apple Bread Pudding 88
T Apple Burritos 87
Apple Crisp 87
Apple Crisp II 87
T Apple Jam 66
Apple-Nut Spread 66
Apple-Oatmeal Muffins 33
Apple Sauce Muffins 33
Apple Pie 85
T Apple Pie Filling 84
T Apple Pockets 96
T Apple-Rice Betty 87
Apple-Rice Dessert 87
Apple-Walnut Spread 66
Apricot Kuchen 95
T Apricot-Pineapple Sauce 31
Apricot Treats 93
Apricot-Walnut Treats 93
T Asparagus 73
Avocado Dressing 62
Avocado Dressing and Dip 62
T Baked Beans 48
Baked Nut Rice 54
Baked Nut Rice II 54
T Baked Oatmeal 27
Baked Oatmeal 27
Baked Rice and Soymeat 54
T Baked Stuffed Potatoes 71
T Banana Ice Cream 89
Banana Logs 88
Banana Nut Cake 94
Banana Nut Cookies 91
Banana Oatmeal Bars 92
Banana-Pumpkin Ice Cream 89
T Barley Casserole 49
T Barley Garbanzo Patties 49
T Barley Patties 49
T Barley and Pinto Beans 82
T Barley Salad 77
T Basic Rice Milk 36
T Bean Burgers 47
T Bean-Corn Chowder 82
Bean Oat Patties 47
T Bean Spread 63
T Beets 73
T Best Barley Soup 79
Blender Strawberry Ice Cream 89
Blueberry Dessert 96
T Blueberry Syrup 31
Boiling Method 26
Brazil Nut Casserole 49
T Bread Dressing 49
Bread Pudding 86
T Breakfast Beans 30
T Broccoli Italian Style 72

Broccoli Soup 81
T Brown Bread 40
T Brown Bread Muffins 43
T Brown Chicken-like Gravy 59
T Brown Rice 56
Brown Rice Casserole 54
Brown Rice Cereal 26
T Bulghur Wheat 51
T Burritos or Wheat Lefse 33
T Bushnell Beans 46
T Cabbage-Carrot Cole Slaw 76
Cabbage Rolls 74
T California Fruit Soup 90
T California Fruit Soup II 90
Carob Fruit Bars 91
Carob Fudge 93
Carob Fudge II 97
Carob Ice Cream 88
Carob Millet Pudding Pie Filling 96
Carob-Nut-Fruit Bars 97
Carob Pie Filling, Pudding 84
Carob Snowballs 93
Carrot Bean Croquettes 48
Carrot Loaf 73
T Carrot Roast 70
Cashew Banana Cream Pie 84
Cashew Cream 37
Cashew French Toast Batter 28
Cashew Gravy (white sauce) 59
Cashew Jack Cheese 65
Cashew Mayonnaise 61
Cashew Nut Cream 36
Cashew Pimiento Cheese 64
Cashew Sweet Basil Dressing 61
T Cashew-Tofu Stir Fry 75
Cashew Topping 93
Celery Loaf 70
Cheese-A-Roni 57
Cheese-Broccoli Casserole 72
T Cherries on Toast 30
Chicken-like Seasoning 99
T Chili 46
T Chili Powder Substitute 99
T Chili Beans 48
T Chinese Vegetables 74
Chip-Oatmeal Cookies 92
Cinnamon Substitute 99
Coconut Cream 37
Coconut Cream Topping 94
Coconut Milk 36
Cocohut-Millet Waffles 28
Coconut Pie Shell 86
Coconut or Sesame Sticks 32
Cole Slaw Dressing 62
Communion Bread 99
Cookie Haystacks 91
T Corn Bread 34
T Corn Bread 40
Corn Bread II 43

Corn Butter 65
Corn Chowder 80
T Corn Chowder II 83
T Corn Crackers 32
Corn Crisps 34
Corn Dodgers 34
T Cornmeal Delight 27
Cornmeal Rice Cakes 34
Cornmeal with Corn 28
T Corn-Oat Muffins 43
T Corn and Zucchini 71
T Cottage Fries 30
T Country Potato Patties 70
T Cracked Wheat Bread 40
Crackers 32
T Cranberry Fruit Sauce 30
Cranberry Relish 100
T Creamed Celery 70
T Cream of Celery Soup 82
Cream of Potato Soup 80
Creamy Coconut Fruit Salad 94
Creamy Lemon Dressing 61
Creamy Millet Spread 63
Creamy Tomato Gravy 59
T Creole Corn 72
T Crepes 96
T Crepes with Broccoli 74
Crispy Cornbread 34
Crispy Corn Chips 35
Crock Pot Method 26
Crumb Crust 86
Crumbly Crust 96
Crunchy Granola 29
T Cucumber Salad 78
Cucumber Soup 81
T Currant Delight 31
Dark Fruit Soup 90
T Date-Banana Blender Ice Cream 89
Date Bars 91
T Date Butter 65
T Date Muffins 18
Date Muffins 43
T Date Rolls 42
T Delicious Millet 26
Delicious Millet 27
Dextrinizing Cereals 98
T Dough for Cobblers 42
Dried Fruit Balls 93
T Dried Fruit Jam 66
T Dried Lima Beans and Rice 46
T Dumplings 57
T Early Morning Pancakes 35
East Indian Rice Pudding 87
T Eggplant 70
T Eggplant Casserole 73
T Eggplant Casserole II 73
T Eggplant Casserole Deluxe 74
Enchiladas 72
Esau's Pottage 79
Escalloped Potatoes 71
T Fast Whole Wheat Bread 40
Favorite Desserts 90
Fig Jam 66
Fig Walnut Bars 91
Filbert Spread 66

French Fried Potatoes 99
T French-type Salad Dressing 62
Fresh Apple Desserts 84
T Fresh Broccoli, Cauliflower Salad 76
T Fresh Corn Saute 70
Fresh Fruit Muffins 33
T Fresh Fruit Pie 84
Fresh Fruit Pie II 97
T Fresh Fruit Salad 94
Fresh Garden Vegetable Soup 82
T Friday Stew 81
T Frozen Banana Logs 89
T Frozen Peaches 96
Frozen Pie Crust 85
T Frozen Strawberries 95
T Fruit Bars 92
T Fruit Braid Spread 92
Fruit Cake 94
Fruit Chews 92
Fruit Crisps 92
T Fruit Leather 95
Fruit Milk 37
Fruit Nut Granola 29
T Fruit Pie Filling 85
T Fruit Plate 94
T Fruit Pockets 42
T Fruit Punch 95
Fruit Shakes 89
T Fruit Soup 90
T Fruit Soups 90
T Fruit Spread 66
T Fruit Toast 30
Fruit Topping 93
T Garbanzos 57
T Garbanzo Burgers 49
T Garbanzo Flour Gravy (brown flour) . . . 59
T Garbanzo Noodle Casserole 49
Garbanzo Nuts 101
Garbanzo-Pimiento Spread 65
T Garbanzo Pot Pie 50
T Garbanzo Roast 45
T Garbanzos 57
T Garbanzo Salad 76
Garbanzo Sauce 50
T Garbanzo Soup 81
T Garbanzo Spread 63
T Garden Soup 82
T Garden Vegetable Pie 74
T Garden Vegetable Soup 79
T Garlic Butter 65
T Garlic French Bread 40
T Gazpacho Soup-Salad 80
T Golden Breakfast Potatoes 30
T Golden Fruit Soup 90
Golden Macaroons 92
T Golden Sauce 59
T Granola 29
Granola 29
T Grape Jam 66
T Green Beans Almondine 70
T Green Beans and Tomatoes 73
Green Onion Dressing 61
T Green and White Beans 48
T Ground Grain Type Cereal 27
Guacamole Spread 64

T Hash Brown Potatoes 30
T Haystacks 50
Herb Bread 39
T Herbed Cabbage Medley 72
Hommus Tahini (Garbanzo) 63
T Hot Fudge Sundae 88
How to Cook Dry Beans 45
T Ice Cream 88
T Indian Corn Crackers or Corn Chips 32
Individual Strawberry Ice Cream Pie 86
T Italian-Type Dressing 62
Jean's Crackers 32
Jiffy Mushroom Soup 80
T Ketchup 65
Kuchen 95
Lasagna 50
T Lebanese Salad (Tabouli) 77
T Legume Spread 63
Lemon Juice Pickles 100
T Lemon Pie 85
T Lemon Pie Filling 84
T Lemon Sauce 31
Lentil Patties 51
Lentil Patties or Roast 52
Lentil Roast 51
T Lentil Soup 80
T Lima Bean-Tomato Casserole 46
T Macaroni and Cabbage Dinner 70
Macaroni with Peanuts 57
Maple Pecan Ice Cream 89
T Marinated Zucchini-Cauliflower 77
Mashed Potatoes and Turnips 72
T Melon Ball Rainbow 94
Melty Cheese 60
Millet Breakfast Dish 27
Millet Butter 65
Millet Casserole 53
T Millet Delight 52
Millet Lentil Casserole 52
Millet Loaf 53
Millet Mayonnaise 62
Millet Patties 52
T Millet Pudding 86
Millet Pudding or Cereal 87
T Millet or Rice Pudding 86
Minty Peas 100
T Multi-Grain Bread 39
T Multi-Grain Waffle 29
Museli 28
Natural Corn Chips 30
T Navy Bean Soup 82
T Navy Bean Soup-Dumplings 57,58
No-Cook Fig Sweet 92
No Knead Bread 43
No Oil Artificial Cheese 65
No Oil Pie Crust 85
No Oil Soy Mayonnaise 61
Nut Milks-Almond, Cashew 36
Nut or Seed Butter 67
Nut Spread 64
Oat Burgers 53
T Oatmeal 27
Oatmeal-Almond Pie Crust 86
Oatmeal Carob Bars 96
T Oatmeal Crackers 42

Oatmeal Gems 33
T Oatmeal Milk 36
Oatmeal Patties 53
Oatmeal Pie Crust 85
Oatmeal Raisin Bread 41
T Olive Rice Ring 55
Onion Bread 43
T Onion Crisps 31
Onion French Toast Batter 27
T Orange Date Sauce 31
T Orange Ice Cream 88
Parched Wheat 99
T Parsley Sauce 59
T Pat's Fruit Soup 90
T Peach-Berry Sauce 31
Peachy Crumb Cake 87
Peanut-Pineapple Jam 67
Peanut Soy Spread 64
T Pear Bread 41
T Pear Jam 66
T Peasant Bread 40
T Pie Crust 86
Pimiento-Parsley Sauce 59
Pimiento Spread or Olive Spread 64
T Pineapple-Apricot Jam 66
Pineapple Ice Cream 89
T Pineapple-Orange Sauce 31
T Pineapple Slush 88
Piquant Beans 73
T Pita 42
Pita Filling 42
T Pizza 51
Pizza Bun Topping 64
Pizza Sauce 51
Polynesian Bars 91
Popped Corn 99
T Potato Balls 71
T Potato Boats 72
T Potato Rice Casserole 71
Potato Salad 77
Potatoes Au Gratin 72
Potatoes and Rice Patties 54
Preparation of Raw Cashews 98
Prune Jam 66
Pumpkin Pie or Custard 84
T Pumpkin Pockets 96
Quick Corn Bread 34
T Quick Pinto Beans 45
T Quick Tomato Catsup 65
T Refried Beans I 48
T Refried Beans II 48
T Ribbon Macaroni and Broccoli 71
T Rice Balls 75
T Rice Breakfast Patties 30
T Rice Crackers 31
T Rice and Lentils 52
Rice Milk 36
Rice Oriental 54
T Rice Oriental 52
T Rice Soup 79
Rice and Soymeat 55
T Rice Spread 64
T Rice and Tomato Dish 55
Roasted Chestnuts 103
T Rolled Four-Grain Cereal 26

T	Rolled Wheat and Oats	26
T	Roman Beans on Rice	56
	Rosy Crunch Salad	76
T	Rumanian Eggplant Dip	62
	Sallie's Navy Bean Soup	79
	Sandwich Spread	63
	Sauer Kraut	100
	Sautéing Vegetables Without Oil	98
	Savory Sauce	75
	Savory Sauce or Spread	64
	Scottish Oat Crisps	42
	Scrambled Soy Cheese	29
	Scrambled Tofu	30
	Sesame Bars	91
	Sesame Crackers	32
	Sesame Crisps	32
	Sesame Milk	36
	Sesame Milk for Cooking	36
	Sesame Rice	55
	Sesame Seasoning	100
	Sesame Spinach Salad	76
	Sesame Spread	65
	Seven Grain Patties	56
	Sherbet	88
	Simple Desserts	95
	Simple Pickles	100
T	Skillet Spaghetti	57
	Southern Pancakes	35
	Soy Bean Base	98
	Soybean Casserole	75
	Soybean Loaf	46
	Soybean Loaf II	47
	Soybean Omelette	47
T	Soybean Patties	47
	Soybeans	46
	Soybean Souffle	46
	Soy Cheese	98
	Soy Mayonnaise	61
	Soy Milk	98
	Soy Oat Patties and Tomato Sauce	47,48
	Soy-Oat Waffles with Topping	28
	Soyteena	47
	Spaghetti Sauce	57
T	Spanish Brown Rice	55
	Spanish Bulghur Salad	77
T	Spicy-Apple Syrup	31
	Split Pea Soup	80
	Sprouted Lentil Casserole	52
T	Sprouted Wheat Bread	33
	Sprouted Wheat Wafers	100
	Sprouting	102
	Sprouting Sunflower Seeds	103
T	Sprout Salad	77
	Sprout Treats	93
	Squash or Pumpkin Pie	85
	Squash Soup	81
	Strawberry Cream	37
	Strawberry Ice Cream Pie	86
T	Strawberry Jam	66
T	Strawberry-Pineapple Banana Sauce	31
T	Strawberry Sauce	31
	Stuffed Green Peppers	55
T	Summer Squash	72
	Summer Squash Casserole	73
	Sunburgers	53
	Sunflower Seed Casserole	56
	Sunflower Seed Loaf	58
	Sunflower Seed Milk	36
	Sunny Spread	63
T	Swedish Limpe Bread	39
T	Sweet and Sour Sauce	59
	Sweet Sour Sauce for Brown Rice	74
T	Taco Chip Seasoning	33
	Taco Salad	77
T	Tamale Pie	56
	Thermos Method	26
	Thick Cream Sauce	59
	Toasted Coconut Chips	96
	Tofu	98
	Tofu Cheese Cake	94
T	Tofu in Pita Bread	74
	Tofu Vegetable Quiche	58
T	Tomato-Lentil Delight	51
	Tomato-Nut Spread	63
T	Tomato Salad Dressing	62
	Tomato Sauce	48
	Tomato Soup	30
	Tomato Soup II	79
T	Tomato Soup	82
T	Topping for Waffles	28
T	Tortillas	34
	Toastada with Beans	48
T	Triticale	27
	Vanilla Freezer Ice Cream	96
T	Vegetable Bean Soup	82
	Vegetable Broth Powder	99
T	Vegetable Chowder	83
	Waffle Perfect	28
	Walnut Tofu Balls	56
T	Wheat Berries	27
T	Wheat Casserole	56
T	Wheat with Lentils	51
	Wheat Oat Muffins	43
	Whipped Topping	93
	Whole Barley Cereal	27
T	Whole Grain Bread	38
T	Whole Millet Cereal	27
T	Whole Oats, Barley, Rice	26
T	Whole Rye Cereal	26
T	Whole Wheat Bread	38
	Whole Wheat Bread II	39
T	Whole Wheat Bread III	41
T	Whole Wheat Cereal	26
	Whole Wheat English Muffins	41
T	Whole Wheat Spaghetti with Broccoli Sauce	57
T	Yellow Split Pea Soup	80
	Yummy Granola	29
T	Zucchini Dinner Salad	76
T	Zucchini Patties	71
	Zucchini Rice	73
T	Zucchini and Tomatoes	71
T	Zucchini Vegetable Stew	81

AVAILABLE for your convenience and cooking pleasure:

COOKING WITH NATURAL FOODS - cookbook

COOKING WITH NATURAL FOODS II - cookbook

COOKING WITH NATURAL FOODS RECIPE CARD COLLECTION in an attractive ACRYLIC BOX with a protective shield for the recipe when in use.

COOKING WITH NATURAL FOODS II, RECIPE CARD COLLECTION that will fit in the box with the other recipes.

ORDER BLANKS:

I would like _____ copy or copies of *COOKING WITH NATURAL FOODS* at $14.95, plus $3.00 Shipping and Handling.

I would like _____ copy or copies of *COOKING WITH NATURAL FOODS II* at $14.95, plus $3.00 Shipping and Handling.

I would like _____ set or sets of *COOKING WITH NATURAL FOODS RECIPE CARD COLLECTION* in **the attractive acrylic box** at $29.95 (plus postage of $5.00). Cards only— $24.95, postpaid.

I would like _____ set or sets of *COOKING WITH NATURAL FOODS II RECIPE CARD COLLECTION* at $24.95, postpaid. (These will fit in the box with the first set of recipes.)

Please send them as soon as possible. My check ☐ or money order ☐ in the amount of _____ is enclosed.

Date _____ Signed_____

Name *(PLEASE PRINT)* _____

Mailing Address _____

City _____ State _____ Zip _____ Phone _____

Please remit U.S. currency.

Make check to **B.H.H.E.C.** and send with the order to:

Muriel Beltz, Black Hills Health and Education Center, HCR 89, Box 167, Hermosa, South Dakota 57744 Telephone: 605-255-4789, 255-4101 or 255-9717

I would like _____ copy or copies of *COOKING WITH NATURAL FOODS* at $14.95, plus $3.00 Shipping and Handling.

I would like _____ copy or copies of *COOKING WITH NATURAL FOODS II* at $14.95, plus $3.00 Shipping and Handling.

I would like _____ set or sets of *COOKING WITH NATURAL FOODS RECIPE CARD COLLECTION* in **the attractive acrylic box** at $29.95 (plus postage of $5.00). Cards only— $24.95, postpaid.

I would like _____ set or sets of *COOKING WITH NATURAL FOODS II RECIPE CARD COLLECTION* at $24.95, postpaid. (These will fit in the box with the first set of recipes.)

Please send them as soon as possible. My check ☐ or money order ☐ in the amount of _____ is enclosed.

Date _____ Signed_____

Name *(PLEASE PRINT)* _____

Mailing Address _____

City _____ State _____ Zip _____ Phone _____

Please remit U.S. currency.

Make check to **B.H.H.E.C.** and send with the order to:

Muriel Beltz, Black Hills Health and Education Center, HCR 89, Box 167, Hermosa, South Dakota 57744 Telephone: 605-255-4789, 255-4101 or 255-9717

LOVE NOTES: What others have said -

"Please send me a copy of your cookbook, **COOKING WITH NATURAL FOODS.** I've borrowed one from my friends many times and I am really anxious to have my own. We have cooked and eaten naturally for several years and yours is the best cookbook on the market. Thank you! You have done well to make recipes visually appealing and tasty." Washington

"My clients find **COOKING WITH NATURAL FOODS** very helpful." California

"We are continuing to sell many of your cookbooks. It is our favorite. We do cooking classes for two physicians. They send their heart and diabetic patients here." Louisiana

"Thank your for the marvelous work you are doing. We are very interested in purchasing the book **COOKING WITH NATURAL FOODS.** In fact, many people here are anxious to get copies of this fine book. Please send current price." Maryland

"I am enjoying the meals I prepare according to your book **COOKING WITH NATURAL FOODS.** I would appreciate your sending a copy to each of the following and indicate that the book is a gift from me. I have already purchased several books and have made other homemakers happy!" New Jersey

"I just saw your cookbook yesterday and it is super! I can hardly wait to get my own copy." Ohio.

"*COOKING WITH NATURAL FOODS* is a wonderful cookbook. Please rush order. Would like to use at childbirth workshop." Ohio

"Thank you for your cookbook, **COOKING WITH NATURAL FOODS.** I will put it to good use. God bless you for taking your time and effort to compile such a helpful book. I have learned so much from it. Praise the Lord!" Florida

"I attended your nutrition seminar and enjoyed it very much. Your gift of service has helped me greatly after many years of confusion and not really knowing why I should eat natural foods. Please send me two books, **COOKING WITH NATURAL FOODS.**" Minnesota